THE RADIANCE OF BEING
Dimensions of Cosmic Christianity

Stratford Caldecott

THE RADIANCE OF BEING

Dimensions of Cosmic Christianity

⊕

Foreword by
ADRIAN WALKER

 Angelico Press

For information, address:
Angelico Press
4619 Slayden Rd. NE, Tacoma, WA 98422
angelicopress.com

978-1-62138-030-6 pb
978-1-62138-032-0 cloth

Cover design: Michael Schrauzer
Cover image: Andreas Achenbach,
Sunset after a Storm on the Coast of Sicily, 1853

CONTENTS

For Léonie

Foreword

Thomas Aquinas once wrote that being pertains to light. In this new book, Stratford Caldecott shows us that the converse is equally true. Light pertains to being, and its radiance—like the splendor of created wisdom—plays over the face of all that is. Caldecott's masterful guidance in refocusing our gaze on this jubilant and serene light makes the present work indispensable reading. The *Radiance of Being* shines so brightly because its author constantly reminds us of the "one thing necessary": not the indubitable brilliance of his own mind, but the beautiful brilliance of being itself.

Caldecott's literary *persona* reflects the very quality of being's own radiance. He does not hector or preach, nor does he try to prove. He simply *shows*—deftly opening a series of windows through which the reader may behold the light of being with his own eyes. *The Radiance of Being* is a highly personal work, echoing with a unique voice, but it does not seek to overwhelm us with any merely private vision. Instead of just persuading us to see things from the author's point of view, it performs the nobler service of freeing us to look at things as they truly are.

The secret of Caldecott's persuasiveness lies partly in his solid but subtle sense of reality, his cheerful freedom from any urge to imprison the radiance of being in some hasty, one-sided, or reductive human construction. But Caldecott's realism, like Chesterton's, is an ever-renewed wonderment over the unexpected, yet appropriate correspondence between the surprising coherence of the world and the even more surprising coherence of Christ. Jesus of Nazareth, who is the "light that enlightens every man" *because* he is a jealously consuming fire, is the source, measure, and end of Caldecott's entire contemplation of reality.

The Radiance of Being treats an impressive variety of topics, but all of them fit snugly within the tripartite pattern of the whole. The first part of the book is appropriately devoted to a contemplation of the radiance of being shining through the inexhaustibly various order of the cosmos. Even contemporary physics, Caldecott suggests here, can help us relearn to see Nature as a prism refracting being's single radiance in a kaleidoscopic interplay of manifold form. Yet the endless fecundity of this display raises the question addressed in the book's second part: Can Nature's sportive delight in "all things counter, original, spare, strange" (Hopkins) really be the manifestation of an ultimately undifferentiated One, as Perennialists such as Schuon and Guénon insist? Or mustn't the unity of the First Principle be essentially Trinitarian "all the way down"? Caldecott's argument for the latter option is reminiscent of Chesterton, but also of Balthasar: It is because paganism cannot account for all that is true in the revelation of the Trinity that the revelation of the Trinity can account for all that is true in paganism. The long passion of *homo religiosus* finds its end, not in esoteric gnosis, but in the Catholic Church, for only the *Catholica* can glory in being "the sewer of history, the tumultuous flowing of human impurity towards immaculate seas" (Nicolás Gómez Dávila).

The third part of *The Radiance of Being* circles back to the first in light of the second: If the divine nature is constitutively triune, what does this radically Trinitarian character imply about the ultimate significance of creaturely nature? Caldecott's answer is both traditional and surprising, for it locates the goal of the divine creative act in the *connubium* between God and man in Christ. The book thus fittingly closes with an orthodox retrieval of Bulgakov's sophiology. *Sophia*, Caldecott argues, is nothing other than the splendor of triune love answered by the glory of the *Assumpta*, who, in the words of Nicholas Cabasilas, is "the fruit of creatures" and the finest "bloom of Nature." *Sophia* is the "analogy of being" manifested as spousal love between God and the world.

The Radiance of Being is a symphony whose master theme is the Trinity, and its pages bear constant witness to the same inexhaustibly simple truth: Being is radiant because it is a gift, not only *from* the Trinity, but also *within* the Trinity itself. In its Infinite Source, in the fathomless abyss of Deity, being is already always one with (triune) love:

I have said that the act of being is an act of giving, an act of knowing, an act of love. It is Trinitarian. The same cluster of metaphors illuminates the nature of created being, the dynamic relationship to God which is intrinsic to all existing things. Giftedness is the signature of God upon creation. But our being is not simply a gift to us; it is God's gift to himself. Created human nature is a gift that the Father gives to the Son, along with his divine nature. And it is a gift that the Son gives the Father, by being born as Man, dying on the Cross, and rising to new life. Creation is therefore gift both in relation to God, and in relation specifically to each of the Persons. Filled with the Holy Spirit in order to be given to the Father by the Son, it is transformed into the Son's Eucharist or "thanksgiving." The world indwelt by the Spirit is therefore now infinitely more than it was when it was created. It speaks not only with its own voice, but with the voice of the Son, who gives glory to his Father with this transformed creation.

This passage (from chapter ten of the book) illustrates Caldecott's talent for keeping his feet planted firmly on the ground even when soaring up to the loftiest heights of speculation. His ability to combine elf-like vision with hobbit-like common sense lends further credibility to the main thesis of his new book, for if the radiance of being is *gift*, then the first place to look for its (esoteric) depth is precisely on its (exoteric) surface. This is true of the surface of Caldecott's own writing, which is radiant with the joy of being one voice in the multitudinous chorus of creation. The author of *The Radiance of Being* is one of the most important living exponents of Catholic metaphysics, but his vision of being's "publicly sacred mystery" (Goethe) is not just the expression of his own genius. It is first the fruit of his participation in the universal communion of the *Catholica*.

ADRIAN WALKER

Preface

In the Beautiful Logos all things cohere. In the Word of words all threads of meaning are drawn together, and the notes and noises of our lives add up to parts of a symphony or a song we could never have guessed. The truth that has been revealed to us in Christ is the beginning of our eternal life.

The present book is based on essays written in many places and times, now revised and developed in a new context. At my publisher's invitation I took an opportunity to revisit this material and try to weave it into an ordered whole—to bring my scattered thoughts towards some kind of conclusion. The resulting book is in three parts, concerned respectively with the nature of nature, the nature of God, and the nature of divine Wisdom. It opens in Part One with some reflections on the history of science and cosmology, using the metaphor of "light" to suggest a bridge between scientific and religious thought. Part Two, about our conceptions of God, is largely concerned with the notion of the Trinity, which makes Christianity so unique among the religions of the world. Part Three explores the intimate relationship between God and man—man viewed as the link or mediator between God and the rest of creation.

The doctrine of the Trinity emerges as the overarching theme of the book. Year after year, Christian preachers get up in the pulpit and try to deliver a sermon on Trinity Sunday. Sometimes it is a lamentable failure. Occasionally it seems they are embarrassed about the wonderful doctrine of the Trinity. They certainly seem to struggle to put into words how one God can be three persons. Perhaps they feel a bit like quantum physicists, trying to explain to laymen how light can be a particle at the same time as being a wave.

But the doctrine of the Trinity does not just make sense of a few experimental observations in a laboratory. It makes sense of human life as a whole. It is the key that opens every lock, an insight that reveals the center of the universe. It shows us the pattern that underlies physics, history, psychology, economics, and the arts. It is the most beautiful, elegant, and simple doctrine in the world—a true "theory of everything."

That is why the central part of this book is my attempt to think through, as a Catholic layman, the doctrine of the Trinity and its implications for cosmology. There is also an important element of inter-religious dialogue in the book, because no theologian, amateur or professional, can ignore the challenge posed by these other great living traditions—a challenge, in some ways, directly to our understanding of the Christian Trinity.

A word is therefore needed concerning my attitude to the other world religions and my approach to dialogue. I believe in the truth of the Catholic faith as taught by the Church, and have since I was baptized into her at the age of twenty-seven. However, our circumstances today do not encourage triumphalism. Of course, many Christians are dying for their faith. This is a fact we should not minimize or ignore. But just as shocking in another way is the fact that many more Christians are living a lie—they are not living in a Christian way. And there are many who can stand the hypocrisy not a moment longer. A friend wrote to me:

> Please, in these ugly days, make a plea for tolerance, for the integrity of the piety of nature and piety of Being that motivates those who, like me, have been so torn up or offended by Christianity/Catholicism as to no longer feel able to stand within it. Please make a plea for tolerance and the Catholic responsibility to seek always the heart of goodwill in others. Call your fellow Catholics to do what only they can do (doctrinally, theologically speaking)—defend the integrity of natural piety, and the integrity of dialogue and diversity.

I have tried to do so. But tolerance and integrity are the virtues of love and freedom, both of which must be aroused, grown into; and sometimes they come more gradually and more painfully than we would have expected. Much of the time we think we are loving and free when in reality we do not even know what these words imply. For example, the whole world currently seems to believe that freedom grows with the number of options placed before us. But God's love teaches us something different. "Perfect freedom is the total inability to make any evil choice," says Thomas Merton. "Therefore, the simplest definition of freedom is this; it means the ability to do the will of God."[1]

To do the will of God: indeed that does sound simple. And how do we know the will of God? Jean-Pierre de Caussade reminds us that it is revealed to us in every moment of every day. God's words to us take the form of all that we see and hear. They change moment by moment. They are addressed uniquely to us, and call for the unique response that God hopes for. God himself does not "choose," he simply "is," and he "creates." For our part, made in God's image, we too must learn to create, bringing into the world possibilities that are not already laid before us. We can only astonish God by participating in God's own creative life. But nevertheless, we have a revelation of our own to make, one that no one can make for us. The importance of this will come to the fore later in the book, as we delve deeper into the meaning of freedom, God's creation of the world, and the relationship between nature and grace.

Influences, Sources, and Acknowledgements

Some chapters of the present book are based on material first developed as articles in journals such as *Communio* and *Second Spring*, or booklets I have written for CTS, and I am grateful to the original publishers. The material has all been extensively reworked. If at times the text resembles a mosaic of quotations and the footnotes start to grow wings, I can only say that it is good to be able to quote others when they say something more eloquently or authoritatively than oneself. A book like this can be nothing more than a work in progress, and many loose threads remain.

I write not as a professional theologian, but as an editor of theology, and an interested observer. I want especially to thank the following (in no particular order) for their encouragement and fellowship over the years in the development of the thoughts expressed in these pages: among them Adrian Walker, Wolfgang

---

1. Thomas Merton, *Seeds of Contemplation* (London: Hollis & Carter, 1949), 120, 122.

Smith, Robert Bolton, Philip Zaleski, Mary Taylor, David L. Schindler, Connie Lasher, Tim Mahoney, Francesca Murphy, Karim Lahham, Jane Clark, Conor Cunningham, David Clayton, Barry R. Pearlman, Christian Moevs, Jim Clarage, and of course my editors, John Riess and James Wetmore of Angelico Press and Sophia Perennis. Special thanks to Anna Maria Mendell for her skillful editing in the final stages, and to Léonie Caldecott, who has been my support and inspiration throughout.

PART I

NATURE

The old Catholic religion-culture of Europe is dead and is being carried out to burial. It cannot be raised from the tomb. Its world year is over, has ended with midwinter. For its matter the inheritance of classical culture no longer exists. It has been destroyed, overwhelmed by a vast influx of new knowledge, by the scientific mass civilization of the modern world.... [But] already in the winter there are signs of the approaching spring.... The abiding and immutable truth of metaphysics and revealed religion must be re-clad in new garments woven by a scientific and historical knowledge incomparably vaster than was ever before possessed by man.

E. I. Watkin[1]

1. E. I. Watkin, *Catholic Art and Culture* (London: Hollis & Carter, 1947), 159–69.

Let There Be Light

The scientific enterprise could be said to have begun when the Greeks tried to account for physical observations by means of theoretical constructions—the harmonies of music, for example, by means of mathematical relations between the notes. Sacred numbers, Platonic and Archimedean solids, circles, squares, and triangles became the building blocks for a theory of natural order that remained unchallenged for two millennia. These are not far removed from everyday experience. When the ancient notion of order was finally challenged (by Galileo, Kepler, Newton, *et al.*), it became clear that the principles governing the universe were more complex than this, and could not be easily deduced from the basic axioms that seem most natural to our imaginations. The planetary orbits form ellipses not circles, for example.

In the course of a few years at the beginning of the 20th century, everything changed again. In 1900, Max Planck laid the foundations of quantum mechanics. In 1905, Albert Einstein came up with special relativity and the equivalence of matter and energy, and two years later extended the principle of relativity to gravitational fields. These breakthroughs were based not on calculation or experimental observations but on acts of the imagination, affecting the most basic assumptions of physics. (This does not mean, as Fritjof Capra suggested in his book *The Tao of Physics*, that "geometry is not inherent in nature, but is imposed upon it by the mind."[1] We still believe there is an objective geometrical order, even if it is not Euclidean.)

The human imagination is naturally influenced by the way things appear to the senses (the sun rises and sets, light appears to travel instantaneously, and the angles of a triangle add up to 180°). But the

---

1. F. Capra, *The Tao of Physics: An Exploration of the Parallels between Modern Physics and Eastern Mysticism* (London: Fontana, 1983), 178.

intellect and imagination together are not so restricted, and one such assumption after another can be suspended or replaced by others. If the resulting theory is hard to visualize, it is nevertheless based on concepts that can be explained, in principle, to anybody, and thus remains rooted in a common world of human experience. It is rooted in that world in another way too, namely by the fact that all the empirical observations on which it depends are necessarily made in the world as we experience it.

Imagining Light

We have all been taught that the speed of light in a vacuum is a constant 186,000 miles or just under 300,000 kilometers per second—that nothing can break that barrier. Unlike the speed of anything else we observe, it is not relative to anything else. So the speed of a car may be 70 mph in relation to the surface of the road, and 5 mph in relation to the car I am overtaking which is traveling at 65 mph. But light is different. It is always traveling at the *same speed* in relation to me, no matter where I am or how fast I am going.

That is bizarre. How did Einstein come up with the idea? In the early 19th century, Michael Faraday had to invent the notion of a "field" as a way of explaining the mysterious action at a distance between electricity and magnetism. If you put an electric current through a wire, it affects a nearby compass needle. If you push a magnet through a coil of wire, an electric current starts to flow in the coil. Building on this discovery, James Clerk Maxwell was able to show that the speed with which the influence travels is exactly determined by the ratio of the *strengths* of the electric field and the magnetic field. Being dependent solely on this ratio, the number does not vary with the *movement* of the wire or the magnet—hence the absoluteness of the speed, which is the observed speed of light.

Light was in this way revealed to consist of vibrations in a unified "electromagnetic" field, which is a description of the way energy propagates through space. The movement of electrons in a wire (which constitutes an electric current) is induced by the energy transmitted by the field, and vice versa. This discovery enabled the manipulation and generation of electricity on a large scale and powered the second phase of the Industrial Revolution. (One important question remained: light or radiant energy in general is a vibration, but a vibration of what? The Michelson-Morley experiment showed it could not be a vibration in any kind of universal "ether." Einstein later showed that it also has a particulate nature— it consists of particles or packets of something.)[2]

It is worth noting the role of *theology* in this breakthrough by Faraday and Maxwell. Thomas Torrance writes:

> Clerk Maxwell's belief in the God who became incarnate in Jesus Christ made him question whether the universe created by the Wisdom of God did really behave in the way described by Newtonian mechanics. The crisis came when he failed again and again to find a Newtonian mechanistic explanation for the behavior of electromagnetism and light. It was through allowing Christian thought (such as the understanding of interpersonal relations derived from the doctrine of the Holy Trinity) to bear upon his scientific thinking that he came up with the conception of the continuous dynamic field, to which Einstein was to point as introducing the most far-reaching change in the rational structure of science and our understanding of nature.[3]

The implications of the identification of light as an excitation of a universally pervasive electromagnetic field are rarely in the forefront of our minds. But when a scientist pauses to express himself in imaginative terms we can be astounded. In a book of essays dedicated to the science and theology of light, Andrew M. Steane pauses to describe how his view of ordinary, everyday objects such as chairs

---

2. The 1887 "ether-wind" experiment of Michelson and Morley undermined the hypothesis of a universal etheric fluid or "luminiferous ether" within which light waves were the vibrations. An attempt to save the hypothesis was devised by FitzGerald, Lawrence, and Larmor, involving a complex mathematical transformation that was later accounted for and incorporated in Special Relativity. Today the space-time continuum itself has taken the place of the "ether," as we see later.

3. Thomas F. Torrance in Robert J. Russell *et al.*, *John Paul II on Science and Religion: Reflections on the New View from Rome* (South Bend, IN: University of Notre Dame Press, 1990), 106–112. Maxwell was not the originator of the field concept, which emerged from the observations and speculations of Michael Faraday. However, Faraday was also a devout Christian.

and coffee cups has changed under the impact of quantum electro-dynamics ("QED"). Since electrical charge itself is essentially a "propensity to emit or absorb" photons, those photons exist in the interior even of solid objects, "enabling them to hold themselves together." Thus: "The table before me is full of light. We don't see that light because it is mostly not coming up out of the table, but passing to and fro within it, hidden inside, each photon glimmering just long enough to pass from one particle to another."[4] In fact, the world is even more luminous than that, because reflected light itself is not what we assume—a collection of photons bouncing off a hard surface. Rather it is a collection of photons being absorbed by the surface and *another collection* of photons radiated back (in wave-lengths, i.e. colors, determined by the properties of the surface itself). In reality, everything is glowing.

And, as Dr. Steane puts it, "if it were not for this dance of energy and light, I would fall through the surface of the road into the interior of planet Earth—or to be more thorough and accurate, my body would dissipate entirely into a vapor of dust, and so would Earth."[5] Add to this fact that the very particles of which we are made, and which are performing this constant dance to keep us in existence, were themselves (that is, these identical atoms) forged in the hearts of exploding stars millions of years ago, and it is hard not to be overwhelmed by wonder.

The existence of every particle implies the existence of a "field of force" within which the particle may be interpreted as a vibration. The discovery of what appeared to be a Higgs boson in 2012 con-firms that even the atoms of matter are only possible because the particles that compose them (leptons and quarks) have interacted with the Higgs field, like bullets ploughing through a vat of treacle. It is this interaction that mainly causes them to have mass or momentum, and therefore not to exist at the speed of light, and to be capable of "settling down" in the form of atoms into the universe

4. Gerald O'Collins SJ and Mary Ann Meyers (eds), *Light from Light: Scientists and Theologians in Dialogue* (Grand Rapids, MI: Eerdmans, 2012), 47.

5. Ibid.

we know. In other words the universe is entirely made of energy interacting with itself.[6]

Imagining Time

One thing that follows from the invariability of the speed of electromagnetic radiation is a weird relationship with time. For if the speed of light is constant regardless of the speed of the observer, *time must slow down* as one accelerates. Einstein tried to imagine observer A trying to catch up with a vehicle traveling at light speed. A fails to do so, no matter how fast he goes, since the speed of light in relation to any observer is a constant. Observer B, however, who is traveling much slower than A, sees him getting faster and faster, and therefore he *must* be approaching the speed of light. The only way to reconcile these two observations is if the rate of time for A has changed when compared to that for B (and *vice versa*).

The faster A travels, the slower his clock runs compared to B, until at light speed it appears to have stopped altogether. Similarly, A sees his own clock as running normally, but to him it seems that B's clock has slowed down. If A then slows down to the same speed as B, his own time continues to flow as normal but he will observe B's time speeding up until the two are matched. However, comparing the two clocks they will find that less time has elapsed for A than for B.

What Einstein realized is that both the speed of light and the flow of time cannot be constant—one of them has to give. The rate of time, or the speed of a clock, must be "relative," in the sense that it depends on where it is measured from, and how fast the observer

---

6. "Modern science has come to the understanding that matter is only condensed energy—which, moreover, was known [in principle] by alchemists and Hermeticists thousands of years ago. Sooner or later science will also discover the fact that what it calls 'energy' is only condensed psychic force—which discovery will lead in the end to the establishment of the fact that all psychic force is the 'condensation', purely and simply, of consciousness, i.e., spirit. Thus it will be known for certain that we walk not thanks to the existence of legs, but rather than legs exist thanks to the will for movement, i.e. that it is the will for movement that has fashioned the legs so as to serve as its instrument. Similarly, it will be known that the brain does not engender consciousness but that it is the latter's instrument of action." (Anon., *Meditations on the Tarot: A Journey into Christian Hermeticism* [Amity, NY: Amity House, 1985], 574.)

himself is moving in relation to it. Just as electrical and magnetic force turned out to be different manifestations of "electromagnetism," so space and time are simply different aspects of "space-time." Time is now conceived as another dimension added to the three that define a volume of space. We cannot talk about distance or speed without involving time, or of either without stating the observer's frame of reference.

It also turns out that what we are investigating is not just the relationship between time and space, but between time, space, and *mass*. To have mass, i.e. inertia, is to resist acceleration. That means that it takes time to speed it up by the application of force (according to Newton, $F = ma$). Mass or matter therefore exists in a state of variable motion. Light, on the other hand, has no mass. It is pure energy. It exists in a state of constant motion. That motion, or changing "position," is a function of measurement, and specifically of measurement in relation to something with mass. But this is a measure applied by the world to the photon, and not the other way around—from the photon's point of view, it is not moving at all. Or rather, it is not moving through the "time" dimension of space-time, only the other three spatial dimensions. Its "time" vector is flat. (Of course, our imaginations get confused at this, because we imagine drawing a line on a graph in two-or three-dimensional space, not four-dimensional space.)

As Einstein declared, at the speed of light "all moving bodies—viewed from the 'resting' frame—shrivel up into plane figures."[7] Space as well as time is contracted. Symbolically, therefore, 'c' represents the ontological distance between light and the material universe (the universe of mass and temporal change). If the biblical "garden of Eden" represents a state outside time and entropy—because it was only after we left it that death became necessary and life a struggle—perhaps we could even say, rather whimsically, that man was expelled from Eden at precisely this velocity. But, like the angels in medieval thought, who live not in time but in an intermediate state called the *aevum* or "sempiternity," light still

7. Cited in Arthur Zajonc, *Catching the Light: The Entwined History of Light and Mind* (New York: Bantam Books, 1993), 270.

dwells in this timeless moment from which the rest of us have been expelled.[8]

Creation from Nothing

It is certainly tempting to make such speculative connections between the hypotheses of modern science and ancient metaphysics. Tempting, but dangerous. In this chapter, so far, I have tried to avoid it. But my somewhat haphazard survey of the current theories about light and space-time cannot but bring us to the threshold of a very big metaphysical question indeed: that of the creation itself. It gives us the background we need to appreciate the most well-established cosmogonic theory of modern times, but one that on the face of it appears to endorse the ancient doctrine of creation found in the first chapter of Genesis.

The Big Bang hypothesis is based on the idea that the entire material universe originated in an infinitely small point called a "singularity," and expanded from there to its present dimensions. The expansion continues—not just in the sense of an ordinary explosion, which affects the things contained within space-time, but as an expansion of space-time itself, along with all its contents. The hypothesis of this explosion, revealed in the progressive "red shift" or elongation of light waves sent out by more distant galaxies, was first put forward in 1927 by the Belgian physicist and Catholic priest Georges Lemaître, and soon after reinforced by the work of Edwin Hubble. It was eventually acclaimed by Einstein and became established as the standard model after 1933.

Interestingly, Lemaître's theory—the disintegration of a "primeval quantum of energy"—was in some ways the revival of a medieval idea put forward by the Oxford Franciscan Robert Grosseteste in the 13th century.[9] Following Aristotle, Grosseteste saw the world as based upon two principles: first form, and first matter. He speculated that the universe was created as a single point of light in mat-

8. See Wolfgang Smith, "Celestial Corporeality," in *Ancient Wisdom and Modern Misconceptions* (Tacoma, WA: Angelico Press / Sophia Perennis, 2013), 68–91.

9. See Marco Bersanelli, "Light in the Beginning," in O'Collins and Meyers, *Light from Light*, 82–5.

ter, a point which instantaneously propagated or multiplied itself in all directions as an expanding sphere, dragging first matter after itself to form the material universe in three dimensions, and rebounding from the point of maximum extension (the celestial firmament) to create the progressively denser planetary spheres and the four elements.

It was not a bad intuition.[10] Current thinking places the initial singularity at 13.77 billion years ago. The first phase of the universe was completely dark, but very dense and intensely hot—corresponding perhaps to the Bible's "formless void" with darkness over the deep (Gen. 1:2). The second phase was one of extremely rapid inflation—"a wind from God swept over the face of the waters"— with the waters in this case representing a primordial soup of electrons, photons, and protons that had condensed out of energy during inflation. The third phase took place 380,000 years after the bursting of the initial singularity: "Let there be light." The universe had by now cooled enough (to below 3000 K) to allow atoms to form, and thus became transparent to the large number of photons that were present. The resulting blaze of light would have shone in all directions, and is still visible today in the form of the Cosmic Microwave Background, the wavelength of this "fossil light" having since that time, by continuing expansion, been stretched into the microwave range, which is invisible to the human eye. (This, incidentally, explains why the night sky appears black rather than luminous.) Interestingly, the first seeds of "structure" in the universe are caused by sound vibrations—akin to music—developing out of the unevenness in the primordial soup of light and matter.[11]

10. Grosseteste, of course, could not know that the speed of light was not infinite, nor that light was electromagnetic radiation extending over a vast range of frequencies outside the capacity of the human eye, nor that time and space were two aspects of a single mathematical continuum.

11. See Bersanelli, "Light in the Beginning," 88–100. Since light takes time to travel, our telescopes are able to look back in time, and are able to see the "surface" where the first light was scattered by the first matter, a surface that encloses our entire universe although it is "much smaller than the regions of space that it contains" because, being earlier in time, it belongs to a smaller universe (Bersanelli, 98–99).

From Nothing

What does it mean, though, for light—or anything—to be created "out of nothing"? Where did the singularity "come from"? The very question is meaningless. If time and space both began with the singularity, there was no before and no elsewhere. As we confront this question, we are standing on the very threshold between physics and metaphysics.[12]

For Grosseteste, as in a more systematically worked-out way for Thomas Aquinas, the existence of a thing simply *is* its dependence upon God. To be created is to be ontologically dependent. It is not to be changed from a state of non-existence to a state of existence. Creation is not a change; it is a more radical beginning than that. It takes place "outside time," because time itself is a creature, or a dimension of created things—as Einstein saw, but not Newton, for whom space and time were in a sense "absolute"—an eternal receptacle into which certain things had been placed by God at a certain time. (It is this way of thinking of time that still to a large extent shapes our imagination, even though we are supposed to know better.)

There are consequently many mysteries around this notion of a "beginning" of time, and of tracing things back in the direction of—but never quite arriving at—an initial singularity. Science has no way of describing the beginning of things. The Bible uses poetry and metaphor, and is perhaps more accurate.

Even the word "nothing" (*nihil*), out of which the world is said by theologians to have been created, needs careful handling if we are not to mistake it for "something," namely an empty box into which something is put.

Even for modern physics, there is no such thing as complete "nothingness." Even a complete vacuum is said to be permeated by "fields of force" (electromagnetic, gravitational, etc.), or perhaps a "dark energy," shaping the space-time continuum. Put this together with the Uncertainty Principle, which means that the value or intensity of the field and its direction cannot both be fixed, and it

---

12. Strictly speaking, science cannot establish the existence of this (infinitely dense) singularity because the laws of nature as we know them break down as we approach t = 0.

follows that quantum field activity can never be reduced to zero but is always subject to random fluctuation.

In fact the energy in a "complete vacuum" is potentially infinite—assuming that space is a continuum and that all the variations in this fluctuating field cancel each other out overall. The existence of such "zero-point energy" in a vacuum has even been experimentally demonstrated (the Casimir effect). According to the inflationary universe model, the birth of the cosmos is based on such a quantum fluctuation in the field-value of nothingness.

You could say that the whole world—according to this theory—is a product of zero and infinity, in a sense poised between these two extremes. What can be manifested is not the infinite itself, but only the differences in energy between the "virtual particles" (quantum fluctuations) that happen to appear there. This enables scientists to handle the calculations without involving infinite quantities.

The theory again bears a strange resemblance to many ancient metaphysical theories that were advanced to explain the world as the result of an interplay between two Principles; such as (in Plato) the One and the Unlimited, or, in Grosseteste, Light and *Materia Prima*. The world of Being was the result of Form (the Form of the One or the Good) having been imposed upon something—Chaos perhaps.

In that case, however, the "infinite" principle was the lower one, which seems odd to us because of the notion of "positive infinity" that matured after Aristotle under the impact of Christian thought about God, and which we now take for granted. The concept of divinity as an "infinite oneness" or an "absolute maximum" than which nothing greater can be conceived was developed by Plotinus in the third century, Gregory of Nyssa in the fourth, Augustine and Dionysius in the fifth, John Scotus Eriugena in the ninth, Saint Anselm of Bec in the late twelfth, and in the fifteenth Cardinal Nicholas of Cusa (who introduced it into the realm of mathematics and geometry). Infinity, applied now to actuality rather than potentiality, was used to express the utter transcendence of God over creation.

For Aquinas, God is the unlimited act of Being (or supra-Being), inexhaustible "isness," unknowable by us directly until we come in the Beatific Vision to share by grace in God's knowledge of himself. God is "infinite" in the strict etymological sense, meaning without limits of any kind. If we wish (anachronistically) to reconcile this idea with Plato's original conception, we might say that the limits we wish to deny God are in this case merely any limitations imposed from without. As pure isness, he does in fact have "limit" in the (Platonic) sense of form—he is "the Form of the Good" or the One. All else, including everything created and everything numerical, is limited in the sense that its existence is "restricted" in relation to the divine plenitude: it participates or shares in one aspect or another of that plenitude but never completely. It may be indefinitely prolonged or extended in one respect or another, making it "indefinite," but it cannot be said to be infinite in the same sense as God. To the most limited of all we now give the name "zero."

To Infinity—and Beyond

The mathematician Georg Cantor (d. 1918) uses the word *infinite* to refer to a number defined as being greater than any finite number. In this sense of the word, the number of whole integers and the number of rational fractions are both "infinite" in the same degree. This is because for every fraction, no matter how many there may be of them, a new integer can always be assigned to it without ever running out of integers, and vice versa. In other words, you can use whole integers to number each item in a series of fractions.

The irrational numbers are rather different. Both integers and rational fractions of integers possess an inherent "graininess" because they are essentially definite, i.e. discontinuous with each other. Irrational numbers, on the other hand, occupy the spaces between each of the rationals, and fill them up continuously. The number of irrationals always exceeds that of the rationals, and therefore, according to Cantor, the "infinity" of the irrationals is of a different order.

The discovery of *orders of infinity* is highly significant for us. In fact Grosseteste had already anticipated this to some extent in his own theory of unequal infinities, but Cantor's set theory proves that there is an *infinite series* of infinities, each of a higher order than the last, right up to an "absolute" infinite, transcending all sets, which he identified with God. As he wrote: "The fear of infinity is a form of myopia that destroys the possibility of seeing the actual infinite, even though it in its highest form has created and sustains us, and in its secondary transfinite forms occurs all around us and even inhabits our minds."[13]

Cantor's analogical account creates a possible way to understand the reality of the world as distinct from that of God. He himself believed that his discoveries would be of great help to theologians; indeed he found support among Catholic scholars, and at one time appealed to Pope Leo XIII for support when his academic and Lutheran colleagues opposed his ideas. His work was one of those developments (like that of the non-Euclidean geometries) that helped to undermine a closed Kantian conception of the universe, and strengthened the sense of creation as contingent—that is to say, in order to find out how it is, we need to observe it, rather than deduce its nature or project our own conceptions upon it.

This also helps to answer a question that has been bubbling just under the surface: is the world some kind of automatic or "random" product or is there a meaning to it? Does the existence of the cosmos "add anything" to that of God? If it does not, why would God create it? Was it even possible that the world might not have existed?

---

13. Cantor himself was aware of the fact that one cannot consistently define a set of all transfinite sets, and for him this implied that "absolute infinity" was something that could only be approached by intuition or revelation. But David Hilbert and others made another objection, seeming to prove that even an infinity such as that of the irrationals cannot exist within a finite structure, such as the circumference of a circle or the diagonal of a rectangle, without bringing down the whole edifice of mathematics. Such infinities, which they term C-infinities, must be notional only. On the other hand, A-infinities and B-infinities—meaning negatively defined infinities (*un*-limited) and *potential* infinities—can exist. Robert J. Spitzer constructs from this an argument for God. Since no universe can be infinitely old, though it may *continue* indefinitely, the world must have had a beginning, if not an end. This points us to its dependence on an infinity that actually transcends the universe and time, namely the A-infinity (defined apophatically) we call "God." See Robert J. Spitzer, *New Proofs for the Existence of God: Contributions of Contemporary Physics and Philosophy* (Grand Rapids, MI: Eerdmans, 2010), 177–215.

Does it really come from "nothing"? (We will return to this later, because the fundamental Christian insight into creation is at stake.)

Monistic philosophies assume that the finite is strictly nothing in relation to the infinite, but this is not the case. Since there are orders of infinity, everything that exists can partake of infinity in a certain respect. In modern mathematics the multiplication of zero by infinity results not in zero, as one might expect, but in an *indefinite* quantity (reminiscent of Plato's *Apeiron*). As Robert Bolton puts it,

> Every finite quantity is in fact infinitely more than nothing, as one may illustrate from the way in which the equation $n \div \infty = 0$ gives rise to $\infty \times 0 = n$, where the finite quantity differs from zero by a factor of infinity. (This does not contradict the meaning of $n \div \infty = 0$ because this form of the equation establishes only the *relative* nullity of n, like that of a surface in relation to a volume, whether the surface and volume are both finite or both infinite.) . . . In all such cases, nullity in relation to a higher-order reality is all of a piece with the possession of a real degree of infinity. Because of this, there is a real sense in which the finite can add something to the infinite.[14]

The "infinite" is not in fact the "maximal conceivable quantity," he adds, for the *true infinite* (which represents Cantor's absolute infinite) is a combination of the infinite and the finite. "Thus the essential nature of the infinite is one of an inherent passing-beyond itself, while the infinite is also a primal reality whose nature is participated in by all forms of being as much as they participate the finite."

By introducing such distinctions into the concept of infinity, we begin to understand how instead of dissolving into God, the world may achieve in him an eternal existence ("the finite can add something to the infinite").[15] The ultimate resolution of the manifold

14. Robert Bolton, *The Order of the Ages: World History in the Light of a Universal Cosmogony* (Ghent, NY: Sophia Perennis, 2001), 32–3.

15. And yet at the same time, it can be true that in a sense, as Eckhart states, "people think that they have more if they have things together with God, than if they had God without things. But this is wrong, for all things added to God are not more than God alone" (cited in C.F. Kelley, *Meister Eckhart on Divine Knowledge* [New Haven: Yale University Press, 1977], 149). This is one paradox of "A-Infinity."

tensions of existence is not the silence of the One, but the music of the Trinity. At the same time, it overcomes the worry we had that the world's creation might be nothing but an arbitrary or "random" act. For if the world has some real existence of its own, an *infinity of its own degree,* by virtue of its participation in God's *actus purus,* then it too is "good" (as God pronounces it in Genesis) and the motivation for its creation is nothing other than love.

Let There Be…

We seem to have wandered some distance from thinking about light, but it is not so. It is simply that light has disappeared into the act of existence, the act of creation. The blaze of light that (perhaps) corresponds in the early universe to the moment of light's creation in Genesis is deceptive. The vast majority of the universe before that moment consisted already of photons, or light energy, even though it was locked in darkness. Light had already been created. *The light shone in darkness; but the darkness received it not.*[16]

When we employ physical metaphors to describe or allude to a spiritual reality—and light is one of the most popular of metaphors the world over—we tend to think of the physical referent as the most real of the two. In reality, the spiritual is higher in the scale of reality, and physical light is nothing but a shadow of God's intelligible self-communication. The true light, the light of heaven, is the archetype of which the light of the stars, and the light of torches and candles, the light that we can measure and manipulate, is a participating symbol.

Once this is understood, we look at the world in a different way. Even before the creation or first appearance of light in space and time, God's eternal light filled the heavens. The light we see is manifested for a purpose. It exists to turn our souls towards the glory of the infinite, which we cannot see until we become united with it. *Let the light of your face shine upon us, O Lord* (Ps. 4:6).

---

16. John 1:5. The translation is by John Lingard.

A Science of the Real

Throughout the past century the "new physics" of Bohr, Planck, Einstein, Heisenberg, and Schrödinger provided a congenial breeding-ground for mystical philosophies of all description.[1] Some of these are bizarre. Many are deeply flawed. But to some of us it seems that the door of science is again open to the idea of levels of being, to ontology and final causation—elements in ancient cosmology that remain perennially valid. This possibility is important not least because of the urgent need to uncover (and treat) the deep roots of the environmental crisis, and to foster in our culture a less aggressive, more harmonious relationship with nature.

Among the distinguished Catholic theologians of the past century it is probably Hans Urs von Balthasar who most clearly saw the need not just for a *nouvelle théologie* but for a new kind of science, a science that is more at peace with metaphysics. This science in fact "has its ready-made metaphysics in Aquinas' doctrine of order and relation," though to make that true Thomism needs to be developed in certain important respects.[2] In the second decade of the 21st century, the thinkers associated with the journal *Communio* (founded in 1972 by Balthasar, along with Joseph Ratzinger, Henri de Lubac, and Louis Bouyer) and with the Radical Orthodoxy movement both

---

1. See Ken Wilber, *Quantum Questions: Mystical Writings of the World's Great Physicists* (Boulder, CO: Shambhala, 1984). Most such speculations fall into pantheism, fail to take account of the Fall, and negate the importance of the human, according to Antoine Faivre in *Access to Western Esotericism* (State University of New York Press, 1994), 275–96.

2. Hans Urs von Balthasar, *The Glory of the Lord: A Theological Aesthetics, Volumes I–VII*, IV (Edinburgh and San Francisco: T&T Clark and Ignatius Press, 1982–91), 411. For one view of the differences between Balthasar and Thomas see James M. Buckley, "Balthasar's Use of the Theology of Aquinas," *The Thomist* (October 1995). Cf. James P. Kow, "The Christian Distinction: The Others," in *Communio* (Winter 1993).

within and outside the Catholic Church, seem to be best character-ized as a new flowering of "Christian Platonism" or "Postmodern Augustinian Thomism"; and as far as I can see this is the most promising basis for a renewed Christian cosmology. In the words of Adrian Pabst, an able exponent of this emerging consensus, "Even though medieval Christendom was divided and ultimately lost, Christian Neo-Platonist theology was never refuted. The unrealized potential of this tradition contrasts with the crisis of liberalism in its secular or religious guise."[3]

In the first chapter I tried to explore the notion of light or "radi-ance" in modern physics and came up against certain metaphysical barriers. But what I found was already intriguing. What I have not done is present a very complete view of modern physics. Our mean-dering path has been concerned mostly with the theory of relativity and less with quantum mechanics—both, in a sense, the children of Einstein, but to a large extent at odds with one another. This ten-sion needs to be explained, and it will better set the scene for the next step in our journey.

Relativity gives us a very distinctive account of gravity. In the cos-mos as described by Einstein, to be at rest is to be following a path called a "geodesic" in space-time. The geodesic at its most basic involves extension through time but not space. If I am at rest, I am simply existing through time and not moving spatially. But the presence of matter causes the shape of space-time to be curved (intriguingly, the reason for this remains unclear). The effect of a large mass like the earth on the geodesics is such as to redefine my state of rest as one of movement "downwards," towards the center of the mass. This is where I would naturally go if no other force was acting upon me. In fact, another force is acting to prevent me, namely all the atomic forces composing the matter that is blocking my way to the center of the earth. The force of gravity that I feel pinning me to the ground is not in fact a force attracting me down-wards, but one forcing me upwards.

---

3. Adrian Pabst *Metaphysics: The Creation of Hierarchy* (Grand Rapids, MI: Eer-dmans, 2012), 443. See also Tracey Rowland, *Benedict XVI: A Guide for the Perplexed* (London: T&T Clark, 2010).

All very counter-intuitive, and rather exciting for that reason. The problem is that, despite the accuracy with which distortions in space-time can be measured, this "geometrical" account of the large scale does not fit with the other main branch of modern physics just mentioned, namely quantum field theory, which has also proved to be an extremely accurate description of the universe on the small scale (that is, of the particles and energies that make it up). A book called *On Space and Time*[4] refers to this uncomfortable fact as the big "hole in the heart of science"—the fact that we "do not honestly know the true nature of space and time." The editor admits that we not only do not know, we "do not even have a theory to test about this deepest layer of physics." Physicists are struggling to unify the two halves of physics in a "quantum theory of gravity," as Einstein himself struggled to do till the end of his life, but the problem seems intractable. (A recent proposal involves situating space-time itself in something higher: an 8-dimensional "phase space" containing all possible values of position, time, energy, and momentum.)

Nor is this the only hole in science, since 96% of the mass of the universe seems to be missing, or (another way of putting it) is made up of "dark energy" and "dark matter" that no one knows much about.[5] That is quite a large gap. It may indicate that some radical thinking is required to arrive at a new paradigm. But even "thinking" may not be enough. What is really needed is thinking in conjunction with imagining. It was by trying to imagine catching up with light that Einstein was led to relativity. The theory did not simply emerge from a mathematical deduction; it involved a new way of looking at things.

The editor of *On Space and Time*, Shahn Majid, suggests that a dialogue is needed on the most fundamental questions not simply among physicists, but between scientists and the wider public—

---

4. Shahn Majid (ed.), *On Space and Time* (Cambridge University Press, 2008).

5. Dark energy supposedly accounts for the fact that the universal expansion is speeding up—until eventually stars and galaxies are moving apart faster than light, since the speed-of-light barrier does not apply when space itself is expanding.

because the big ideas in science come from "sitting in cafes, from art, from life."[6]

In order to foster that conversation, I want to step back in this chapter, albeit briefly, from the question of light and its creation, and look at the history of science more broadly, and where it might be going. This will prepare us in the next chapter to focus on the biological sciences and the theory of evolution, and more general considerations about the nature of life and of nature herself.

The Rise and Fall of Mechanism

Modern science arose within a Christian milieu, bringing in its train a multitude of benefits, as well as the ecological and other crises for which Christians (therefore) must bear some considerable responsibility. That the birth of science in Europe was not a matter of mere chance but was intrinsically related to the nature of the synthesis of Biblical faith and Greek philosophy has been argued persuasively by Pierre Duhem and Stanley Jaki.[7] In order for anything like modern science to arise, it was necessary to believe in both the intelligibility of the cosmos and its contingency—both the fact that it *made sense*, and the fact that it *might not have existed*. Intelligibility alone would lead to the priority of deduction over induction, as in the ancient philosophies of nature where an observed reality (such as the motion of the planets) had to be conformed to *a priori* structures (such as the perfect circle). Contingency, or the dependence of the cosmos on the decision of a Creator to bring into existence one of many equally possible worlds, meant that a certain priority had to be given to empirical observation, in order to find out what form this particular cosmos had in fact taken. The structure and harmony of the world thus revealed could shed light on the wisdom of its Creator. Aspects of that wisdom could be known, perhaps, in no other way.

The seeds of the modern scientific enterprise were sown in the

6. Majid's thoughts then move in the direction of what he calls "Relative Realism," in which the observed reality and the observer are mutually determined in what he calls a "self-representing universe."

7. See, e.g., S.L. Jaki, *The Road of Science and the Ways to God* (University of Chicago Press, 1978).

thought of Scholastics such as Albert, Thomas, and Bonaventure. God, who made the human eye and all that it looks out upon, did so (they believed) in order to reveal something of himself—as it might be, some thought, to prepare us for the fuller revelation he would make in Christ. The universe as observed by the naked senses is a book of symbols waiting to be read; it is an act of self-expression by God, a theophany imbued throughout with the intelligibility of the divine Logos. To be real, to exist at all, is therefore to participate in a divine act of communication.[8] Josef Pieper, a twentieth-century follower of St. Thomas, puts it this way: "All that exists, because it exists, is ordered towards a knowing mind, even towards the finite human mind. This means, not only is the eye sun-related, the sun as well is eye-related; all that has being is mind-related in its most intrinsic core. Mind and being are interconnected."[9] All things are therefore intrinsically "knowable." At the same time, they are *unfathomable* because they are rooted in God: their full truth is their nature as creatively known not by us, but by God.

The intellectual and spiritual balance evident in this attitude was not preserved. By separating real from rational entities, science from faith and God from nature, the *via moderna* of the nominalist philosophers from the 14th century onwards undermined natural theology and metaphysics. By arguing that nothing can exist but individual objects, it effectively eliminated the "vertical" or "interior" dimension of reality—the dimension of metaphysical form, final causality, and divine providence—and with that the last remaining possibility of a contemplative science. The world's

---

8. Seyyed Hossein Nasr points out that, as a contemplative or symbolic cosmology, Ptolemaic astronomy was never fully invalidated by the discovery that the earth moves round the sun. As conscious beings, we stand at the center of the world looking out: that is part of what it means to be a created reflection of divinity. To extend the range of our vision does not make a *symbolic* cosmology impossible, although to interpret correctly what is found calls for a spiritual preparation that is lacking in modern science. See his *The Encounter of Man and Nature* (London: George Allen & Unwin, 1968) and *Religion and the Order of Nature* (Oxford University Press, 1996).

9. J. Pieper, *Living the Truth* (San Francisco: Ignatius Press, 1989), 59.

rational coherence could thereafter only be maintained by supposing a strict conformity with mathematical laws, imposed from without by the Creator or else subsisting without reason (as, later, in postmodernism). After Galileo, the *consciousness of the observer* could no longer be recognized as an intrinsic part of reality, and was relegated to the realm of the merely subjective, along with all those "secondary qualities" that did not lend themselves to objective measurement. Science had been transformed into a search for the mathematical models sufficient to account for the motion and transformation of matter. The divorce of faith and reason was consolidated by the Reformation, while the sense of God's presence in nature became increasingly tenuous and ghostly with the erosion of the concept of sacrament.[10]

By the seventeenth century science was an activity with a definite practical purpose. Its goal, as formulated by Francis Bacon, was the subjugation of the whole natural realm to the service of man. Scientific method offered results of such an eminently practical kind that it appealed not only to the scientists themselves, but to the new patrons of science, namely merchants and bankers, for whom the most important reality consisted in that which could be accumulated and counted.[11] The last three hundred years have consequently been an increasingly empirical rather than metaphysical

---

10. For the role particularly of nominalism and voluntarism in the shaping of modern science and attitudes to nature see Louis Dupré, *Passage to Modernity* (New Haven and London: Yale University Press, 1993); E. Gilson, *History of Christian Philosophy in the Middle Ages* (London: Sheed & Ward, 1955), Part 11; Kenneth L. Schmitz, *At the Center of the Human Drama* (Washington, DC: Catholic University of America Press, 1993), 130–37; Balthasar, *Glory of the Lord*, V, 28–9, 452; Jeremy Naydler, "The Regeneration of Realism and the Recovery of a Science of Qualities" (*International Philosophical Quarterly*, 23, 1983, 155–72); and Peter Henrici, S.J., "Modernity and Christianity," *Communio* (Summer 1990). Cf. Harold P. Nebelsick, *Renaissance and Reformation and the Rise of Science* (Edinburgh: T&T Clark, 1992). For Nebelsick, as a Protestant, the symbolic "sacramental" value of nature is merely a hangover from Platonist otherworldliness; science must assert the *intrinsic* value of particulars (17).

11. Louis Bouyer, *Cosmos: The World and the Glory of God* (Petersham, MA: St. Bede's Publications, 1988), 115.

age: priority has been accorded to externals, to quantities, to experimental evidence (although this emphasis on the material externals masked a parallel absolutization of human consciousness as the sole source of certitude and value).

Once Charles Darwin had extended the reductionistic method of the new sciences to the human and social realm, emphasizing the continuity between animate and inanimate matter, between animal and human life, the final triumph of nominalism seemed to be only a matter of time. The various animal species were merely *names*: nothing prevented a gradual drift from one category to another, as each new generation diverged from its predecessors. Hence the fervor with which Darwin in his correspondence with Charles Lyell defended "gradualism" against any suggestion that species might have originated by sudden mutation. The controversy resurfaces today: Stephen Jay Gould's "punctuated equilibrium" seems to imply a reality to the species as distinct from the individual. Gould's neo-Darwinist opponents, such as Daniel Dennett, view this reintroduction of the "intelligible essence" with great suspicion—even when it is couched in terms that suggest a purely material explanation for the essence itself.

It is notable also that, when faced with evidence against a purely Darwinian evolutionary process, Dennett's strategy is to respond with the following admission: "I cannot (yet) see how to refute this objection, or overcome this difficulty, but since I cannot imagine how anything other than natural selection could be the cause of the effects, I will have to assume that the objection is spurious; somehow natural selection must be sufficient to explain the effects."[12]

Of course, this is standard scientific procedure: you cannot abandon a good working hypothesis at the first sign of difficulty. However, more lies behind his enthusiasm for Darwinism than this: it is bound up with an emotional commitment to materialist atheism. If there is a place for the great religious traditions, he writes, it is in "cultural zoos" for those who still need them. Similarly, for Richard

---

12. Daniel Dennett, *Darwin's Dangerous Idea: Evolution and the Meanings of Life* (Harmondsworth: Allen Lane, The Penguin Press, 1995), 47.

Dawkins it is clear that DNA is the bedrock of reality, and needs no ultimate explanation in terms of final or formal cause: in an abdication of reason that amounts to an unconscious parody of existential Thomism he asserts that "DNA itself just *is*."[13] We will return to the question of evolution in the next chapter.

The modern critics of Darwin, or at least of the reductionistic sociobiology that grew from his work, have drawn strength and inspiration from recent developments in the physical sciences, and particularly from the new physics.[14] According to the view of "classical" (nineteenth-century) physics (setting aside the reaction of the Romantics to this state of affairs), the universe was like a giant machine. It could best be studied by analyzing it into component parts, and isolating these as far as possible under controlled laboratory conditions. Since Galileo, the scientist was supposed to be a detached observer, recording what took place in any experiment without personal bias and without interfering in any way with the result. The twentieth century changed this completely, bringing the consciousness of the observer back into the picture.

The Quantum World

The uncertainty principle formulated by Werner Heisenberg in 1927 established a new paradigm for scientific knowledge, making it axiomatic that any act of observation will change what is being observed. No one can establish by observation both the position and momentum of a given particle: determine location and you affect velocity. At this sub-microscopic level, at least, the observer is no longer detached: he or she has become a *participant* in the sys-

13. Cited in Colin Grant, "The Gregarious Metaphor of the Selfish Gene," *Religious Studies* 27, 431–450.

14. M. Polanyi's critique of neo-Darwinism in *Personal Knowledge: Towards a Post-Critical Philosophy* (University of Chicago Press, 1958)—see especially Chapter 13 on "emergence"—foreshadowed that in S.J. Gould's *The Panda's Thumb* (New York: W.W. Norton, 1980) and the provocative question posed in 1981 by the British paleontologist Colin Patterson at the American Museum of Natural History: "Can you tell me anything about evolution, any one thing, that is true?" Patterson is an exponent of "transformed cladistics": the systematic classification of the hierarchies of organisms in nature without regard for the theory of evolution.

tem. The consciousness of the observer, exiled from the realm of reality after Galileo, had returned with a vengeance. The idea of "participation" now runs all the way through physics. According to quantum theory, particles are not solid objects resembling billiard balls; they may act as solids in some circumstances but like waves in others. What they are in themselves, we are now told, is not our concern, for we can know them only insofar as they participate in events with us. Matter is a form of energy; time is inseparable from space; and as we have seen, gravity results from the curvature of space-time by matter.

This participatory physics, however, raises the question of "reality" in an acute form. According to the Copenhagen interpretation of quantum mechanics, physics is not concerned with a supposed underlying reality, only with hypotheses or theories designed to correlate the observed results of experiments. "There is no quantum world. There is only an abstract quantum description" (Niels Bohr, 1927). This interpretation was strenuously resisted by Albert Einstein, the discoverer of the Quantum, who, with colleagues Boris Podolsky and Nathan Rosen devised in 1935 a thought experiment to place physicists on the horns of a painful dilemma. In the "EPR" experiment, two particles are correlated by an interaction that takes place before their separation. Thereafter, according to Heisenberg's principle, the position of one particle cannot be determined without instantly determining also the position of the other, no matter where it happens to be—even on the other side of the universe. It is as though information could fly faster than light from one particle to another, "telling" the second particle where to be. Thus Einstein confronted his fellow-physicists with the choice of either positing some kind of "spooky action at a distance," or abandoning the interpretation that led to it.

Unfortunately for Einstein, not only was "non-locality" eventually established (by Bell's Theorem) as an intrinsic feature of the quantum world at a theoretical level, but in the early 1980s it was proved by Alain Aspect and others that such "spooky" correlations do in fact occur; moreover the design of the experiment eliminated the possibility that this could be the result of the particles *having a definite position before they were measured*. Apparently, before being measured a particle was "neither here nor there": it was in what came to be called a "superposition" of states, and only the act of measurement "collapsed the probability wave" into one state or the other. The absurdity of this is illustrated by another thought-experiment, the Cat Paradox devised by Erwin Schrödinger. If the life of a cat is made dependent upon the decay of an atomic nucleus, but that nucleus exists in a superposition of states, then the cat itself must be in a superposition of states, neither alive nor dead, until it happens to be observed.[15]

The solution to the problem of non-locality that seems to be gaining most traction—and which offers some hope of reconciling relativity with quantum mechanics in a quantum theory of gravity (the current golden prize of physics)—involves "non-commutative geometry," a kind of "pregeometry" that describes space not in terms of a continuum made up of points, but of algebraic equations. It makes things impossible to visualize, but neatly bypasses the problematic aspect of non-locality, which depends on space-time being made up of points in a coordinate system. For Michael Heller,

---

15. One significant but controversial attempt to counter the anti-realism coming out of Bohr's Copenhagen school was the ontological interpretation of quantum theory developed by David Bohm, *Wholeness and the Implicate Order* (London: RKP, 1980), who posited hidden variables to account for apparent indeterminacy, and an "undivided wholeness" or state of unity prior to all division across time and space to account for non-locality. For theological commentary see David L. Schindler (ed.), *Beyond Mechanism: The Universe in Recent Physics and Catholic Thought* (Lanham, MD: University Press of America, 1986). Other significant Catholic commentators on this theory (and quantum physics in general) are Stanley Jaki OSB and Peter Hodgson, who defended traditional realism against the Copenhagen philosophy of "probabilistic truth," Jaki writing for example (in a 1985 review of John Polkinghorne), "It still remains a colossal fallacy in logic to argue, with an eye on Heisenberg's uncertainty principle, that if an interaction cannot be measured exactly, it cannot take place exactly. The fallacy is the confusion of the operational and ontological levels." Jaki was fond of Einstein's 1931 statement, "Belief in an external world independent of the perceiving subject is the basis of all natural science." Peter Hodgson in *Science and Belief in the Nuclear Age* (Ave Maria, FL: Sapientia Press, 2005) pins his hopes on the further refinement of realist rather than positivist accounts of the quantum world, such as stochastic electrodynamics (203–6). On all these questions, see Stephen M. Barr, *Modern Physics and Ancient Faith* (South Bend, IN: University of Notre Dame Press, 2003).

it can give us an insight into the "timeless dynamics" of a world in some sense prior to the one we see—the world of God's creation.[16]

The Catholic mathematical physicist Wolfgang Smith traces these extreme examples of so-called "quantum strangeness" to the loss of the Aristotelian-Thomistic distinction between form and matter, and more fundamentally to that between actuality and potency. Like A.N. Whitehead, he attributes the shipwreck of modern thought to the Cartesian bifurcation between subjective and objective, between *res cogitans* and *res extensa*. This took the place of St. Thomas' subtler metaphysical distinction, and the result was a physical reductionism quite simply incompatible with reality. The incompatibility reveals itself both in the various quantum paradoxes and in the need to construct ever more bizarre ontologies to escape from these. Smith shows that the paradoxes in question simply disappear once we realize that the "physical" world—by which he means the quantitative world, as conceived and measured by the physicist—is mere potentiality in relation to the "corporeal" world perceived in human consciousness.

Roughly, according to Smith the "physical" world discovered and described by modern science occupies a distinct ontological level in a spectrum that runs from pure Act (God) to Potency (*materia prima*, or the "lower waters" of Genesis). It is below the corporeal world of everyday experience, within which our measuring instruments are situated, but above the *materia prima*. In fact Smith identifies it with the *materia secunda signata quantitate*, as Werner Heisenberg himself put it, "just in the middle between possibility and reality." The indetermination and chaos that have been made so much of in the quantum world pertain to the element of potency in all things, and the relationship between potency and act is illustrated by the "collapse of the wave function" which takes place when

---

16. Heller concludes, after a discussion of this approach, "It would be ridiculous even to try to construct a model of God's interaction with the world on the basis of our attempts to create a theory of quantum gravity (or any other mathematical model), but it would be equally unreasonable not to notice that the above theological speculations seem less extravagant if read with the consciousness that even more abstract ideas can be found in the most exact among exact sciences" (Majid [ed.], *On Space and Time* [Cambridge University Press, 2008], 268).

an observation is made. The corporeal domain itself is determined by substantial forms of a higher order, including those of living organisms and of Life as such.

Smith's work may not be widely known or accepted, but it has the merit of avoiding another absurdity: that of multiple universes. This fashionable theory is based on the idea that every quantum discontinuity engenders two parallel but diverging realities: for every two possible but mutually exclusive outcomes both occur, and every possible universe exists. The fact that this would violate one of the core principles of science, the conservation of energy, remains a problem for its supporters, but like the "inflationary universe" theory (that the world originated as a random fluctuation in a primal vacuum) or the "no boundary" hypothesis (that the world, though finite, has no temporal boundary or beginning), it is regularly seized upon as a way to dispense with the unacceptable conclusion that the world needs a cause or a Creator. The laws of this universe appear to be fine-tuned to permit human life (more than forty such cases of fine-tuning have been identified): if a multitude of lifeless universes exist, each governed by other laws, it would no longer seem so surprising. All such attempts to undermine theism suffer from the same flaw, which we have already touched upon: a failure to understand that the doctrine of Creation is designed to account for *existence as such*, not for the beginning of a process, and for the existence of the laws of physics as much as that of the things we see and touch.[17]

In Smith's account, the act of measuring (of course basic to modern science) is itself not somehow "neutral" but a *creative act* and a determination of reality. For the physicist must always employ a corporeal instrument that is "in act" to decide which of two possible states or positions of a particle applies. In so doing he necessarily collapses what was merely potential into a single definite outcome.

17. See W. Smith, *The Quantum Enigma: Finding the Hidden Key* (Tacoma, WA: Angelico Press/Sophia Perennis, 2011). William A. Wallace published a sympathetic response in "Thomism and the Quantum Enigma," *The Thomist* (July 1997), as did Kenneth M. Batinovich in *The Chesterton Review* (November 1997) and S. H. Nasr in *Sophia: A Journal of Traditional Studies* (Summer 1997). Cf. William E. Carroll, "Thomas Aquinas and Big Bang Cosmology," *Sapientia* 53 (1998).

Every such collapse of probability into actuality echoes by analogy the divine act of creation *in principio*: that ultimate discontinuity which forever grounds the unity of the two ontological domains. Our participation in this "open" universe reflects, in its own way, the creative involvement of God in its creation and conservation. Indeterminacy is resolved in favor of "vertical causation" rather than randomness. Indeed, Smith writes, quantum discontinuity "can now be understood by analogy to the phenomenon of artistic production" (96). Given a further distinction between ontological realms "below" and "above" the corporeal, Smith suggests that the denial of bifurcation would lead to the recovery of the concept of (non-mathematical) substantial forms in science, and thus a renewed appreciation of the role of "qualities" in the generation of order and design.[18]

A New Science of Living Nature?

In general terms we may say that in the new physics the world is increasingly compared to an *organism*, rather than a machine. That is to say, it is a pattern of relationships, preserving itself in a meaningful homeostasis or equilibrium in the midst of change, while the matter of which it is composed is in constant flux. The development of the sciences of organization—cybernetics and General Systems Theory—established a conceptual framework for the study of systems as such: that is, of wholes whose properties depend not just on the sum of their parts but on their interrelationships.[19] But this in turn made theoreticians increasingly aware of the need for some kind of metaphysics; hence the various attempts to find illumination from Eastern religious philosophy, Western Hermeticism, and

---

18. According to Smith's interpretation of Bohm, the pilot wave associated with every quantum particle must belong not to the "physical" realm as he has previously defined it, but to a "supra-"corporeal level of being, beyond which lie the spiritual archetypes and the Logos at the center of creation.

19. Morris Berman, in *The Reenchantment of the World* (Ithaca, NY: Cornell University Press, 1981), looks to cybernetics and the thought of Gregory Bateson for a scientific holism capable of overcoming bifurcation. Fritjof Capra, in *The Web of Life* (London: HarperCollins, 1996), turns to Bateson and Humberto Maturana.

German Romanticism.[20] It led also, in a few cases, to the re-application of certain key ideas from the Aristotelian-Thomistic tradition.

What we are considering is the possibility of what C.S. Lewis in *The Abolition of Man* calls "a new Natural Philosophy, continually conscious that the 'natural object' produced by analysis and abstraction [Smith's "physical" as distinct from "corporeal" world] is not reality but only a view, and always correcting the abstraction."[21] In this very same line of thought, Hans Urs von Balthasar aims to unite the aesthetics of St. Thomas with Goethe's "gentle empiricism." He believes that a "true science of living nature as, for instance, Goethe strove for in his morphology" is possible; it would "combine the cool precision of scientific research with a constant awareness of the totality apparent only to the eye of reverence, the poetic-religious eye, the ancient sense for the cosmos."[22]

There can be no question of theology dictating to physics (or biology) what it will find. Physical theories cannot be deduced from the data of Revelation: faith cannot simply take over from reason, or muscle it aside. Nevertheless, theology may not be written off by science as having no bearing on its own methodology, or its conception of an objective world. As David Schindler puts it: "an *anticipation of the truth of something like an organismic understanding of the cosmos*

---

20. An interesting attempt has been made by physicist Basarab Nicolescu in *Science, Meaning and Evolution* (New York: Parabola Books, 1991) to understand the ontology of the quantum world in terms of Jacob Boehme's "sevenfold cycle" (reading him not as a theologian, but as a cosmographer expressing himself mythologically). Wolfgang Smith is in sympathy with this reading of Boehme. More pertinent here is the growing interest in Goethe's scientific method. J. von Goethe (1749–1832), best known as a poet, was also a leading figure in the Romantic reaction against Newtonian science. His theory of color and work on plant morphology has long been ridiculed by the scientific establishment, but is now being reassessed: see H. Bortoft, *The Wholeness of Nature: Goethe's Way of Science* (Hudson, NY, and Edinburgh: Lindisfarne and Floris Books, 1996), 214–15; A. Zajonc, *Catching the Light* (New York: Bantam, 1993); J. Naydler (ed.), *Goethe on Science: An Anthology of Goethe's Scientific Writings* (Edinburgh: Floris Books, 1996). See also the article by Naydler mentioned previously.

21. C.S. Lewis, *The Abolition of Man* (London: Geoffrey Bles, 1946), 47.

22. Balthasar, *Glory of the Lord*, I, 447; V, 363.

is already given in our christological faith."[23] The whole point of the perspective described here is that the connection between subjective and objective is no longer arbitrary (as for Cartesian science)[24] but *intrinsic*: knower and known, while eternally distinct, belong to one single reality, and the meaning at the centre of that reality is the Person of the Logos. The unity-in-distinction of the Trinity is the basis for an analogy that runs right through creation as a kind of watermark: the analogy of "spousal" union between subject and object, self and other. The life of love revealed in Christ promises to each of us no mere absorption into the Beloved, but our own integrity and fulfillment in the very measure we give ourselves away.

The cultural implications of this principle are endless. In particular, it guarantees the legitimate autonomy of reason, and of scientific research, even as it overcomes the separation between science and religion.[25] If love is the deepest meaning of the objective universe, the scientist and the mathematician are fully vindicated in their intuition that beauty (or "elegance") must somehow be the signature of truth. Central to Balthasar's thought is the *Gestalt* that enables a recovery of the notion of substantial form, and it is this which makes beauty possible.[26] In the first volume of *The Glory of the Lord*, he writes: "every created thing is a manifestation of itself (the more intensively the higher it ranks): the representation of its own depths, the surface of its own ground, the word from its essential core; and upon this essential movement of being (from its interior to its exterior) are founded the good, the true, and the beautiful."[27] Beauty unites not only truth with goodness, but also observer with

23. David L. Schindler, *Heart of the World, Center of the Church* (Grand Rapids and Edinburgh: Eerdmans and T&T Clark, 1996), 214.

24. The Cartesian error has been unmasked by several modern authors, including Michael Polanyi in the work already mentioned, and more recently by Catherine Pickstock in her book *After Writing* (Oxford: Blackwell, 1998), 57–74: for Descartes, she says, "Representation is now prior to ontology."

25. See Schindler, *Heart of the World*, e.g., 19–29, 212–20.

26. He was influenced here not only by Goethe but by Brentano's pupil, the musician C. von Ehrenfels: see Francesca A. Murphy, *Christ the Form of Beauty* (Edinburgh: T&T Clark, 1995), 134.

27. Balthasar, *Glory of the Lord*, I, 610.

observed. Knowledge in its full sense is found only in this marriage or compenetration of knower and known. Beauty is what makes the true attractive to us; what draws the will towards it. But this means that it is a function of *love*, a response of love called forth by what is received in *the given* by one who is disposed to gratitude.

This implies a restoration of the sense of natural interiority, of the metaphysical "depth" to all things, by which the Giver is in the Gift.[28] The world must be given back this sacramental quality, its dimension of mystery, which was too hastily stripped from it by the successors of nominalism. All identities—from that of numbers in mathematics to that of corporeal objects such as apples and pears, and above all human persons—are fundamentally identities-in-relation, existing as gifts one to another, and ultimately as gifts from one divine Person to another. Such a reorientation, he thinks, would spell the final demise of mechanism as the paradigm of cosmic order: the end of seeking to understand a thing by breaking it into parts and reassembling these in a purely extrinsic order.

"We have to feel our way back," he writes; "we have to overcome a certain blindness to the primal value of being. This sick blindness is called Positivism, and it arises from regarding reality as raising no questions, being 'just there'; for the phrase 'the given' already says too much, since there is no one who 'gives.' In fact (from a Positivist point of view) the only question that arises is: what can we do with this material?"[29]

Thus the secular conception of the world culminates no longer in contemplation, but in technology, and with the whole gamut of

---

28. K.L. Schmitz, *The Gift* (Marquette University Press, 1982), 58, 90; also "The First Principle of Personal Becoming," in *Review of Metaphysics* 47 (June 1994). As we shall see later, this sheds light also on *transubstantiation*, which has been wrongly regarded as making sense only within the metaphysics of Aristotle.

29. Hans Urs von Balthasar, *Theo-Drama: Theological Dramatic Theory, Volumes I–V*, II (San Francisco: Ignatius Press, 1988-98), 286. In Vol. IV he writes that human power unintegrated with the fundamental act of prayer "becomes a tyranny over the earth, exploiting it and heedlessly laying it waste" (159). These remarks on "technocracy," which he relates to the "Battle of the Logos" in world history, may be expanded and applied to other areas of culture, from art to economics. Cf. Schindler, *Heart of the World*, 161–76.

problems caused by the Baconian will to power. Against the "sick blindness" of positivism Balthasar projects the possibility of a visionary science in which empirical observation and quantitative description would be integrated within a metaphysics of gift. The attitude of a science that takes this insight seriously would have to be completely changed; fascination with technology need not usurp the place of contemplative wonder. The power granted to such a science would no longer be the power to degrade and destroy, but the power of beauty to heal and unite.

Vertical Evolution

According to John Locke, writing in 1690, it is impossible to conceive that "bare incogitative Matter should produce a thinking intelligent Being," such as Man. A century later, the Scottish philosopher David Hume played with the idea that what he called the "continual motion of matter" might produce all the appearances of "wisdom and contrivance" in the universe—but in the end, when it came right down to it, he could not take his own idea seriously.

It was another century before the European Enlightenment finally gave birth to what we now call the theory of *evolution by natural selection*, associated primarily with the name of Charles Darwin (although the word "evolution" itself came from Herbert Spencer). Articulated, clarified, qualified and deepened by others, this idea has swept aside the essentialist, dualistic, and teleological philosophies of the Middle Ages, and attempted to explain the origins of mind and morality in a blind, purposeless, and mechanical process starting from nothing at all.

As if in order to remove the last leg on which a religious believer or creationist might try to stand, Daniel Dennett in his bestselling book *Darwin's Dangerous Idea* suggests that even the *laws of nature* governing the origin of species may have themselves evolved from absolute chaos through a process of trial and error, extending through a series of alternative and successive universes governed by quite different laws and constants, in many of which the evolution of life would have been impossible. Design can emerge from order and order from chaos "via an algorithmic process that makes no use of pre-existing Mind." Thus for Dennett, the idea of evolution by natural selection at least potentially "unifies all of biology and the history of our planet into a single grand story."

Despite the anti-religious virulence of such writers, Catholics generally, from the Pope down, prefer to avoid head-on confrontation. Most have been happy to accept the current scientific view that the world is millions of years old, and find relief in the fact that the Big Bang hypothesis seems to chime so well with the Genesis account of creation from nothing.[1] The only non-negotiable items on which the authorities of the Church have continued to insist in recent years are the direct creation by God of the human soul,[2] and the derivation of the whole human race from a single couple (Adam and Eve). For the moment, neither of these Catholic dogmas seem particularly problematic. The empirical evidence seems to be in favor of monogenism (the genetic origin of the present human race from one ancestral couple rather than several), while the divine creation of the soul is open to a conveniently wide range of interpretations.

This friendly truce, however, is not likely to continue. The tendency in the evolutionist camp is always to turn the theory of evolution into something more than it is, indeed to transform it into a substitute for religion, as the philosopher Mary Midgley showed in her book *Evolution as a Religion*. E.F. Schumacher wrote in *A Guide for the Perplexed* (1977), "Evolutionism is not science; it is science fiction, even a kind of hoax. It is a hoax that has succeeded too well and has imprisoned modern man in what looks like an irreconcilable conflict between 'science' and 'religion.'" Furthermore, on the Catholic side there persists an uneasy feeling that something important has been lost or forgotten; that the Church Fathers would perhaps not have looked so kindly on the present compromise.

As we saw earlier, the quasi-religious fervor with which Darwin's "grand story" has been promoted by some sectors of the intellectual establishment suggests that what is at stake here is more than meets the eye. The theory does not merely happen to be true: in a sense, for many people, it *has to be true*, for no other type of explanation

---

1. We should remember, however, that all scientific theories are provisional. Those who tie their theology too closely to the latest consensus in science usually live to regret it. The arguments for creation *ex nihilo* (out of nothing) are quite independent of the duration of the created order.

2. "Theories of evolution which, in accordance with the philosophies inspiring them, consider the spirit as emerging from the forces of living matter or as a mere epiphenomenon of this matter, are incompatible with the truth about man," according to Pope John Paul II in 1996.

43

would be acceptable to the modern mind. What is at stake is modernity itself, for which evolution provides an overarching paradigm. For that reason it deserves more detailed (and critical) examination here.

The Mainstream Theory

Evolutionary theory aims to explain the origin of life and all its present variety of forms: that is, the whole range of individual organisms normally categorized into species, genus, family, and kingdom. It postulates the emergence of complex living organisms from non-living matter by way of a much smaller number of less complex ancestors. It claims that all life on earth can be traced back to one primitive organism, developing spontaneously and by chance, probably from a primordial soup of electrified chemicals.

This account has a certain intuitive appeal. After all, it is a matter of common observation that offspring are rarely if ever exactly the same as their parents. Variations on species-type naturally occur, some of them quite radical, a few of them perhaps making the individual stronger or fitter or cleverer. A variation that favors survival or reproduction in a generally hostile, competitive environment may be more likely to be passed on to the next generation. One can imagine those variations gradually, over long periods of time, resulting in the emergence of new strains. If so, why not whole new species?

The precise mechanism by which variations occur and may be passed on from one generation to another was not known to Darwin. The discovery of chromosomes and the development of the science of genetics seemed at first to supply that need. However, gaps in the fossil record (in popular parlance "missing links") remained troubling to some throughout the 19th and 20th centuries. Some evolutionists suggested that the various species we know today did not emerge slowly but rapidly, in jumps that took place over thousands or perhaps even just hundreds of years, rather than the millions hypothesized by Darwin. The original theory was therefore adapted by suggesting ways in which variations could be brought about more rapidly through genetic mutation and/or environmental pressure (the inheritance of acquired characteristics being ruled out by the lack of an appropriate mechanism). Stephen Jay Gould has been the best-known exponent of this theory of "punctuated equilibrium."[3] As for the attempts to replicate the creation of life under laboratory conditions, these have not so far been successful.

The best known opponents of the evolutionary account (whether fast or slow) are the *biblical creationists*, who believe that God created the various separate species in a sequence of distinct acts described in the Book of Genesis, perhaps even in six days of twenty-four hours each. This does away with the difficulty of explaining incredible variations between different forms of life in terms of environmental pressures working on spontaneous genetic variation, but introduces a whole series of other problems, not least the existence of the fossil record. It has to be said that the methods and arguments of "creation science" do little to allay the fears of irrationalism that haunt this debate. It has been rightly said that a simplistic creationism "is the best thing that could have happened to Darwinism, the caricature of religion that has seemed to justify Darwinist contempt for the whole of religion."[4]

God of the Gaps?

A more sophisticated critique of the Darwinian paradigm on the basis of science alone is provided by exponents of "Intelligent Design" (ID), a theory promoted by the Discovery Institute and the Access Research Institute in the United States.[5]

Intelligent Design claims that biological systems at the molecular level are "irreducibly complex." This means that they are made up of many complicated parts and subsystems, all of which have to be

3. The theory has been severely criticized by, among others, Simon Conway Morris.

4. Marilynne Robinson, cited in Michael Hanby's important article, "Creation without Creationism: Toward a Theological Critique of Darwinism," *Communio* 30:4 (Winter 2003), 679.

5. This attack on scientific orthodoxy is presented in a series of books by Philip R. Johnson (*Darwin on Trial*, 1991), Michael Behe (*Darwin's Black Box*, 1996), Lee Spetner (*Not By Chance*, 1997) and William A. Dembski (*The Design Inference*, 1998). (Users of the Internet can find the case laid out at http://www.arn.org/.)

in place in order for the system as a whole to perform a useful function—such as enabling the organism to survive and reproduce. Its exponents rely on complex technical arguments in biochemistry and probability theory, but the argument resembles one that has often been made by opponents of evolution (including G.K. Chesterton). How could a complex organ such as the eye emerge by a series of stages, each of which would have to have been selected by evolution, when the eye itself is only of any benefit to the organism when it is functioning *as an eye*? Transposed to the biomolecular level, the argument allegedly becomes even stronger. Perhaps the complexity of life does not get built up from simple components at all, but exists from the beginning.

It is important to note that the proponents of Intelligent Design claim to make their case without appeal to divine revelation, even though the exponents of ID tend to be Christians, and some at least have joined the Orthodox Church.[6] The Access Research Network website carefully distinguishes ID from so-called "scientific creationism." And rather than proposing to infer God's existence or character from the natural world, ID simply claims "that intelligent causes are necessary to explain the complex, information-rich structures of biology and that these causes are empirically detectable." In fact, the fundamental argument is mathematical. It is argued that certain transformations cannot occur in the process of natural development because "complex specified information" cannot be produced by any natural process, be it deterministic, random, or stochastic.[7] In the tradition of William Paley, the failure of science to explain complex structures easily leads to a single conclusion: the existence of God—or at least of an Intelligent Designer responsible for the existence of those structures.

Most scientists, it seems fair to say, do not accept the mathematical impossibility of explaining biological complexity. Cambridge

6. The link is made explicitly by Philip E. Johnson in his Introduction to *Genesis, Creation and Early Man*, by Seraphim Rose.

7. This claim to mathematical rigor is not something I am qualified to judge, but its importance is emphasized by Wolfgang Smith (see e.g., *The Quantum Enigma*, 116).

46

palaeontologist Simon Conway Morris is one. Unimpressed by the ID argument for impossible jumps in biochemical evolution, in *Life's Solution* he observes the tendency of different species to arrive at the same structural solution to a similar need. Thus despite the lack of any direct genetic connection, wings or eyes or limbs may resemble each other without any need for a designer to intervene in the process. Conway Morris, though, is a Christian. What he is reaching towards is an understanding of evolution not as a random, wandering process, but as highly ordered—shaped by an underlying logical structure that makes certain developments (eyes, arms, wings, feathers) almost inevitable. God creates a world that unfolds in time according to these deep biological structures.[8]

The Holistic Model

The last few decades have also seen the gradual emergence of a new field in developmental and evolutionary biology called *epigenetics*. This focuses less on the genetic mechanism itself, than on the surrounding influences on the genome. It takes a more holistic view of evolutionary biology, suggesting that emergent properties are not entirely caused by the component parts of the organism, but that interaction between parts also plays a major role.

Epigenetics is the latest scientific manifestation of an organicism that itself has a long ancestry. Other attempts to establish an organicist view of evolution have been made on the basis of systems theory. Organicists argue against Intelligent Design on the grounds that, like the genetic determinism of Richard Dawkins, it assumes an unfolding order based entirely upon genetic control—even if the two theories differ on where that order ultimately comes from. Life is still reduced by ID to a mechanism, albeit one that has been designed. The epigeneticists prefer the view of life as a *process* in which new and complex properties may emerge as the result of interactions between the various parts.

Organicist writers look for the secret of emergent order in the *sci-*

---

8. Conway Morris is followed by Conor Cunningham, whose book *Darwin's Pious Idea* critiques both ID and the "ultra-Darwinism" of Richard Dawkins *et al.* in the name of a more moderate, theistic theory of evolution.

ence of complexity, a branch of systems theory. Leading exponents such as Humberto Maturana, Ilya Prigogine, and Fritjof Capra argue that greater complexity develops less through environmental pressure or selection from outside than through self-organization from within. A living organism may be viewed as a dynamic system, an open or "dissipative" structure (absorbing energy and dissipating entropy to its environment) which maintains its own stability through positive and negative feedback—the flow of information. "Life" is defined as a process found in some, though not all, types of dissipative structure (a hurricane and a whirlpool would be examples of non-living dissipative structures). Following Gregory Bateson and Maturana, Fritjof Capra goes one step further, and identifies the life process with cognition itself, proposing thereby to overcome the Cartesian split between mind and body.

Organicism and the scientific theories of emergence are compatible with a belief in evolution, but are they resonant or consonant with a Christian understanding of how God works in the world? Although the systems thinkers I have just mentioned are opposed to reductionism and materialism as well as to Cartesian dualism, it is possible to argue that they are reductionistic in a new sense. What they oppose is "mechanistic reductionism," or the view that organisms are machines that can be completely understood by analyzing them into their component parts. But some of them, at least, appear to be replacing this with a kind of "information reductionism." The word *autopoesis* (self-making) applied to emergence sounds scientific enough, but if all it really signifies is that new forms of order appear from nowhere it looks very like an appeal to magic.

By reducing mental processes to the flow of information, these organicists are also ignoring the spiritual or interior dimension of consciousness. Jerry Fodor once strikingly commented that "Nobody has the slightest idea how anything material could be conscious. Nobody even knows what it would be *like* to have the slightest idea about how anything material could be conscious." In fact, as Erwin Schrödinger argued in 1946, consciousness can never be the external object of scientific investigation because it is always interior to the observer. It cannot be reached by the methods of science. It is something completely other than matter, energy, or even the flow of

48

information. It has no color, shape, or weight. Unless we recognize this, the human person will dissolve in the dance of information just as surely as it dissolved into the flux of matter and energy during an earlier phase of modern science.

Yet the organicists are surely moving in the right direction. From a religious, or a specifically Christian, point of view there is much scope in the epigenetic approach for a richer understanding of God's relationship with the world. It moves away from the reductionism that deadens the religious spirit. "All of the perversions that human freedom can inflict upon being and its qualities always aim at one thing: the annihilation of the depth dimension of being, thanks to which being remains a mystery even, indeed precisely in its unveiling."[9]

Hans Urs von Balthasar, from whom this quotation is taken, is by no means averse to the scientific unveiling of reality. He simply wants to insist that this unveiling not destroy the "depth" out of which reality emerges. To equate the brain with the mind, or the substance of consciousness with the transmission of information, is one more way of trying to eliminate this "depth dimension" of being. Only within this vertical dimension does it make sense to seek for God, and for a divine influence on the unfolding or evolution of creation. Any other attempt to combine religion and science will lead to a "process" God so identified with creation that he loses all transcendence.[10]

---

9. Hans Urs von Balthasar, *Theo-Logic: Theological Logical Theory Volumes I–III,* I (San Francisco: Ignatius Press, 2000-2005), 16–17.

10. For further, more sophisticated discussion of epigenetics and the links to Christian theology see W. Malcolm Byrnes, "Epigenetics, Evolution and Us," *The National Catholic Bioethics Quarterly* 3:3 (Autumn 2003), 489–500. This article is also available in the Archive of the *Second Spring* website http://www.second-spring.co.uk/. See also Rudolf B. Brun, "Principles of Morphogenesis in Embryonic Development, Music and Evolution," *Communio* 20:3 (Fall, 1993). Balthasar transcends the "process" view by means of his concept of "theo-drama." Historical developments are due to the dramatic interaction of created with uncreated freedom. Freedom is real because, from the point of view of anyone within time, the future is not yet determined. Theo-drama is applied to evolution in Celia Deane-Drummond, *Christ and Evolution: Wonder and Wisdom* (London: SCM Press, 2009).

Levels of Reality

In the 19th century, St. George Jackson Mivart, a Catholic opponent of Charles Darwin, argued along lines similar to Balthasar's, and was praised by Cardinal Newman for exposing the logical insufficiency of Darwin's theory.[11] In the 20th century, Michael Polanyi analyzed the phenomenon of emergence and concluded that evolution, and life itself, must have been originated by the action of an "orderly innovating principle" of a higher order, the action of which is "released" by random fluctuations and "sustained" by fortunate environmental conditions.[12] Arthur M. Young defines four levels of being, each possessing different degrees of freedom and constraint, linking them to the four causes of Aristotle.[13]

More recently, the Faith Movement in Britain has also been aiming to reconcile the theory of evolution with Catholicism in what it calls a "new synthesis." Its founder, the late Father Edward Holloway, posits that God works through evolution to bring about an ordered cosmos. Christ is the embodiment and master of a Law of Unity and Direction, the center of human and universal history. In the words of Fr. David Barrett to a Faith Theological Symposium in 2003, the Mind of God is "actively and dynamically knowing and willing the creation as a unity in development, an evolving whole.

11. As a Catholic organicist, Mivart believed that "an internal power is a great, perhaps the main, determining agent" for directing changes in organisms and producing convergence to common structures" (J. Brook and G. Cantor, *Reconstructing Nature: The Engagement of Science and Religion* [T&T Clark, 1998], 258). Unfortunately, Mivart was marginalized in the debate, drawn into Modernism and excommunicated by the Church for reasons unconnected with his opposition to Darwinism.

12. Polanyi, *Personal Knowledge*, 386. See also Brian Goodwin, *How the Leopard Changed its Spots* (London: Weidenfeld & Nicolson, 1994). Goodwin argues that Darwin's fundamental mistake was to lose sight of the very organisms whose existence and variety were his original interest. He draws on the sciences of complexity and emergent order to show that organisms "are as real, as fundamental, as irreducible, as the molecules out of which they are made"—in which case the metaphor of evolution by competition gives way to a metaphor of cooperation. Polanyi's metaphysics and theology are usefully analyzed in John F. Haught and D.M. Yeager, "Polanyi's Finalism," *Zygon* 32:4 (December 1997).

13. For an introduction to Young's theory see Frank Barr online at http://www.arthuryoung.com/barr.html.

So the Unity-Law is identified with and through every aspect of the material universe, and is at the same time the relationship of all these parts as a unity to the Mind of God." Thus, "Control and direction, space and time, meaning and purpose are descriptions of how evolving matter is constituted by Mind in one perpetual act of knowing and willing."[14]

All of these approaches want to introduce a "depth dimension" of being, and move on from there to the possibility of an evolutionary science that would take account of a distinction between different levels of reality. We have already touched upon it in the discussion of relationality, which applies both horizontally (between creatures) and vertically (between creatures and God) through the gift of being.[15] Everything owes its existence to the God who brings it (along with all its physical and temporal causes) out of nothing, and it belongs to an order that only becomes evident when the ultimate purpose of God is revealed.

Christians have a robust intuition of how this works in everyday life in the concept of divine Providence. No matter how accidental a series of events may appear to be, Christians often believe them to be foreseen and permitted, if not positively intended, by Providence, and to be unfolding according to an eternal plan. (The problem of whether divine foreknowledge of human action deprives us of free will need not detain us, since it was adequately answered long ago. If God exists, he exists above time, and so he does not see our decisions before we make them, but rather sees them eternally *as we make them*. Since he plans the world in eternity, he can take into account every free act that will ever be made.)

References to Providence are, however, normally found in discussions of spirituality rather than science. The language of spirituality, moreover, tends to be personal rather than impersonal, thus removing it from the realm of scientific discourse. According to J.-P. de

14. David Barrett, "The Unity Law Throughout the Plan of Creation," *Faith* 35:4 (July/August 2003), 6. Unfortunately, the new synthesis makes the human soul an exception to the process of evolution but without explaining how this does not render the whole account incoherent.

15. See Pabst, *Metaphysics*, 246–50.

Caussade in his classic *Sacrament of the Present Moment* (also titled *Abandonment to Divine Providence*), God speaks to us not in human words but through whatever happens to us, moment by moment. Setting aside the implication that God resembles us sufficiently that we can regard him as "speaking,"[16] we may take this as a reference to another kind of causality, at right angles to the kind investigated by science but not in contradiction to it. The events of my everyday life have their normal (efficient, material) causes, the kind studied by science, but they also have a higher explanation in terms of some kind of "divine speech." The Christian therefore has faith in a higher level of order or meaning, supervening upon and assuming the lower-level order of material cause and effect. I know there is a perfectly rational reason for my friend to have phoned at five o'clock. But my friend may also have phoned at five *in answer to a prayer*, or because God knew that I needed to hear what that friend would say precisely then, rather than two hours earlier.

It may seem at first sight that we have discovered in this notion of Providence and the "depth dimension" an easy way to reconcile evolution with religious or Christian belief. All we need to do is attribute the mutations that lead to speciation to the Providence of God instead of regarding them as purely random. But things are not so simple. In order to understand why, we need to probe more deeply into the underpinnings of evolutionism.

The philosophical system that lies behind most forms of evolutionary thought is Nominalism, which first became popular in Europe around the time of the Black Death and with even more devastating effect. It was this philosophical revolution that led to what Wolfgang Smith calls the "eclipse of verticality." The nominalists and their successors (positivists, pragmatists, and members of other schools of thought hostile to traditional metaphysics) believe that the real world consists entirely of individual particles, elements or energies and their relationships, which can be described in a variety of ways. It is only the way in which we *choose to describe* certain

16. Religious believers should know that God cannot be directly known or accurately described, but that we can employ analogies that at least gesture in the right direction.

things that determines whether they belong to one "species" or another. On this assumption there can be no reason to prevent one type of thing turning into another, given the right circumstances and enough time: all that needs to happen is for one collection of particles to be sufficiently restructured for re-description to become necessary.[17]

The World Before Time

It is this *philosophical* theory of nominalism that we are implicitly calling into question with our talk of "levels of reality." In so doing we are undermining the very basis of evolutionism. In fact with this possibility in mind we may return to the Biblical texts and read them in quite a different way than either the creationists or their critics. Genesis hints at quite a complex series of conditions or states existing before our present world, and it may be possible to conceive of these in terms of events taking place at different onto-logical levels rather than simply in an earlier time. Before the Fall, Genesis tells us, animals did not eat each other's flesh. Certain Patristic writers, such as Gregory of Nyssa, assume that in this state, also, sexual reproduction would have been unnecessary, and that the "coats of skins" later given by God to Adam and Eve were not bear-skins, as the modern reader perhaps imagines, but the animal-like flesh in which we now find ourselves. In the Garden, where Man was at first set apart from the rest of creation, death and sickness were unknown, which suggests that this state was even exempt from the entropy which defines our temporal state of existence, putting it right outside the known universe of modern science.

Science has conceded that different physical laws might pertain within the first few nanoseconds of the Big Bang, or in the depths of a black hole where space and time have been forced into a singular-

---

17. As James Le Fanu points out in *Why Us?*, micro-evolution within species is undeniable, but macro-evolution (the evolution of one species or family into another) is still not proven. It tends to be believed simply because an alternative is hard to imagine—because, as one biologist put it, "it is the only possible explana-tion that we can conceive" (104). Nominalist assumptions render the distinction, and therefore this whole debate, meaningless, concealing the vulnerability of neo-Darwinism on this point.

ity. What if the Bible, in its own way, is also trying to describe a very different world to our own, one in which Nature is in the process of formation? St. Augustine's reflections on the days of creation in *De Genesis ad Litteram* may be taken as one example of a Christian interpretation along these lines. For Augustine, time itself is a creature, while the six "Days" represent not periods of time that can be measured in hours, or even millennia, but distinct aspects of an instantaneous creative act as viewed by the angelic intelligences. The creative act of God, he taught, terminates in the "causal ratios" or *seminal reasons*, spiritual seeds of all things projected into prime matter. "Let the earth bring forth living creatures . . . according to their kinds" (Gen. 1:24). These "kinds" then unfold in time as the actual or corporeal existence of individual species or creatures.[18]

I am sure the Book of Genesis still contains many mysteries. We read the story of Adam naming the animals, and then we discover that at least one of the animals in the Garden is an angel. The serpent is that creature of God sometimes called the Archangel Lucifer. What if *all* the animals in the story were angels? In fact, what if the story is about the relationship of archetypal Man with archetypal Animals: and the archetypal Animals are none other than the angels of tradition?

This may seem a startling idea, but I believe it is a possible interpretation of the text. A monk of Holy Trinity Monastery suggests the "cause" of an animal species might be an "angel" in the following passage:

---

18. There is no space here to explore the differences between this conception and that of the *logoi spermatikoi* of the Greek patristic tradition. For Maximus, it appears, the *logoi* are the uncreated divine intentions; as such presumably they would be at the root of Augustine's seminal reasons but cannot be identical with them. See Lars Thunberg, *Man and the Cosmos: The Vision of Maximus the Confessor* (Crestwood, NY: SVS Press, 1985), 137–43. Cf. Alexei V. Nesteruk, *Light from the East: Theology, Science and the Eastern Orthodox Tradition* (Minneapolis, MN: Fortress Press, 2003), e.g., 101–7. It should be noted that for Conor Cunningham in *Darwin's Pious Idea*, Augustine's seminal reasons, like Gregory of Nyssa's "seedlike potencies," point towards a form of material evolution (299), or the unfolding of potentialities that exist within the material creation.

None of the individuals of a species can account for the nature of the species as such. In order to explain the nature or form of any species, we are required to posit a cause which transcends the individuals of the species. Such a cause must contain the form of the species within it in a higher way without being itself part of the species. These are the spiritual substances or angels. The angels contain within themselves in a purely spiritual way the forms of things in the material world. . . . The causality of the angel of sparrows on the young sparrow is more intimate than even the sparrow's own mother. When the mother dies the sparrow continues to exist; but without the angel there would be no sparrows at all.

We will return to this idea in a later chapter, but in the meantime I will just note that the assumptions or the vision behind the monk's statement are spelled out by the Orthodox writer Sergius Bulgakov in his book on the angels. He writes that the angelic world "contains in itself the ideal analogue of the universe in *all* its parts: all ideas or creative themes of this world are present in the angelic world and are realized only when it is present. In this the angelic world is really *the intermediary* between God and the world, the ladder from earth to the heavens without which our world could not endure the immediate proximity of God. It both unites and separates the creature from God."[19]

The "easy" way to reconcile evolution and faith is to think of events as controlled directly by God. Thus the creationist posits the direct creation of species, while the more sophisticated Christian imagines that Providence simply controls the process of mutation in a way that science cannot detect, for divine ends. The atheist scientist, of course, is free to ignore both notions, since they do not affect his own work. But once we have admitted the existence of a vertical dimension, this other possibility needs to be considered—that of *intermediary causes* between the mind of God on the one hand, where all things that might exist are present as ways in which the

19. Sergius Bulgakov, *Jacob's Ladder: On Angels,* transl. Boris Jakim (Grand Rapids, MI: Eerdmans, 2010), 34. He goes on to say: "The world of the ideas, prototypes of being, which Plato gained sight of, only vaguely discerning its real place in God and even mixing it with Divinity, is in reality the angelic world in its relation to being, *Jacob's ladder.* Such is the true sense of Platonic idealism."

divine Essence could be imitated (the Thomistic way of describing the Forms in their highest aspect), and the corporeal world around us on the other, in which certain things exist and others do not.

These intermediary causes are reminiscent of the "implicate" or "generative" orders and "holomovement" hypothesized by physicist David Bohm, initially as a way of accounting for certain quantum phenomena.[20] They would be the true "morphogenetic fields" of each species, the beginning of each evolutionary chain, needed to explain the emergence of new forms in nature. Perhaps, as I have suggested, some of them are angels. Wolfgang Smith in *The Quantum Enigma* calls them "secondary modes" of vertical causality, akin to that bestowal of form effected by the artist when he brings a work of art into existence—an artifact, of course, in that case, rather than a substance. In fact, for Smith, vertical causality is commonplace, not only because in its primary mode everything is the result of God's creative act, but because secondary vertical causation is itself ubiquitous. The spatio-temporal world is *not a closed system*. Horizontal and vertical causality are like the warp and weft making up a single fabric.

All of which, though it does no more than hint at certain possibilities that may have been overlooked in the debate between evolutionists and creationists, brings us back to a remark by Goethe: "One cannot properly speak of many problems in the natural sciences if one does not draw on metaphysics for help; but not that school-and-word wisdom; rather that which was, is, and shall be before, with and after physics."[21] But once metaphysics has been reintroduced, it calls into question the very basis of a science posited on the destruction of metaphysics. The effect on the future direction of science is unpredictable, but it leaves the exponent of atheistic materialism in a very exposed position.

---

20. David Bohm describes how he arrived at his idea in the final chapter of Schindler (ed.), *Beyond Mechanism*. Bohm's language is strikingly reminiscent of the fifteenth-century writer, Cardinal Nicholas of Cusa, who also speaks of the "unfolded" and "enfolded" order, for example in Book 2, Chapter 3 of *On Learned Ignorance*.

21. Naydler (ed.), *Goethe on Science*, 125. This area of metaphysical cosmology may be one in which the various great religious traditions—despite the important differences that divide them in others—may collaborate to the profit of science.

Being Alive

All that came to be had life in him. (John 1:4)
Where subject and object touch, there is life.[1]

In discussing evolution, or the unfolding of life through time, the more fundamental question, "What is life?" has not so far been directly addressed. In biology one considers a whole list of properties that are said to distinguish living organisms from inanimate matter: homeostasis, growth, reproduction, and adaptation to environment being among the most important. Scientists talk about a *local reversal of entropy.* A life-form is an entity whose nature sustains itself (temporarily) against the universal rise of entropy, by means of energy drawn from outside itself. All other things, from sub-atomic particles to galaxies (pebbles on the beach being midway between the two), are unable to resist entropy and are inanimate. But the borderline is sometimes hard to draw: on which side do we place viruses, for example, or the hypothetical machines that may one day be able to perform all the functions at present associated with organisms?

The question cuts deeper than this. What is life, as distinct from death? Of what is death the absence? For someone facing the prospect of his own extinction, the answer must be more than a simple description of what happens when his body turns into a corpse, for it concerns the "I" at the center of his existence. The question of life is nothing less than the question of being. (For Aristotle in *De Anima*, in the case of living creatures their "to be" is "to be alive.")

In another way, the question of life also cuts to the heart of modernity, as Blessed John Paul II noted when he contrasted the "culture of life" with the "culture of death." The latter, referring to a tendency

1. Johann Wolfgang von Goethe, cited in Naydler (ed.), *Goethe on Science*, 123.

within modernity though not modernity *per se*, is not unrelated to the history of science that we have just been discussing, for there is a sense in which the development of Baconian or Cartesian science led us to view the world reductively, to murder by dissection, and so to give priority to death over life. It was as though death had become the norm, and life the strange exception, to be explained by an accumulation of random mutations over vast stretches of time. An emptiness crept into the souls of men, which Balthasar called the *anima technica vacua*. Man took on the characteristics of the machine, which had become the new model of the world.

In this chapter I want to try to understand the culture of death and a possible response to it by focusing on two thinkers in particular, who seem to me helpful in this regard. The first is the Cambridge theologian Catherine Pickstock, and the second, who becomes the main subject of the chapter, is the British-born architect and designer Christopher Alexander.[2]

To Be or Not To Be

The "culture of death" identified by John Paul II finds an echo in *After Writing*, by the Anglican theologian Catherine Pickstock. For Pickstock, when the world of things and people has been reduced to manageable image and information, suitable for human mastery and consumption, existence is effectively closed to transcendence. She argues that in this situation, life and death have become equivalent. In loving the surface of the beloved, for example, but not the inner depths that have been eliminated by nominalism and its successors, we are loving the beloved *as a body separated from its soul*. This leads to her dramatic (and no doubt exaggerated) characterization of modernity in terms of *necrophilia*.

> [In] seeking *only* life, in the form of a pseudo-eternal permanence, the "modern" gesture is secretly doomed to necrophilia, love of what has to die, can only die. In seeking only life, modernity gives life over to death, removing all traces of death only to find that life

2. The discussion of Alexander is largely based on my article in *Second Spring*, issue 13 (2011), and my paper "Is Life a Transcendental?" in *Radical Orthodoxy: Theology, Philosophy, Politics*, vol. 1, no. 1 & 2 (2012).

has vanished with it. And so there is a nihilistic logic to this necro-philiac gesture, this sacrificing of life to a living death so as to ensure that when death arrives to unmask life of its tinsel, he finds only the presence of absence, life reduced to the deathliness of equivalence.

For Pickstock, then, "necrophilia" has become a metaphor describing what becomes of human love and human desire in a world deprived of the dimension of metaphysical depth, of soul and personality. The world of Richard Dawkins and the reductionists is a soul-less world, and the love of someone who is merely a set of selfish genes walking around is macabre and in some sense absurd.[3] With the loss of the "I" we had lost also the "Thou" and the contem-plative relationship of the two.

The project of modernity, as Pickstock describes it, is an attempt to turn time into space (*mathesis*), precisely because the sense of *eternity* as subsuming both time and space has been lost. The foun-dations of the polity of death, she thinks, were laid by Peter Ramus in the sixteenth century, whose spatialized logic, like that of Des-cartes later, tried to reduce all knowledge to a kind of diagram, to place everything real on a map or grid, within a universal calculus. The project was only to come close to being fully realized in the late twentieth century, with the development of the computer and arti-ficial intelligence, but already by 1600 its lineaments are clear. The world was thought to be intelligible only if it could be surveyed at a

---

3. The central claim of the book is that whereas Derrida's postmodern Gnosti-cism, in which everything evaporates into a groundless "sign" of something else, "evacuates the body," a realistic construal of the event of the Eucharist "allows us to ground a view of language which does not evacuate the body, and does not give way to necrophilia." As she puts it herself, "the event of transubstantiation in the Eucha-rist is the condition of the possibility for all human meaning" (xv). Thus, in the fourth chapter of her book, Catherine Pickstock sets up against the "polity of death" what she calls the "sacred polis" of the medieval Roman Rite, in which meaning finds a home. The dimensions of this sacred polis, she writes, are "articu-lated through the signs of speech, gesture, art, music, figures, vestment, color, fire, water, smoke, bread, wine, and relationality" in such a way that language and sub-jectivity are "consummated" in the transformation of space and time as "gift" and "sacrifice" (169). It is important that these signs are things (*res*) as well as signs, and signs both "of one another and of that which exceeds appearance."

glance and read like words on a page. Reality must be capable of being "owned," and therefore controlled and infinitely manipulated, by man—or rather by a "detached, 'spiritualized' human self" (xiii); a self aspiring to be liberated from matter altogether.

This contrasts with the Christian understanding of the world, in which the possibility of transcendence is held open by the sacraments, or more broadly a religious understanding in which things in this world are but tokens of a reality that exceeds them infinitely. An interior relation to the mystery of Being gives things a depth that should never permit us to treat them merely as tools bereft of intrinsic value of their own. In their wholeness and intelligibility they speak of God, arousing amazement and wonder. It is in this spirit that they should be treated, and are so treated in the traditional crafts, so different in spirit from the industrial production-line.[4]

It seems to me that death is not merely an absence of life, but its essence lies in a process of *separation*. Soul is separated from body, and the parts of the soul and the body from each other. It is the dissolution of wholeness and unity that we face when we face our own death. As for life, it is that which unites, binding many parts into a single whole. As such, it is memory, understanding, and love to which we must look for the secret of life. When Christians speak of immortality, we are referring to the existence we receive when God remembers, understands, and loves us. And in our own love for others is revealed that interior dimension through which we ourselves are renewed and resurrected. In fact all experience, when carefully attended to, arouses this sense of an interior.[5]

But a culture that has succeeded in eliminating sacraments and even the sense of transcendence views individual human beings as it views everything else: they become means to a human end, or else

---

4. See Brian Keeble, *God and Work: Aspects of Art and Tradition* (Bloomington, IN: World Wisdom Books, 2009).

5. David L. Schindler in "Living and Thinking Reality in Its Integrity: Originary Experience, God, and the Task of Education," (*Communio* 37, Summer 2010, 167–85), argues that primordial or "originary" experience "implies a dynamic in the creature for saying forever" (173); that is, a stirring up of the heart's core, inspiring fidelity to a whole that transcends time.

obstacles to its achievement. That is why the spirit of this age, unchecked, can so easily permit the killing of the very young, the very old, or the very sick, when their continued existence becomes inconvenient.

The Nature of Order

I said that to the extent we fall under the sway of the "culture of death" we tend to view the world as fundamentally dead, unconscious matter, with life the exception—and that a phenomenon to be explained mechanically, as the meaningless operation of parts (forces and particles) resulting in behavior complex enough to be called animate. But there is another way of viewing the world, and another way of doing science. We find it in the following quotation from Christopher Alexander, in a monumental study called *The Nature of Order*.[6] Alexander believes that "life" is a quality not just of organisms, but of space, and therefore in some sense universal.

> There is a sense in which the distinction between something alive and something lifeless is much more general, and far more profound, than the distinction between living things and nonliving things, or between life and death. Things which are living may be lifeless; nonliving things may be alive. A man who is walking and talking can be alive; or he can be lifeless. Beethoven's last quartets are alive; so are the waves at the ocean shore; so is a candle flame; a tiger may be more alive, because more in tune with its own inner forces, than a man.[7]

Alexander claims that the balance of forces and forms evident in a great cathedral of stone and glass, or in a peaceful garden or courtyard where the light falls just right and the benches are exactly where they are needed, brings something to life by making explicit (actual) something that had been merely implicit (potential) in existence itself. Biological life is the same thing happening at a higher level, more intensively.

6. Four volumes, available from the Center for Environmental Structure, at http://www.natureoforder.com/.

7. Christopher Alexander, *The Timeless Way of Building* (Oxford University Press, 1979), 29.

Is there, as Alexander suggests, a broader sense of "livingness" in which everything that exists is more or less alive, though in varying degrees? Would a sliding scale or spectrum of "aliveness" enable us to preserve the appropriate distinctions between organisms, machines, and minerals? And would this be this enough to identify "life" as a transcendental property of all being, in the sense given to this term by Christian philosophers? I'll come back to that question shortly, but first let's consider Alexander's approach on its own terms.

The antecedents and parallels lie in Romantic, holistic, and eco-logical thought, *gestalt* psychology and systems theory. As already mentioned, Goethe tried to reconcile poetry and science through his study of plant morphology and color. David Bohm's *Wholeness and the Implicate Order* based on the new physics reaches similar conclusions to Alexander, who could also be seen as fleshing out the idea of "quality" we find in Robert Pirsig's *Zen and the Art of Motor-cycle Maintenance*. And so *The Nature of Order* opens with an assault on the mechanistic idea of order, or simplistic reductionism. Alexander argues that matter and space are not "dead" but possess *degrees of life*, because the elements of which they are made relate to each other not as mere parts but as mutually supporting "centers." (The whole is therefore more than the sum of its parts, because the parts in this case interact together making a system that possesses its own integrity.)

The first stage of the argument is to define the concept of "degrees of life," based on a survey of living systems and traditional cultures. But he begins his argument with *feelings*, because he is aiming to overcome the separation of feeling and thought, subject and object, associated with the scientific Enlightenment. We "feel" that there are different degrees of life in things, not only in organ-isms and ecological systems but also in traditional buildings and designs. Why is this? The second stage of the argument uncovers the objective correlates of this commonly shared feeling, both physical and mathematical.

What Alexander calls a "center" is a *focus of attention* that makes us aware of relations within a wider configuration. (It is a useful concept because it already implicitly overcomes the separation of subjective and objective.) The "wholeness" to which such centers contribute is a field-like structure (*gestalt*) that is somehow ontologically prior to the features of which it appears to be composed. A center can only be defined in terms of other centers (the mathematical term he introduces here is "recursive"). Alexander draws attention to this circularity as an essential feature of the argument. A center "functions as an organized field of force in space" (119), and the field is made up of other centers in structural relation to each other. Each gives life to the others. He illustrates this by means of the pattern in a Turkish carpet and the architectural and decorative features of the Alhambra. In fact, the life of a whole "arises mutually as a result of the way the centers prop each other up. No one of them comes first; each helps to support the others. Together they all raise themselves to life" (126).

Coherence, beauty, intensity of life, depth of structure, are all connected. So far the argument appears very abstract. Then, in the heart of the book, Alexander defines fifteen specific structural features that correlate with degrees of life.[8] This enables him to become quite practical in his recommendations. Each describes "one of the possible ways in which centers can intensify each other" (241). They are the "glue, through which space is able to be unified." These are illustrated first in drawings and human designs, and then in natural forms, contrasting in each case examples of designs that fail to "live" because they do not possess these features. The examples he chooses are eclectic, ranging from mud huts to palaces, from Shaker furniture to Persian glassware, from electrical discharges to cell walls, from the branches of plants to the cracking of mud and the formation of crystals and feathers.[9]

---

8. The fifteen interacting features he calls levels of scale, strong centers, boundaries, alternating repetition, positive space, good shape, local symmetries, deep interlock and ambiguity, contrast, gradients, roughness, echoes, the void, simplicity and inner calm, and non-separateness.

9. By adapting the fifteen features to the categories of music—such as rhythm, tone, melody, harmony, and so forth—one might easily derive from this a theory of musical form, alongside a telling critique of the "modernist music" that developed in parallel with modernist architecture and painting in the first half of the twentieth century. In fact he does something of the sort for painting and color theory in

The breadth of his examples lends weight to Alexander's claim that these features are universal. But why do they occur in nature as well as in man-made objects, and indeed *more often* in the latter than the former? He answers this by saying that these are simply the ways things work most effectively. In other words, they are functional, but in a deep sense of the word. Biological life is one example of a universal tendency of nature, all of which, animate and inanimate, is a great process of unfolding wholeness. The fact that human beings can break from this pattern and create objects or environments that lack life is due to the fact that we are "not constrained by this unfolding" (294). Though a part of the process of life, we clearly also transcend it.

The second part of Book One is more philosophical in tone. In the first part Alexander had already suggested that his approach offered a way beyond Hume's fact-value distinction and Whitehead's "bifurcation of nature." Chapter 7, "The Personal Nature of Order," establishes that as space becomes more deeply functional, or better organized according to the criteria he has already described, it also begins to resemble *the human person*. And in the following chapter he presents an empirical test (the "mirror-of-the-self" test) that demonstrates the objectivity of our deepest likings; that is, of our liking something "from the heart." He found that when people are asked to pay attention to the way they feel when they compare any two things (he starts with a glass salt-cellar and a plastic ketchup bottle), and specifically to attend *to what degree each thing could function as a picture of their whole self*, they quickly come to agree on which object they prefer, on which is the more wholesome and nourishing to their humanity.

Beauty, Alexander argues, though it is perceived in the mind, must therefore be an objective property of things. It corresponds, in

---

Book Four. The same features would be applicable in economics, where a more intensely "living" economy is one—like that described by G.K. Chesterton, E.F. Schumacher *et al.*—in which strong centers, such as small businesses and the various elements of civil society, act to support each other in a whole that is more than the sum of its parts. By contrast, the monolithic consumerism or the growth-addicted economy of modern times is both mechanistic in its structure and ugly in its results.

fact, to their degree of life, as previously discussed. What Alexander has proposed is nothing less than an extension of scientific method in which the self is used as a measuring instrument.[10] This is complicated by the fact that in order to judge the objective value in things we have at the same time to refine (that is, educate) the instrument with which we measure, the faculty of discernment itself. His mirror-of-the-self test is also a method by which to teach people to discriminate between what they have been taught (by fashion or ideology or habit) to like, and what truly moves, attracts, and inspires them at a deeper level. These are not always, or even usually, the same thing. As Alexander states:

> Our apparent liking for fashions, post-modern images, and modernist shapes and fantasies is an aberration, a whimsical and temporary liking at best, which has no permanence and no lasting value. It is wholeness in the structure that we really like in the long run, and that establishes in us a deep sense of calmness and permanent connection.

> But the peculiar fact is that it is not so easy to find out what we really like. It is a skill and an art to become sensitive enough to living structure so that we see it accurately and become sufficiently aware of it, so that our liking, as we experience it superficially, is in tune with the real liking that has permanence in us. That is why we need a mirror-of-the-self test. It is an instrument that not only helps us discover living structure and see living structure accurately: it also helps us to discover what we truly like. (343)

After conducting tests with hundreds of subjects drawn from many different cultures, Alexander is convinced that he has devel-

---

10. We should note that he does not reject the Cartesian method, indeed he claims to "revere" Descartes. "In any situation where the relevant facts have to do with things that can be viewed in a machine-like fashion, the method of Descartes is best. Pretend the unknown thing is a machine, and find a model which represents its behavior. But in any situation where the relative wholeness of different systems is the most relevant issue, then the method of Descartes, by itself, will not work. We then need a method which can *explicitly*, and objectively, recognize the relative degree of wholeness in different systems" (369). He adds that if we follow both methods, we arrive at a world-picture "which includes the self and which is able to recognize the personal nature of the universe."

oped an empirical method that yields sharable, repeatable, predictable, objective results; but it is a method that exists outside the Cartesian paradigm based on the elimination of the self of the observer (in accordance with the assumption that "everything is a machine"). What it points towards is precisely that "science of qualities" prophesied by Goethe, based on the accurate observation of inner feeling in relation to the parts of the world. Alexander's "second empiricism" overcomes the bifurcation of subject and object by discovering that our feeling-response to things, properly discerned, is an objective measure of their structural wholeness—in other words that "feeling and wholeness are two sides of a single thing" (312).

Furthermore, "Centers which have life increase our own life because we ourselves are centers too. We feel more wholesome in the presence of things which have wholesomeness in them because we, like other centers, are intensified by them." This has implications for ethics—since the "good" is what nourishes, expands, and frees our genuine humanity—and even our worship. (One version of Alexander's test asks the subject which of the two objects inspires most devotion, or makes him more aware of God or feel closer to God.) The fourth book will argue that interior freedom, which Alexander also describes as "the wholesomeness and integrity of a person's existence," is directly dependent on "the extent to which that person is able to sustain an *inner* relatedness with the world in its entirety" (402).

The power of Christopher Alexander's approach is based on the fact that everything is so thoroughly and exhaustively documented from a lifetime of practical experience in architecture and design around the world. The practical dimension of his work is evident in the final chapter of the first Book, with section headings like "How a Chisel Works" and "How a Living Room Works." Alexander's architecture enables an integration of beauty (including ornament) and function, for function is simply the "dynamic aspect of wholeness" (405). Functional life consists in the interaction of centers. But in order to discuss function, one has to be aware of *needs*; that is, not manufactured but authentic needs. Human beings require communication, relationship, privacy, silence, and music as well as food, water, and light. He grounds this discussion in a couple of examples drawn from the Shaker communities, where functional, aesthetic, and spiritual cannot be separated. "If a Shaker room was a machine at all, it was a machine for inducing and intensifying [a] spiritual state in a person who is in the room" (420). Yet it is not that "form follows function," so that if you seek the most efficient use of space it will turn out also to be beautiful. Rather, Alexander argues, the discovery of functionality derives from a search for beauty, for an intensification of the field of centers, of the *life* of centers.

Alexander's startling conclusion from all this is that life is a property of space itself. He bypasses the conventional understanding of life as a self-sustaining biological process, developed through an evolution from simple elements, and opts for a more general description. Biological life, capable of resisting entropy by drawing energy from the environment, is a special case of something that occurs universally. Life is not "an accidental thing which happens in organisms as matter gets highly organized. It is in the very nature of order for matter to be alive," to a greater or lesser degree (438). Space "awakens" into life, like a bud opening into a flower. (Balthasar, operating within a similar *gestalt*-based perspective, writes that "In a flower, a certain interior reality opens its eye and reveals something beyond and more profound than a form which delights us by its proportion and color.")[11]

The final step, which Alexander anticipates here but only fleshes out in Book Four, is to show that the awakening of space in a given geometrical center is measured by the degree to which that center becomes associated with the human "I" or self. The entire cosmos and every process within it has a natural goal or *telos*, which is personality. "When a building works, when the world enters the blissful state which makes us fully comfortable, the space itself awakens. We awaken. The garden awakens. The windows awaken. We and our plants and animals and fellow creatures and the walls and light together wake" (439). But "in order to make it possible to have an idea like this, we need to understand space as a material which is *capable* of awakening."

11. Balthasar, *The Glory of the Lord*, I, 444.

Building for Life

In the second volume of his series, Alexander concentrates more attention on the "Process of Creating Life"—his own version of the theory of evolution, if you like. He argues that the emergence in nature of pattern and order, even in such relatively simple things as snowflakes, is not adequately explained by the three principles normally invoked to account for it: least action, natural selection, and geometric attractors. Rather than turn directly to a notion of vertical causation, he argues for the addition of a fourth natural principle, the "principle of unfolding wholeness." That is, every natural system will tend to *preserve wholeness*, to destroy symmetries and centers as little as possible. With the inclusion of this fourth principle, the emergence of life and living structure in the world, he thinks, becomes inevitable. The geometric properties of space give rise to structure that reinforces wholeness (47). This notion of wholeness, if not the same as the traditional notion of form, is at least compatible with it, being the manifestation of a unity that subsists at a deeper level.[12]

Nature therefore proceeds by means of "structure-preserving transformations" (201), the nature of which he analyzes in some detail. These are the process-equivalents of the fifteen structural features or properties of life, and they are fundamental to the creation of living, beautiful structure in every field, from biology to poetry and music (429). They apply in particular to architecture, of course. What he now claims is that a living order, even in architecture, *cannot be designed*. It can only be generated, as a cumulative and responsive process of developing centers that preserve existing wholeness. At a stroke, then, he has set himself against all mainstream design education. It is his view that the process of designing out of one's own head and onto the drawing-board must inevitably be both life- and structure-destroying.

---

12. In *The Nature of Order* he remarks, that in conversation, David Bohm had identified it with his own "implicate order." The failure of Darwinian evolution on its own to explain morphogenesis is noted by Alexander in pp. 42–43 of Book Two, where he seeks an additional "pattern-like tendency" that lies behind these coherent transformations.

Book Two therefore contains a critique of certain aspects of modernity and a proposal for their eventual rectification. Alexander traces the twentieth century's destruction of living process back to one individual: Frederick Taylor, who was employed as a consultant by the entrepreneur Henry Ford. It was his time and motion studies that lay behind the modern organization, with its machinelike repetition of processes. Taylor deliberately set out to make labor independent of craft, tradition, and knowledge, reducing the worker to a cog in the machine of industry who could be replaced at will for the sake of efficiency and cashflow. Modernist architecture is largely the result of the application of Taylor's idea, which Alexander calls "the source of monsters." Modernism is bureaucratic, not personal. Whether capitalist or socialist, he says, it is all the same.

What is his solution? The fact that so much damage could be done by one man (Taylor) encourages Alexander to think that the undoing of that damage, the establishment of a "new paradigm," could also be accomplished by one man, or a small group. So in the final chapters of Book Two he outlines the way our present society and methods of construction can be transformed, not "top down" by command, but by setting good examples, and by "injecting *morphogenetic* sequences into the mainstream" (he also calls these "genetic snippets").[13] He ends Book Two with an inspiring, perhaps grandiose vision of architecture in the future, and the role of architects as "healers of the ravaged earth."

Vision of a Living World
Book Three examines the impact and application of living processes in architecture, design, and planning, both on a small and on a large

---

13. One of the examples he gives is that of the Grameen Bank, which started to lend money to low-income families without collateral in Bangladesh based on trust and feelings in face-to-face relationships. Another example is Alexander's own book, *A Pattern Language*, which transformed the way houses were designed in the 1980s. "Snippets" have to be kept small and simple if they are to catch on. Alexander and his colleagues have been posting examples of "life-creating sequences" that can be adapted and applied by others at his website, http://www.patternlanguage.com/, whether to create a kitchen, or plan a pedestrian-friendly street, or regenerate the ecology of a beach.

scale. Alexander uses hundreds of examples of buildings, plans, and designs that conform to the general principles and architectural "style" he has outlined. A lot of this involves learning from nature. His description of the fundamental process begins as follows:

> At each step, the process begins with a perception of the whole. At every step (whether it is conceiving, designing, making, maintaining or repairing) we start by looking at and thinking about the whole of that part of the world where we are working. We look at this whole, absorb it, try to feel its deep structure. (4)

His "textbook" of the new architecture (rooms, buildings, neighborhoods, massive projects, etc.) concludes with sections on color and ornament. Most of us assume that ornament is separate from function; that it is, perhaps, a luxury, or extraneous. Alexander's view is that ornament is itself functional, that it is an intrinsic part of the process of unfolding. It is essential "to complete and perfect the field of centers" (582). Furthermore it need not add to the overall costs of a project, provided it is integrated within the building and designing process. He even says that we should understand the *whole building* as an ornament. The same applies in nature. "A person's face, in the eyes of God, is an ornament to the world; the eyes ornament the face; the face ornaments the body" (613).

If architects apply these ideas, their buildings will be the "continuation and completion of the land," and buildings will be a part of nature instead of representing a brutal rejection of it. Alexander's advice to the modern architect is worth repeating: "What has been lost is the inner language which connects you to your own soul, which makes you know, with certainty, which way is likely to be right, and which way is likely to be wrong. To be more clear about it. To feel it, as a real thing. To know, listen to, the voice that is in your own heart" (683).

In Book Four, Alexander moves onto the dangerous ground of metaphysics. Religion as a system of beliefs and behavior, he thinks, will not improve our situation if we continue to assume that the world is made of machinelike matter, and he believes that even "the Pope and the Dalai Lama today have a mechanical view of the nature of matter" (18). Piety and theological orthodoxy is no protection against the mental habits instilled by modern education. Nevertheless, he observes that most of the profoundly living structures and most objectively beautiful works of art in the world's history have been created "within the cultural context of some religion." The reason was that these belief-systems all fostered a sense of relatedness between ourselves and the universe, or rather the Self that is the ground of the universe. "They all emphasized the need to abandon concern with one's own ego. They all emphasized the importance of hard work and repeated simple, even menial tasks. Above all, they all emphasized the desire to reach God, or the ground of all things, directly, face to face" (35).

Seeing God "face to face" is a Christian aspiration. However, in other places Alexander sounds more like a Theosophist. He tells us in his opening remarks that whenever he makes a building he is always reaching for the same thing. "In some form, it is the personal nature of existence, revealed in the building, that I am searching for. It is 'I,' the I-myself, lying within all things. It is that shining something which draws me on, which I feel in the bones of the world, which comes out of the earth and makes our existence luminous." The question that will immediately strike a Christian reader is whether Alexander ultimately dissolves all differences between self and other into one universal Self.[14]

In order to discern the underlying tendency of Alexander's thought we need to focus on the concrete, even empirical, meaning he gives to his "universal Self." Building on the "mirror-of-the self" experiments reported earlier, he shows that we all can be brought to recognize a deep connection between our self and something that is present in all things to different degrees, which he calls the "I." This I, he says, is not subjective, imagined, but a reality in matter itself—

14. The danger is spelled out amusingly by G. K. Chesterton in *Orthodoxy:* "Of all conceivable forms of enlightenment the worst is what these people call the Inner Light. Of all horrible religions the most horrible is the worship of the god within. Anyone who knows anybody knows how it would work; anyone who knows anyone from the Higher Thought Center knows how it does work. That Jones shall worship the god within him turns out ultimately to mean that Jones shall worship Jones. Let Jones worship the sun or moon—anything rather than the Inner Light; let Jones worship cats or crocodiles, if he can find any in his street, but not the god within."

matter understood to be (as indeed modern physics understands it) a certain configuration of space, rather than something *in* space.

> For every artist, every builder, this must be true: as I work I must try to create a structure which appears like I to me. I must try to arrange the colors in a painting in such a way that living breathing I appears in it. This effort makes the centers live; it makes me communicate with the ultimate beyond all things; and at the same time it mobilizes myself, animates me, makes my person, my being, awaken, because I am then more present. It is this mobilizing of my self in the great work which chills me, devastates me, wakes me to the bone. And this, which is personal because it reaches the personal in me, also connects me to the great ultimate beyond all things: to the ocean and the wind and the fire. (70)

My own individual self and the universal Self are not necessarily one and the same, but they are connected. In the sixth chapter, "The Blazing One," Alexander says that the creation of structure in space, and especially living structure in the sense he has defined, opens a kind of "tunnel" to this underlying Ground. Every beautiful object, *to the extent it is beautiful,* "begins to open the door towards the I-stuff or the self." When I look at the Parthenon, he suggests, I am literally glimpsing heaven. Any beautiful thing has something luminous within it: I am seeing into the glow of the Blazing One. Furthermore, "the I which one of us experiences as his own self is not a private and individual thing, as most of us imagine it to be, but a partial connection of our *own* physical matter (my body) to this very great, and single, plenum of I-stuff."

But what does it mean to say that my "I" is not "private and individual" to me? This certainly does sound like "the god within." But Alexander adds one very significant comment. The more connected we are to this "I-stuff," the more whole, the more free, the more childlike, the more *uniquely ourselves,* we become. "This is, perhaps, the central mystery of the universe: that as things become more unified, less separate, so also they become most individual, and most precious" (309). And he returns to the more "dualistic mode" in the final chapter when he describes the "necessary state of mind" in which we can make a living and beautiful structure as one in which "you make each building in a way which is a gift to God." "It belongs to God. It does not belong to you. It is made to serve God, to glorify God. It is not made to glorify you. Perhaps, if anything, it humbles you."

The apparent contradiction between these two tendencies—the Christian and the pantheist—in Alexander's thought is due to a fundamental paradox that his metaphysics is unable to resolve. He does not, in the end, *want* to merge everything into one reality, but rather to affirm the real existence, value, and life of the particular and the individual, especially human beings. To show how this is true, how things become *more themselves* the more deeply they are unified, he would need to be able to draw upon a metaphysics of love that is more than merely sentimental or aspirational. In my view such a metaphysics would need to be based on a concept of the Trinity as the "form" of love and the ultimate meaning of being. As we shall see in a later chapter, only the "dual unity" of the Trinity provides a home for otherness that can survive the end of the world. But in the meantime, Alexander has shown us the beginnings of a way from modern science, not only to a reconciliation with the arts, but towards a reconciliation with metaphysics. The "unfolding wholeness" that he seeks in everything is not to be found except in what we earlier called the dimension of vertical causality, in the *logoi* that rest in the Logos.[15]

Life as a Transcendental

In terms of the traditional Christian metaphysics that Alexander seems, unconsciously, to be seeking, when we talk about "beauty" or "wholeness" we are talking of transcendental properties that apply to everything in the world to some degree or another—these properties are coextensive with being. Our very humanity is bound up with our capacity to realize that being is one, good, true, and

---

15. "All that came to be had life in him and that life was the light of men" (John 1:4). Origen, commenting on one possible translation of John 1:3–4 ("That which has been made was life in him"), writes: *"That which was made in him*; and then, *was life*; the sense being, that all things that were made by him and in him, are life in him, and are one in him. They *were*, that is, in him; they exist as the cause, before they exist in themselves as effects" (Aquinas, *Catena Aurea*, 4, Part 1, 16).

beautiful. For *Unity* is the property of being oneself and not another. But the unity of a thing does not isolate it; instead it gives it an interior relation to everything else. *Goodness* is being as willed, or as loved; it is the end in which things are fulfilled or completed. *Truth* is concordance with reality, with what is. Perfect truth is perfect concordance, amounting to identity and so unity. *Beauty* is being as enjoyed, as rejoiced in. Or we could say with Aidan Nichols that "The beautiful *is* reality under the aspect of form, known as such by imaginative intuition, just as truth is reality as best known through propositions, by the intelligence, and goodness is reality as best known through values, by the moral sense."[16]

Each transcendental tells us something about God, since he is their source; he is the utterly real in which all existing things are given to participate. It is possible to describe other properties, too, as transcendentals. For example, Aquinas adds *res* and *aliquid* along with *ens* (being), *unum*, *verum*, and *bonum*, and Gustav Siewerth describes *love* as "more comprehensive than being itself; it is the 'transcendental' par excellence that comprehends the reality of being, of truth, of goodness."[17]

Could "life" be a transcendental, as Christopher Alexander seems to imply? We are today under enormous mental pressure to regard life as a mere biological, or perhaps even a mechanical, phenomenon devoid of deeper significance. We forget the metaphysical dimension of life, of nature herself. If we can discover that, our whole approach not only to biology, but to architecture and design, and perhaps even to ethics, will indeed have to change along the

16. Aidan Nichols OP, *A Key to Balthasar: Hans Urs von Balthasar on Beauty, Goodness, and Truth* (London: Darton, Longman & Todd, 2011), 25.

17. Cited by Balthasar in *Theo-Logic*, II, 176–7. The citation occurs in a section of Balthasar's text where he discusses the relationship of the transcendentals to the Trinity. At the beginning of *De Veritate* Aquinas argues against the identification of particular transcendentals with one or other divine Person, on the grounds that they are one in reality (unlike, say, wisdom and power), and that their unity in God is even more perfect than their unity in creatures. However, in the *Summa*, I, Q. 39, art. 8, he is more flexible. In general he tends to view *pulchrum* as an aspect of *bonum*.

lines Alexander suggests. (To ethics because modern decision-making is consequentialist and utilitarian, whereas a "transcendentalist" approach would include the dimension of reverence and piety towards being.)[18] Of course, for life to be regarded as a transcendental, it would have to be in everything, not just in biological organisms. Does such a suggestion even make sense?

In Question 18 of the First Part of the *Summa*, St. Thomas defines life as self-movement, and ranks creatures according to the degree of this ability they possess. On that basis he denies life to minerals and the material elements, which are passively moved by another. But the same definition of life would seem to leave him with a problem. If life is self-movement, God cannot be alive, since there is no "movement" in God. He gets around this objection in Article 3 by arguing that there is *understanding* in God, and that understanding is itself *a higher kind of movement*. He concludes: "In the sense, therefore, in which understanding is movement, that which understands itself is said to move itself. It is in this sense that Plato also taught that God moves himself; not in the sense in which movement is an act of the imperfect."

Perhaps, then, we can broaden the concept of movement in a slightly different way, in order to capture the sense in which, as Alexander puts it, a work of art or a candle flame is "alive." If God is life in the highest sense, rather than focus on the act of *self-understanding* in order to describe what being alive means for God, we might take a more Trinitarian line and say that, in God "life is *kenosis*."[19] The whole life of God is self-giving and self-receiving, which is another way of describing the fact that the divine Persons are not

18. As Schmitz says in *The Recovery of Wonder: The New Freedom and the Asceticism of Power* (McGill-Queen's University Press, 2005), 48, after summarizing the traditional metaphysics, it was the sense even of inanimate things as "deep and luminous" that made their misuse seem terrible.

19. I owe this formulation to Christopher Mitchell. The Greek word *kenosis* originally means "emptiness," and refers to the self-emptying that allows God's will to become present in us, based on Philippians 2:7, where Jesus "made himself nothing" or "emptied himself," becoming humble through obedience to the point of death.

substances but subsistent relations.[20] This act of *kenosis*, which is the characteristic "activity" of God, must be reflected analogically throughout the creation. The existence of a thing is a receiving and a giving of itself. Thus C.S. Lewis, who knew and loved the medieval conception of the cosmos, described it as "tingling with anthropomorphic life, dancing, a ceremonial, a festival not a machine." The steps of the dance are learned from the Trinity, and performed by angels.

The quality of *livingness* that Alexander finds in things, I suggest, is precisely this universal movement welling up from within— although only in the case of animate and particularly *conscious* animate beings does the creature's own will play a part in that movement. A stone, in other words, possesses a kind of interior life of low degree, which is related to the fact that God creates it from within, not without. It has a nature, on which God bestows existence: it receives the power of self-gift in the measure of its own essence. It plays a part in the whole, and it may be fashioned into a statue or a building whose form is given to it by another. Its degree of aliveness increases depending on the ways in which it receives and gives itself. A beautiful, harmonious pattern contains more self-gift than an ugly or broken one. An animal contains more *kenosis* than a stone, or even a statue. Thus life, for Alexander, is the radiance of being.

And of course, a creature that is able not only to grow and to move around but to reflect upon itself, to imagine, to will and know, possesses an even higher or more intensive participation in being, in the activity of God. And only men, with their refusal to give, may fail to be fully what they are or should be, what they are called to be, and fall short of the real. The type of life possessed by creatures such as ourselves, which is not simply to exist passively, and not merely to resist entropy, but to know and to will and to love, implies the possibility of failure or refusal.

As Alexander points out, whereas an atom is "so simple that there is never any question whether it is true to its own nature," this is not

20. Presupposed here is a theology of gift, and receptivity as a perfection, which will be discussed later.

the case with more complex systems, and most men "are not fully true to their own inner natures or fully 'real.' In fact, for many people, the effort to be true to themselves is the central problem of life. When you meet a person who is true to himself, you feel at once that he is 'more real' than other people are."[21]

Parts and Wholes

I have broadened the notion of life so that it can apply to everything that exists. As in the case of beauty or goodness, a thing may possess this property in various degrees. A heap of refuse or a bloody corpse is not beautiful, compared to a Greek statue, but some kind or degree of beauty is present in everything. To call beauty a "transcendental" implies that ugliness is simply a deprivation and never reaches absolute zero in anything that exists. The same would have to apply to the quality of livingness, or self-givingness, if this is a transcendental property. And yet the argument up to now, I must admit, is not entirely convincing, probably because the concept "life" feels as if it has been stretched a bit too far for comfort. The next stage of the argument may help to strengthen it.

We need to cease conceiving creatures as isolated and only externally related to each other, and begin to see them as interiorly related (through form and finality, relation and participation) to everything else. As we have seen, nothing in the world is completely alone. It is clear that our modern mentality lost a sense of the interconnectedness of things in the community of being, the "cosmos." But my own existence necessarily implies that of others, and my flesh is porous to the influences and elements of the environment around me. It is only for that reason that I am able to live at all, since the war against entropy depends on my not being a closed system. This means that the whole world, in a sense, can be seen as an extension of my own body. The fact that I am alive, and that other creatures are alive, is a function of our connectedness to the world, including the inorganic world.

The inorganic is necessary to the organic; one might even say that it is given a meaning or brought to fruition by the organic, just as

21. Alexander, *The Timeless Way of Building*, 27.

the organic (a Christian philosopher might add) culminates in the *personal* and is given a meaning by man. Which is to say, if I may complete this thought, that the world as a whole must be alive if we are alive, since all inorganic elements are parts, more or less remote but nevertheless essential parts, of an organic process. In themselves, of course, viewed in isolation, these elements lack an animating soul. But this is only one way of viewing them. In reality they are part of something much greater, to which we also belong, and this greater whole is alive. We recall that Plato in the *Timaeus* (30b) describes the world formed by god as "a living being, endowed thanks to his providence with soul and intelligence."

An interior relationality binds the whole world together, and this is made explicit in the liturgy of the Church. It is by participating in man as priest of creation, and in his sacrifice perfected in the Eucharist, that all creatures, including the inanimate elements, achieve the fullness of their own being by giving themselves to God and thus sharing his eternal life. Of course, it is important to note that St. Thomas, in the first part of the *Summa* (Q. 18, Art. 1), rejects Plato's idea that the "whole corporeal universe" is in fact "one animal." One can see why he should do this, and I don't plan to retrace the arguments here. But he does not take fully into account the intimate dependencies that exist between all things, and which have been explored by modern science. Nor does he give the Divine Liturgy the central role that (Eastern theologians have reminded us) was the perspective of the early Church. We can retrieve Plato's insight without falling out with Aquinas, especially if we deepen the liturgical perspective even further in the light of eschatology.

Briefly put, even if the world as a whole cannot convincingly be said to be "alive" right now, it *will* be alive when it attains its end. It is not alive yet, because the cosmic Fall has introduced death into it. Life—the life of God, that is, Trinitarian life—has not yet been fully revealed. Death has not yet been defeated, except in principle, by Christ. It is the *eschaton* that will reveal the true nature of the world that, right now, is still "groaning" to be born (Romans 8). We might speak of a "personalized" cosmos, a world that through union with Christ becomes a kind of theological person—namely the Church in her cosmic extension. And if the world is, or is becoming, a person, it is also, or is becoming, alive. The Holy Spirit is coming to "renew the face of the earth," by filling all things with the life of God—and "death shall be no more" (Rev. 21:4).

Life, one might say, is therefore a transcendental of a peculiar sort. It is an "eschatological" transcendental, pertaining to the perfection of all things in God. Like man himself, the cosmos is an unfinished project, a work in progress, which can only be completed with the cooperation of man, through death and resurrection. The "new heavens and the new earth" reveal the ultimate truth about the world. And this is where I would also see a place for the notion of Sophia, Wisdom, Sapientia, identifying it (with Louis Bouyer and Sergius Bulgakov) as the goal towards which creation tends—God's objective or purpose in creation. Sophia both pre-exists the act of creation (in God's foreknowledge), and does not yet exist (in the ever-moving present), and yet is mysteriously present throughout, accompanying the present as a foreshadowing of what will be. I will return to this topic at the end of the book.[22]

So you could say, paraphrasing Irenaeus, that the glory of God is not just a man fully alive, but the personalized *cosmos* fully alive, filled with life because penetrated by God's Holy Spirit. The reason I find Christopher Alexander so helpful is that his non-theological approach shows us from the side of nature an opening through beauty and life to the supernatural. In the fullness of this light, revealed to the eyes of faith, discussed in theology, and celebrated in the liturgy, we cannot treat nature—our own or anything else's—as we have done in the days of our ignorance, when things seemed to us already dead beneath our hands; for we know that our purpose is to gather them with love into never-ending life.

---

22. But for more on the "reverse causality" by which the shape of things is determined from the end point rather than the beginning, enabling the world to be freed from decay, sin, and death, see John Zizioulas, *Remembering the Future: An Eschatological Ontology* (London: T&T Clark International/ Continuum, 2013).

Saving the Planet

My aim in this chapter is to explore the relation of ecology to the Christian notion of redemption. I will also touch on the question of hope, and hopelessness. More and more ecologists seem to require counseling these days. Despair is a serious issue, and it needs to be addressed.

In the history of the Latin Church, it is, of course, not only the Franciscans who have contributed to the development of Christian ecological awareness. The Celtic saints and the Benedictines are often mentioned in this connection.[1] But Pope John Paul II made St. Francis, not St. Benedict or St. Columba, the patron saint of ecology in 1979, and he did so for understandable reasons. One might ask, however, why more saints and teachers of the Church have not been obvious candidates for this position. Deborah Jones, in her book *The School of Compassion*, points to the disconcerting indifference if not hostility towards the non-human creation on the part of many Christian teachers and authorities, for whom animals and the rest of nature were merely for man's use and would have no part in any resurrection. This applies even to the great Franciscan theologian Bonaventure. In the *Breviloquium*, where he treats of the resurrection, he argues that the animal and vegetable creation will be saved only in man, who "has a likeness to every kind of creature."

Such a conclusion can be seen as the legacy of a misunderstood or imperfectly assimilated Platonism, or even a kind of Gnosticism that values the spiritual at the expense of the corporeal. Rather than criticize the tradition along these lines, however, I prefer to remember

---

1. John Carey's book *A Single Ray of the Sun* discusses this neglected strand of Celtic and Irish thought in the legends of the saints, the writings of Augustinus Hibernicus, *In Tenga Bithnua*, with its prophecy of a resurrected earth, and Eriugena's *Periphyseon*.

that the Church is like "a householder who brings out of his treasure what is new and what is old" (Matt. 13:52). Historical circumstances and the challenges that arise may provoke a development of doctrine. In fact there are at least three areas where it is pretty obvious that Catholic teaching is currently undergoing development. One is the "theology of the body" (the term popularized by John Paul II in his series of Wednesday talks concerning gender, marriage, and sexuality); another is over the question of religious pluralism and the urgent dialogue between traditions of faith, and the third concerns nature and the environment. In my view all three are related, and they each require a "return to metaphysics"; that is, to a renewed appreciation of ontology and symbolism. But this time around, we must find a place for the rest of nature in our philosophy, in the spirit of St. Francis himself, whose instinct was to make special provision for the feeding of birds and cattle on Christmas Day.

The Revealing of the Sons of God

In Paul's Letter to the Romans (8:18–23), the Apostle writes:

> I consider that the sufferings of this present time are not worth comparing with the glory that is to be revealed to us. For the creation waits with eager longing for the revealing of the sons of God. For the creation was subjected to futility, not of its own will but by the will of him who subjected it in hope; because the creation itself will be set free from its bondage to decay and obtain the glorious liberty of the children of God.[2] We know that the whole creation has been groaning in travail together until now; and not only the creation, but we ourselves, who have the first fruits of the Spirit, groan inwardly as we wait for adoption as sons, the redemption of our bodies.

This passage is quite dense, and has been much commented upon. It seems to imply, first, that the "revealing of the sons of God" will liberate the natural creation as a whole from entropy, death, suffering, and decay, and, next, that this revelation of the sons of God is equivalent to our "adoption as sons" and with the "redemp-

---

2. Literally: ". . . the freedom of the glory of the children of God."

tion of our bodies." But what is the link between adoptive sonship and the redemption of our bodies, and how can a spiritual process like this affect the whole of creation? I don't have time here to explore all the eschatological implications of the passage, or the intriguing questions raised by the notion of a "cosmic fall." My emphasis will be on spiritual anthropology. I will interpret the "revealing of the sons of God" in terms of humanity's role as microcosm and mediator.

This idea has a long history. Right up until the time of Francis and Bonaventure and indeed the age of industrialism, the world was viewed as an organic whole, ordered from within, possessing a sacred and spiritual value by virtue of its creation by God and the continued divine presence within it. The stars were thought to be angelic creatures, the movements of their dance helping to determine the pattern of events unfolding below. The physical elements themselves were imagined as conscious beings, participating in a cosmic intelligence. It is quite in keeping with this ancient tradition for the Bible in the Canticle of Daniel to call upon all of creation to bless the Lord, including the sun and moon, stars of the heavens, clouds of the sky, showers and rain.[3] The animals, plants, and minerals, the stars and elements, can be said to "praise" their Maker, either simply by their very existence, or else though man, who gives them a voice they do not possess in themselves. (This is in fact the tradition to which Bonaventure appeals when he describes man as containing the essences of all other creatures.) In this view, the human being occupies a central place in the universe, but he does so as a microcosm containing all the elements of nature, and faculties or powers corresponding to both animals and angels. Adam's role in the cosmos is a priestly and mediatory one, radically compromised by the Fall, but restored in Christ, who by assuming human nature assumed *the whole of nature* by taking on a body.[4]

St. Francis is the "patron saint of the environment" partly because he spoke to the birds and was kind to animals, but also

3. Daniel 3:57–88, 56.
4. Maximus the Confessor, "Ambiguum 7," *On the Cosmic Mystery of Jesus Christ* (Crestwood, NY: SVS Press, 2003), 45–74.

because he understood and lived this mediatory role. The particular originality of his approach was to address not only the animals but even the elements of nature as his brothers and sisters; a spirituality expressed in the Canticle of Brother Sun, and exemplified in the way he spoke to Brother Fire and the other elements on various occasions. This was no mere sentimental romanticism (though he was certainly extremely romantic). His espousal of poverty brought him into the closest contact with the physical elements, and made him intensely aware of his dependence on them, under divine providence. He was conscious both of the presence of God within and through them, and of their infinite difference from God as mere creatures.

This love of nature was different from pagan animism, as G. K. Chesterton writes in the second chapter of his biography of Francis. The Celtic saints and Desert Fathers, and the Benedictine monks, had prepared the ground, but St. Francis was the beginning of a new stage in our relationship with nature (one that, it might be argued, has not yet been totally fulfilled). Chesterton writes of a necessary "purge of paganism" in the early Church, until at last the flowers and stars could recover their first innocence, and fire and water "be worthy to be the brother and sister of a saint":

> For water itself has been washed. Fire itself has been purified as by fire. Water is no longer the water into which slaves were flung to feed the fishes. Fire is no longer that fire through which children were passed to Moloch. Flowers smell no more of the forgotten garlands gathered in the garden of Priapus; stars stand no more as signs of the far frigidity of gods as cold as those cold fires. They are like all new things newly made and awaiting new names, from one who shall come to name them. Neither the universe nor the earth have now any longer the old sinister significance of the world. They await a new reconciliation with man, but they are already capable of being reconciled. Man has stripped from his soul the last rag of nature worship, and can return to nature.[5]

---

5. The passage ends rhetorically as follows: "While it was yet twilight a figure appeared silently and suddenly on a little hill above the city, dark against the fading darkness. For it was the end of a long and stern night, a night of vigil, not unvisited

What Chesterton leaves out of account here is the Eastern Church, which had become separated from the West, but preserved in its liturgical theology and in its iconographic tradition a cosmic vision that we must take into account. Our present historical age requires us to breathe with *two lungs*, if we are to have a hope of responding to the new post-Christian, post-religious mentality to which the West has given birth. And of the Eastern Fathers, St. Maximus the Confessor gave perhaps the most sophisticated theological expression to the view of man as mediator. Pope Benedict summarized the teaching of Maximus as follows:

> God entrusted to man, created in his image and likeness, the mission of unifying the cosmos. And just as Christ unified the human being in himself, the Creator unified the cosmos in man. He showed us how to unify the cosmos in the communion of Christ and thus truly arrived at a redeemed world. Hans Urs von Balthasar, one of the greatest theologians of the 20th century, referred to this powerful saving vision when, "relaunching" Maximus—he defined his thought with the vivid expression *Kosmische Liturgie*, "cosmic liturgy." Jesus, the one Savior of the world, is always at the center of this solemn "liturgy." The efficacy of his saving action which definitively unified the cosmos is guaranteed by the fact that in spite of being God in all things, he is also integrally a man and has the "energy" and will of a man. . . . Jesus Christ is the reference point that gives light to all other values. This was the conclusion of the great Confessor's witness. And it is in this way, ultimately, that Christ indicates that the cosmos must become a liturgy, the glory of God, and that worship is the beginning of true transformation, of the true renewal of the world.[6]

Balthasar's book on Maximus, to which the Pope refers, makes the point that the Confessor overcame the tendency in Christian thought to make the corporeal world of nature merely a ladder to heaven that will one day be kicked away, by positing an indestructi-

---

by stars. He stood with his hands lifted, as in so many statues and pictures, and about him was a burst of birds singing; and behind him was the break of day." G. K. Chesterton, *Collected Works*, vol. 11 (San Francisco: Ignatius Press, 1986), 44–5.

6. Pope Benedict XVI, General Audience, 25 June 2008. (All papal speeches and documents may be found on the web at www.vatican.va.)

ble relationship between spirit and matter, an "apologia for finite, created being in the face of the overwhelming power of the world of ideas."[7] The unity of the many depends on the parts and their relationship to each other. And since God is completely transcendent, the world of intellect takes us, in a sense, no closer to him than does the world disclosed by the senses.[8] This opens the way for a much deeper, less timorous, appreciation of the beauty and goodness of nature in general.

Human Ecology

The phrase "breathing with two lungs," as referring to Eastern and Western Christian traditions, was coined by Pope John Paul II. His own intensive efforts at reconciliation with the East were motivated by the need to bring all the resources of Christianity to bear on the task of evangelization in the modern world. And he gave a new lease of life to the ancient view of man as microcosm and the universe as a sacred cosmos. John Paul affirmed a mystical bond between ourselves and the rest of creation, and sought to recall us to our original mission as stewards and priests of nature, receiving the creation from God's hand, cultivating it or making it fruitful, and giving it back to him in sacrificial worship. The healing of the world around us, he believed, depends on a re-ordering and a healing of the inner world of imagination, intelligence, and will. Man was intended to be the mediator of creation, the one in whom all things connect, through whom all things are reconciled, the image of the invisible God (Col. 1:15–20). This high calling is fulfilled in Christ, the new Adam and incarnate Logos, into whom we are baptized when we receive the Holy Spirit.[9] In his encyclical on the Holy Spirit (*Dominum et Vivificantem*, 50), he puts it like this:

> The Incarnation of God the Son signifies the taking up into unity with God not only of human nature, but in this human nature, in

---

7. Hans Urs von Balthasar, *Cosmic Liturgy: The Universe According to Maximus the Confessor* (San Francisco: Ignatius Press, 2003), 239.

8. Ibid., 172.

9. As background to the present chapter please see the very useful document of the International Theological Commission, "Communion and Stewardship: Human

a sense, of everything that is "flesh": the whole of humanity, the entire visible and material world. The Incarnation, then, also has a cosmic significance, a cosmic dimension. The "first-born of all creation," becoming incarnate in the individual humanity of Christ, unites himself in some way with the entire reality of man, which is also "flesh"—and in this reality with all "flesh," with the whole of creation.

Pope Benedict XVI picked up John Paul's cosmic personalism in *Caritas in Veritate*, which anchors its whole argument in the "centrality of the human person" (*CV*, 47) and the relational nature of man (*CV*, 53–5). For both popes, in fact, "human ecology" is inseparable from environmental ecology, because respect for ourselves, for our sexuality, and for human life in all its stages and manifestations, is the manifestation of a respect for nature as such, which has been created in divine Wisdom:

> The book of nature is one and indivisible: it takes in not only the environment but also life, sexuality, marriage, the family, social relations: in a word, integral human development. Our duties towards the environment are linked to our duties towards the human person, considered in himself and in relation to others. It would be wrong to uphold one set of duties while trampling on the other. (*CV*, 51)

Thinking through this link between human and environmental ecology is no easy matter. To some people the connection is obvious, but the difficulty is demonstrating it to those for whom this is not the case. In a world where everything is assumed to be disconnected from everything else, in which each man is an island, it is so easy to think that political or environmental problems can be treated separately from matters of private or sexual morality.[10]

Persons Created in the Image of God" (2002), available at www.vatican.va. Celia Deane-Drummond provides a useful survey of the literature in *Eco-Theology*. Catholic teaching on ecological responsibility was summarized in *The Compendium of the Social Doctrine of the Church* (Vatican, 2004), and has been consolidated further by Benedict XVI in *Caritas in Veritate* (2009).

10. Mary Taylor makes the point that environmental concern has moved through at least three phases or "trajectories." The first is that of reductive science,

In order to make this point clearer I will try to develop the notion of an "ethical microcosm" as an extension of virtue ethics. By this I mean the type of ethical theory that, unlike accounts of morality that emphasize the necessity of conforming to a set of moral rules (deontological), or deciding the right thing to do entirely on the basis of likely consequences (utilitarian), regards morality as having to do with the development of character and wisdom—conformity, if you like, with a moral nature or norm. The virtue ethics approach is radically at odds with the most common type of ethical thinking in the environmental movement, where the "end" (for example, the survival of the ecosystem) justifies the "means" (for example, artificial or even coercive methods of population control). And yet, the virtue ethics approach does have a certain intuitive appeal, as expressed in this splendid quotation from Dr. Martin Luther King Jr.: "We will never have peace in the world until men everywhere recognize that ends are not cut off from the means, because the means represent the ideal in the making, and the end in process. Ultimately you can't reach good ends through evil means, because the means represent the seed and the end represents the tree."[11]

St. Thomas Aquinas teaches that love or charity is the "form" of the virtues. Virtues are the powers or habits that conform us to that image and likeness of love. To acquire virtue, in the true sense of being *inwardly formed* by love, in such a way that we naturally make our day-to-day practical decisions in harmony with divine wisdom,

and the second that of postmodern idealism (so called "deep ecology" fits here). The third is a "human" or "personalist" ecology that balances and integrates concern for human beings with concern for the wider environment of creatures. See M. Taylor, "A Deeper Ecology: A Catholic Vision of the Person in Nature," *Communio* 38:4 (Winter 2011), 583–620. See also Pablo Martinez, *Environmental Solidarity* (London: Routledge, 2011).

11. I am afraid I do not have a source for this quotation, or for another from Dr. King that may be helpful: "We are tied together in the single garment of destiny, caught in an inescapable network of mutuality. And whatever affects one directly affects all indirectly. For some strange reason I can never be what I ought to be until you are what you ought to be. And you can never be what you ought to be until I am what I ought to be. This is the way God's universe is made; this is the way it is structured."

is to become holy. And the portrait of the virtuous or holy person is given for all time in the Beatitudes of the Sermon on the Mount: the poor in spirit, those who mourn, the meek, those who hunger for righteousness (we remember the "groaning" of creation in Romans 8), the merciful who will have mercy shown them, the pure in heart who will see God, the peacemakers who will be called "sons of God." These Beatitudes are first of all the portrait of Jesus himself, who is the universal norm of ethics—the Good—concretely embodied in a human life.[12] They also describe that "second Christ" who was St. Francis of Assisi. What the Beatitudes give us is an image of man restored to health and sanity. And as such they describe what I am calling the "ethical microcosm": man, reflecting the whole of creation in himself, but now conforming to the inner law and purpose of his own nature.

In simple and practical terms, the notion of an ethical microcosm implies that, more important than codifying a list of rights belonging to nature or to animals, and then legislating to enforce them, and more important than working out exactly how our treatment of nature will damage society's happiness or the planet's chances of survival, is to become the *kind of people* who are never cruel to animals or needlessly destructive. Laws are clearly necessary, but we at least should know that they will not succeed in solving anything (no matter how rigorously they are enforced) if we do not also acquire virtue in ourselves. Thus the one-sided emphasis on moral law which has afflicted us for too long, certainly since Kant, but perhaps since William of Ockham, may be transcended by integrating the notion of duty within an anthropology; that is, an understanding of the human being as called to holiness in the image and likeness of God. We must act in certain ways not because we are ordered to do so by a divine legislator, but because we are yearning

---

12. Christ is the "concrete categorical imperative": see Heinz Schurmann et al., *Principles of Christian Morality* (San Francisco: Ignatius Press, 1986), 79: "Christian ethics must be modelled on Jesus Christ since, as the Son of the Father, he carried out the entire will of God (i.e. every 'ought') in the world. He did this 'for us,' so that from him, the fulfilled concrete norm of all ethical actions, we might receive the freedom to fulfill God's will and to live according to our nature as free children of the Father."

to unite ourselves with the divine Beloved. This anthropology is "nuptial" (to use John Paul II's expression). The purpose of history, you might say, is to bring about the *liturgical consummation of cosmology* in what the Book of Revelation describes as the "wedding feast of the Lamb."

The Three Kinds of Hope

The problem remains, of course. For probably the majority in the environmental movement will not see the relevance of mysticism, or personal virtue and morality, to the great issues of our day. To them it is merely a technological or political challenge. They will try to get their hands on the levers of power, and will be increasingly and everlastingly frustrated to discover that all their attempts come to nothing, or make things worse. I do not mean to say that there is no point in political action, but rather that the assumption that these problems are *primarily* political is a mistake. We need a new kind of politics, a new kind of technology, to solve these problems, namely a politics and a technology that have not been elevated to the level of what the Pope calls "ideological power" (*Caritas in Veritate*, 70). We need the kind of "appropriate technology" that has been developed for use in the poorer regions of the world, and we need a more local politics, in accordance with the Catholic principle of subsidiarity. This would place the emphasis back on the human person and our individual efforts. The belief that we can solve the world's problems by throwing power and money at them does not take account of human nature. It leads to the creation of vast commercial and political empires that inevitably become corrupt.

We need to remember that the call to holiness takes place *in the midst of our fallen state*. This is why our efforts to do good are so often frustrated. There is no immediate return to the conditions preceding our exile from Eden—even if saints like St. Francis give us a glimpse of prelapsarian innocence. Francis may have been able to speak with the animals like Adam, but he was nevertheless afflicted still by illness and eventually death. Christ, though without sin, adopted the condition of fallen man, and as such he was subject to the same human state. We who come after, in the time of the Church, are living within his body and to some extent measuring out the years before his resurrection is fully revealed to all. The Book of Revelation speaks of a "new heavens and new earth" (Rev. 21:1) where mourning and crying will cease, but for now there are tears a-plenty. That is why, in the passage I quoted earlier from Romans 8, there are three references to "groaning": creation groans in travail (v. 22); we groan inwardly as we wait for our adoption as sons in the Son (v. 23); and the Holy Spirit, the personification of God's self-gift to us, groans in supplication on our behalf since we do not know how to pray as we ought (v. 26). This word "groaning" signifies the sadness, suffering, and expectation of the whole world; its longing for liberation and the misery of decay. Groaning expresses the tension between what we are now and what we will become, and is a measure of the distance and difference the overcoming of which is anticipated through the virtue of hope.[13]

The author of *The Lord of the Rings*, J. R. R. Tolkien, in constructing a language for the pre-Christian Elves of Middle-earth, gives them two main words for hope.[14] The word *Amdir*, which means "looking up," refers to optimism, or the expectation that things will turn out well or at least get better. The assumption that the ecological crisis can be solved, that big corporations can be persuaded to change their ways, that the earth can survive whatever we throw at it, these fall under the heading of *Amdir*. The second word, *Estel*, means "trust"—trust in our deepest nature and the being of things, or in their source of being, despite the apparent victory of evils known and experienced. That, I would say, is perfectly valid, and in its own way quite consoling, but in the face of so much evil it is easily overwhelmed. To these two kinds of hope we must add a third, for which there is no Elvish word. Christian hope is not psychological nor metaphysical, but theological. It rests on the gift of faith. This is the

---

13. It is also an expression of desire, of *eros*. So for example, Maximus the Confessor quotes the prophet-king David; "*Crying out I will be satisfied when your glory appears* (Ps. 16:15). And: *My soul thirsts for the strong and living God* (Ps. 42:2)." (*On the Cosmic Mystery of Jesus Christ*, 49.) *Deus Caritas Est*, with its analysis of the close relationship between *eros* and *agape*, could be used to explore in greater depth this aspect of "groaning."

14. See J. R. R. Tolkien, *Morgoth's Ring: The Later Silmarillion, Part One* (Boston: Houghton Mifflin, 1993), 320.

hope with which Benedict is mainly concerned. In section 31 of *Spe Salvi*, his encyclical on Hope, Benedict writes that while "we need the greater and lesser hopes that keep us going day by day . . . these are not enough without the great hope, which must surpass everything else. This great hope can only be God, who encompasses the whole of reality and who can bestow upon us what we, by ourselves, cannot attain."

Today, as I mentioned, many environmentalists are falling into despair. Pope Benedict diagnoses the problem thus:

> All serious and upright human conduct is hope in action. . . . Yet our daily efforts in pursuing our own lives and in working for the world's future either tire us or turn into fanaticism, unless we are enlightened by the radiance of the great hope that cannot be destroyed even by small-scale failures or by a breakdown in matters of historic importance. If we cannot hope for more than is effectively attainable at any given time, or more than is promised by political or economic authorities, our lives will soon be without hope. (35)

Without "the greater hope" that Christianity offers, environmentalism will end in fanaticism or despair. But at the same time the Pope reminds religious believers that secular environmentalists have had good reason to reject them as potential allies—for "modern Christianity, faced with the successes of science in progressively structuring the world, has to a large extent restricted its attention to the individual and his salvation. In so doing it has limited the horizon of its hope and has failed to recognize sufficiently the greatness of its task" (25). This restriction of Christianity to the individual level is, I take it, precisely what we now need to overcome. As Christians we have been too hasty to "limit the horizon of our hope," so that hope has indeed become a feeble-minded excuse for inaction.

The children of God are revealed in a life of holiness, which is a life where love has become tangible. The sign of love is not the creeds we adhere to, or the ideas we carry in our heads, but the spirit in which we behave towards each other and the world, which is a spirit of hope. The liturgy and Eucharist begin where philosophy also begins, in amazement and gratitude, in praise for the sheer existence of so much beauty, so much actuality. Forests and mountains, deserts and stars, animals, plants and insects are here and gone in a day, and their existence is fraught with sorrow, but God made them and pronounced them good. In our mysterious desire to unite ourselves with the Giver, to find the source and thank him, somehow, however inadequately, for the community of being, we begin to recall the reason we were made, and to play our part in the redemption of the world.

St. Francis can be an inspiration and example to those in the ecology movement for the simple reason that he lived his life as an imitation of Christ. Christ's portrait was reproduced in him. And I think we can also see in Francis, Western though he was, the potentiality for a reconciliation of East and West. Though his followers, beginning with Giotto, initiated the departure from the ancient iconographic traditions that would culminate in the Renaissance, Francis himself became a living icon. It was an icon perfected in the vision on Mount Alverna, where he was confronted with the six-winged Seraph in the form of a man crucified, and was imprinted in his own body with the wounds of the Cross. Devotion to the suffering humanity of Christ is a very Western devotion. But the glorified wounds, the idea that they persist in the Resurrection as signs of love, perhaps represents something that the West can contribute to the East.

So Francis is not the end-point, but rather a pointer, a signpost towards the great reconciliation of Christians in one and the same calling. That can only be achieved by the following of Christ in the flesh, through death to resurrection, bringing with us the whole of creation.

The Blessed Earth

Ecology is therefore a serious business; a *theological* business. If (as I suggested) the animals are angels—not each cat or dog, centipede or flamingo a distinct angel, but each species or family of animals the fragmented instantiation of an intelligent, immortal angelic force, a constituent element in the cosmos—then surely we have to recognize a new seriousness in the heinous crime of extinguishing a species from the face of the earth: an angel is being thrust out of God's creation by man.

In the first chapter of the book of Genesis, God "saw all the things that he had made, and they were very good" (1:31). Here is the earliest and best refutation of the philosophical heresy of recent times (that of David Hume and others) that separates facts from values. Implicit in Scripture is the sense that there is something *ontological* about goodness: in other words, that it is an intrinsic attribute of being. If this means anything, it surely means that all creatures are *worthy of love*. They deserve it; it belongs to them. But at the same time we have to remember that in the traditional understanding of the word, to love something is not just to feel warm and friendly towards it: it is to *will its existence*, its life, its fulfillment. We are therefore *obliged*, as free creatures capable of having a moral obligation, to love the creation in something like the way that God loves it. Animals are due that love, whether they are angels or not.

But now we have to ask, can that "debt" be called a "right"—a *right* to be loved, to be respected, to be nourished and helped? Is there such a thing as "animal rights"?

It seems to be generally assumed by Christian and other philosophers that a "right" can only be possessed by someone who is *capable also of assuming obligations*. But it seems to me that it is always obligations, duties, and debts that in the first place create the "rights" which correspond to them. You have a right to the money I owe you because I have a debt to you, or an obligation towards you; I do not first have an obligation to pay the money because you have a right to it. My obligation to you is based on your prior gift to me (or simply your need for the money), coupled with my love for you that leads me to want your good. Gifts naturally evoke gratitude, and the desire to reciprocate. We are all creatures, receiving all that we have, including our existence, from a divine Source as well as from each other. We must recognize that we all start from a position of obligation, of gratitude, of love. Any subsequent debts we incur, as we receive more from each other during life, simply add to this fundamental indebtedness—and the whole moral life, inspired by love, is a joyful repayment of an endless debt.

Rights, then, according to this line of thought, are entirely secondary. They are a way of describing and, ultimately, codifying our debts, both as individuals and as members of a group. To the extent that they enter into positive law, then it can certainly be said that "I owe you because you have a right." But that is only because this is the way we have defined our obligations. Having done so, rights are used to remind us of our duties under the eternal law of God and existence.

From that it seems to follow that there may be creatures that (unlike humans) have rights without having duties—simply because they *generate obligations in us* by their very existence. If that is the case, it would after all make sense to talk about "animal rights." But we are not talking, yet, about rights in law. The codification in law of animal and of human rights might look very different. Animals, and the rest of the natural world, do not enter into legal arrangements, and here the reciprocity that is attributed to rights and duties comes into its own. To the extent that rights are *contractual*, animals are not eligible for them. Perhaps there is a case for keeping the word "rights" for these contractual or positive relationships only. Yet I can't help wondering if "animal rights" might still be a way of describing part of the general obligation we possess towards the world to maintain and preserve it, its integrity and beauty, both for its own sake (as having intrinsic value) and for the sake of our own distant neighbors and unborn descendants.

After all, though animals may not enter into a contract, they do enter into a *covenant*. To be specific, they enter into the "rainbow covenant" that God made with Noah as high priest of creation (Gen. 8:20–22) and with the birds, cattle, and beasts of the earth (Gen. 9:9–17). According to the terms of that covenant, God would not destroy the earth again with a flood like the one that had just taken place. The terms of the covenant also specified that the life of man was sacrosanct, whereas animals were given to man to eat. Vegetarians might quibble with this, but it does at least mean that animals are included as partners in an agreement: for their part, they are required not to attack man (9:5). While the covenant does not assign rights to the parties, it imposes duties. The fact that animals are given to man for food also implies that they are not for abuse. They now come under his stewardship in the way the vegetable world did before: as entrusted to his care. He may use them for his bodily needs; but nothing is said of his luxuries. The Bible does not envisage the grotesque abuse of animals, for example in cosmetic experiments.

So what do we conclude? The other day my friend's pet was put down, after it became too ill to survive and was living in constant pain. The same night I slapped a mosquito that was keeping me awake, and squashed a spider that would have frightened my children (in fact it frightened me). I put antiseptic on a cut to kill any lurking germs. Did these creatures, large and small, have a *right to life*? They certainly had a right not to be treated cruelly, or killed without reason. But nothing I have said actually implies that they have a right to life in the absolute sense: the sense in which we rightly apply it to an innocent human being. The reason for this surely lies in the intrinsic difference between the animal and the human.

The animal is worthy of love, but love must respect the *nature* of the creature in question. If the goodness in things is "ontological," it is proportioned to their being, and to their *level* of being. A dog or a spider is not in itself a person, even if the species, or the angel of the species, is one. A human being is not merely the instantiation of a species, but a unique individual with a unique destiny. He or she is made "in the image of God," not in the image of an angel, and the sacredness of human life (even in the womb) is correspondingly of a different order. Moreover humanity has a "dominion" over the rest of creation that it was simply *not given* over its own nature, this being reserved to God alone. All of this we see reflected in the rainbow covenant.

However we misuse it, our dominion over the animals and over the whole earth in some way persists. The fact that the very survival of the earthly ecosystem is now threatened by industrial and military technology demonstrates the fact. For better or worse, it is not "speciesism" but *realism* to locate human beings at the center of the world, as microcosm. But that centrality, far from implying careless disregard and selfish irresponsibility, implies the exact opposite. That is our fundamental obligation which we are now massively failing to fulfill: the obligation to "dress and keep," to "till and cultivate" the blessed earth which sustains all our lives and speaks to us continually of the glory of God.

PART II

DIVINE NATURE

Having set out in search of the secret of Charity, one day I 'encountered' Trinitarian theology.... I went back to ancient doctrines like a delighted child going from discovery to discovery, from treasure to treasure, from marvel to marvel.... Drinking in the freshness of the ages, I felt my Christian soul revive. Henceforth it was impossible to repudiate the source of our faith, impossible not to offer it to drink.

Jean Borella[1]

If we were more Christian, we would talk about the Trinity all the time, for we would understand that the Trinity is the source and the great secret which helps us understand all things.

Marie-Dominique Philippe OP[2]

---

1. Jean Borella, *The Secret of the Christian Way*, ed. and trans. G. John Champoux (State University of New York Press, 2001), 3.
2. Marie-Dominique Philippe OP, *Wherever He Goes: A Retreat on the Gospel of John* (Laredo, TX: Congregation of St. John, 1998), 124.

One in Three

"For this I was born, and for this I have come into the world, to bear witness to the truth. Everyone who is of the truth hears my voice."

Pilate said to him, "What is truth?" (John 18:37–8)

The fact is, we live in an increasingly pluralistic society. One in three of the world's population is Christian (more than a half of that are Catholic). Muslims account for roughly 21%, Hindus 14%, Buddhists 7%, non-religious for 16%.[1] But believers are scattered across the world, and modern communications and transport have brought about a situation where most people grow up with neighbors and friends or family members belonging to a variety of faiths. Some parts of England are more Muslim than Christian. The biggest Buddhist monastery and research center in Europe is located in the west Scottish lowlands, at Eskdalemuir. I have never been there, but I am told it is big and pink, with paintwork in red, yellow, blue, and gold. Inside are 1000 golden Buddhas, gold-encrusted pillars and silk-screen prints of dragons and birds.

A person trying to make moral and metaphysical sense of a world where the scriptures of every religion are equally accessible on the internet or in any large bookshop may be forgiven for feeling a bit confused about the nature of God, or even about whether there is a God. Every one of these religions offers a complete way of life and claims to answer the question of human and/or cosmic meaning. Apart from their obvious social and cultural expressions, every one of them has the following five components: *scriptures, institutions, doctrines, morality,* and *rituals*. Most if not all of them claim some kind of revelation from heaven, and their holy men and women seem reputedly to perform the same kinds of miracles. Yet if you

1. Statistics from http://www.adherents.com/.

look at the actual teachings of each religion, they are so different from each other that they often appear contradictory.

In order to create a space for religious studies within an increasingly secular academy, Ninian Smart, the exponent of "comparative religion," prescinded from the truth claims made by any religion and argued that they should be studied simply as social and cultural phenomena in their own right. Christians or Muslims or Buddhists would be at liberty to believe what they liked, but religious studies has to be concerned only with the truth of *what they believed*, not with sorting out which of their beliefs was true. Similarly, the philosopher John Hick promotes the idea of religious pluralism: that all religions are (equally inadequate) "human" responses to the ineffable, historically and culturally conditioned and therefore not to be taken as absolute or certain.[2]

Catholics cannot simply dismiss other religions as completely false. We are told in *Nostra Aetate*:

> The Catholic Church rejects nothing of what is true and holy in these religions. She has a high regard for the manner of life and conduct, the precepts and doctrines which, although differing in many ways from her own teaching, nevertheless often reflects a ray of that truth which enlightens all men [John 1:9].... The Church, therefore, exhorts her sons, that through dialogue and collaboration with the followers of other religions, carried out with prudence and love and in witness to the Christian faith and life, they recognize, preserve and promote the good things, spiritual and moral, as well as the socio-cultural values found among them. (n. 2)

Thus the Church recognizes there are "good things," even truths, to be found in other religions. The question is how to "preserve and promote" these good things at the same time as witnessing to Christ; for the sentence I omitted from the quotation I just gave affirms that the Church "proclaims, and ever must proclaim Christ 'the way, the truth, and the life' (John 14:6), in whom men may find the fullness of religious life, in whom God has reconciled all things

---

2. See Gavin D'Costa, *Theology and Religious Pluralism* (Oxford: Blackwell, 1986).

to Himself." Catholics are committed to the belief that our faith is *true*—we cannot drop one part of it simply because another religion disagrees with it.

"Interfaith dialogue," which was one of the themes and achievements of the Second Vatican Council, received an enormous boost from Pope John Paul II. In 1986 he organized an inter-religious prayer meeting in Assisi that may have been one of the inspired moments of his pontificate, although it provoked severe criticism from some Catholic conservatives. In order to take account of these criticisms, the Pope was careful to make a distinction between "praying with" and "praying in the presence of" a member of another religion, given the widely different understandings we have of what it is we do when we pray, and of exactly whom we address in our prayer. It is not possible to pray a common prayer, he said, but only to pray our own prayers in the same place. He also took pains to emphasize that he was not encouraging relativism:

> The fact that we have come here does not imply any intention of seeking a religious consensus among ourselves or of negotiating our faith convictions. Neither does it mean that religions can be reconciled at the level of a common commitment in an earthly project which would surpass them all. Nor is it a concession to relativism in religious beliefs, because every human being must sincerely follow his or her upright conscience with the intention of seeking and obeying the truth.[3]

In making these remarks, he may have had in mind several recent attempts to produce a kind of global religious alliance along the lines of a World Parliament of Religions, such as the United Religions Initiative (www.uri.org). Such attempts are full of good intentions, but risk subordinating the search for truth to the search for peace and social collaboration.[4]

---

3. John Paul II, "Address to the Representatives of the Christian Churches and Ecclesial Communities and of the World Religions Gathered in Assisi for the World Day of Prayer," 27 October 1986.

4. More should be said about dialogue, to distinguish for example the different forms it takes, not all of which involve the confrontation of one theological or doctrinal position with another (see my booklet *Catholicism and Other Religions*). One

An ecumenism that is prepared to gloss over substantial differences for the sake of initiating friendly discussion needs to give way to a more profound engagement. But those who try to engage at this level soon find that the differences are *so* substantial because each religion is actually an answer to a slightly different question.

• The primary question that the religions of India tend to ask is *Who am I?* The answer that emerges from the Upanishads and from the teachings of the Buddha is that the innermost self is one with the Absolute.

• Buddhism asks, *What is the way beyond suffering?* The answer it gives is the Noble Eightfold Path of detachment from the world.

• Judaism asks, *Who are we?* Or *What is our identity as a People?* Being Jewish is being a member of the people who have been called into a Covenant by the One God, a Covenant defined in the Law, the Torah.

• Islam asks simply, *What must I believe and do, in order to be rightly guided?* The answer is that I must worship the one God only, and follow his Prophet.

• The fundamental question Christianity asks is different again: *Who is Christ?* or *What must I do to be saved from sin and death?* The answers are: Christ is the Son of God, the second Person of the Holy Trinity, and to be saved one must believe in him, or entrust oneself to him.

The more deeply one investigates the religious experience of

---

particularly important development is that spearheaded by Angelo Cardinal Scola and his Oasis Foundation, based on the principle of a human "universal," the existence of a common or shared experience of being human, that allows communication and translation across and between cultures. Theological and political differences are often irresolvable, but it is a fact that members of rival religious communities and traditions find themselves sharing a territory, a city, a neighborhood. In this way they build a common culture without ever reaching ideological agreement. The interest of Oasis is in the cultural interpretation of the faith that determines the interaction of these human communities. Here it may be appropriate to speak of "conversation" rather than "dialogue."

mankind, the clearer it becomes that the doctrines of the Incarnation and the Trinity constitute the special and unique treasure that Christians bring to any dialogue with others. Of course, each of the "great religions" can lay claim to uniqueness in respect of the one question to which it is the specific answer. That is why, from the perspective of each, it appears at the center while all the others belong on the periphery. This is the basis for claims of superiority, and lies at the root of much mutual incomprehension.[5] But even the enormous differences between, say, the monotheism of Islam and what we might call the therapeutic agnosticism of Buddhism fade into insignificance when compared to the difference made by the doctrine of the Incarnation. The claim that Christ is God *in person*, not merely a teacher of the truth, a prophet, or a projection of God, and that the Church is imbued with the authority of God through the continuing presence of the Holy Spirit, differentiates Christianity at the deepest level from all the great religious traditions.[6]

In this chapter, therefore, we need to clarify the meaning of these particular doctrines, to explain how they came to be affirmed, and to show how they are related. How did we get from the One God to a God who is Three and One?[7]

God as Such

God is a spirit, or rather is Spirit. The word for "spirit" is derived from the Latin for "breath" or "wind": something that moves other things yet remains essentially invisible. Yet philosophically it would be appropriate to identify "spirit" with inwardness, or interiority.

---

5. See J. A. DiNoia, *The Diversity of Religions: A Christian Perspective* (Washington, DC: Catholic University of America Press, 1992), in which this is the major theme. On what follows, see especially Massimo Serretti, *The Uniqueness and Universality of Jesus Christ: In Dialogue with the Religions*, transl. Teresa Talavera and David C. Schindler (Grand Rapids, MI: Eerdmans, 2001).

6. Frithjof Schuon's doctrine of the "transcendent unity of religions" will be discussed further in the chapter on non-dualism.

7. For a detailed survey of the Trinitarian debates at the high point of the Western scholastic tradition, see Giles Emery OP, "The Threeness and Oneness of God in Twelfth to Fourteenth Century Scholasticism," *Nova et Vetera*, English Edition, vol. 1, no. 1 (2003), 43–74.

That is where intrinsic or essential invisibility comes from. The eye cannot see itself (except indirectly, say in a mirror). Consciousness is not visible to itself; it is that in which all else is seen. It reveals itself by our outward behavior, but its presence is only known certainly to itself and in itself (and perhaps we may say, disagreeing with Descartes, reflexively *in action* rather than as an image or object of the mind).

When I say "I" it is my spirit speaking. The mysteries of the "I" point towards the mystery of God. You and I can both say "I," but I cannot say it on your behalf. I am the center of the entire world, and yet I know that you can legitimately say exactly the same—*for you* all things revolve around you and are situated in relation to you. This experience of selfhood is only a reflection of, or participation in, the selfhood of God. That is where it *comes from*. The "I" of absolute Spirit, of God, is the self or "I" of all things: it is the "I" in relation to which every other self, every existing thing, is situated. Thus God as Spirit is the "absolute 'I'" or center and Principle of all things, the supreme Subject in relation to which all other entities, including all other subjects, are reduced to the position of object.

It is in this way that I make sense of the claim that God, as supreme Principle, is no merely impersonal "Force," as in *Star Wars*, let alone a mere abstraction, but conscious, and indeed the highest consciousness conceivable. God is the supreme spirit, "I," or self. If the Principle were *not* this, then the whole world of human subjectivity, of human experience, which is as real as anything else that exists, would remain unaccounted for. Consciousness, too, must have its archetype.

What else can be said of the divine essence, this Principle or Absolute? There are two distinct approaches, known as the cataphatic (or *via positiva*) and the apophatic (or *via negativa*): the way of immanence—seeing God in everything—and the way of transcendence—seeing God as beyond everything.

Positive statements about God, as in the tradition of the divine Names or Attributes, are based on the principle of analogy—the fact that all that exists must naturally bear some resemblance to its maker, since he draws on knowledge of himself to make these things. Attributes such as Wisdom, Justice, Goodness, Majesty,

Beauty, and so on, which we attribute primarily to things and people in the world, must exist to a supreme degree in God. (Since evil is merely the lack of some good that would otherwise exist, attributes such as Cruelty, Foolishness, and Ugliness do not exist in God but only in creatures.) Once again, this *via positiva* offers only a series of pointers to God, not a clear picture of God as he is in himself, who remains as mysterious as ever. The *via negativa* consequently denies the resemblance between God and creatures on the grounds that God is always going to be more *unlike* than he is *like* the things he has made. Between the finite and the infinite there can be no common measure.

Denys (or Dionysius) the Areopagite combines these two methods into a third, the "superlative" way that praises and celebrates God as the super-eminent and super-excellent lover and creator of all things. That is to say, God is not just majestic, but *super*-majestic—a formulation that preserves the sense that he is both like and unlike the things we can imagine. Nicholas of Cusa, in the same tradition of Christian Platonism, locates God beyond the "coincidence of opposites," knowing him, as it were, in not-knowing him.

And still we are back at the threshold of Christianity, and have not yet broached the question of those Names that are above every name: Father, Son, and Holy Spirit.[8]

Enter the Trinity

The next step is to see that God may choose not to leave us on the threshold, but come to meet us; that he may make himself known within the creation, sharing with us his own knowledge of himself (and this ultimately means sharing *himself*). This is what our tradition calls the "Covenant." The skeptic will object immediately, however, that revealing himself "within" creation (say as a partner in a Covenant or as a provider of miracles) is not at all the kind of thing that the Absolute, as I have so far been describing him, would or could do. To intervene in that way might be a possible course of

---

8. I am not, of course, implying that Dionysius and Nicholas do not cross that threshold—indeed they do, since both are Christian theologians as well as philosophers—merely that the arguments used so far do not take us there.

action for an anthropomorphic God, but not for a Supreme Principle, however "conscious" or super-conscious he might be.

This would be a valid objection were God only *what we have said so far*. That he is more than this is something that philosophy alone cannot show us. It is God who now reveals, not only his own inner nature, but how such a process of self-revelation might be possible, and moreover in a way that does not contradict human philosophy. This is the revelation of the Trinity, which takes place through the Incarnation of one of the three divine persons.

As commentators have shown, on the evidence of the Gospels, the man Jesus did not act merely as a Prophet and Rabbi. He claimed the divine name ("I am"), that is, he identified himself with pure Being and the source of all existence, and for this he was crucified. But though he claimed to be divine, and acted as such by forgiving sins and raising the dead, he also distinguished himself from God the Father, whom he called *Abba* ("Papa"), and from the Holy Spirit whom he promised to send down upon his Apostles from heaven. He prayed to God as though to a Father, although in a more than creaturely intimacy. And yet he claimed to adhere to Jewish monotheism. Finally he rose from the dead to live forever, and announced that all authority in heaven and earth had been entrusted to him.[9]

If a scientist must develop a theory to account for seemingly contradictory results of an experiment with electrons or photons, which perhaps shows them behaving equally as particles and as waves or existing in two places at the same time, so must the theologian reconcile these seemingly contradictory evidences from revelation, in a way that does not contradict human reason.

Reflecting in this way, the early Christians were forced to the conclusion that in order to make sense of the statements and behavior of Jesus, God must (somehow) be Three: Father, Son, and Holy

9. For a summary of the arguments against the "form criticism" that would undermine these claims, and on behalf of a "Jesus of testimony" overcoming the dichotomy of the "Jesus of faith" *vs.* the "Jesus of history," see Barry R. Pearlman, *A Certain Faith: Analogy of Being and the Affirmation of Belief* (Lanham, MD: University Press of America, 2012), Part 2.

Spirit. And yet they could not deny the truth, already perceived by other religions and by the philosophers, and taught most vigorously of all by their own faith (Judaism), that God is One. According to the perennial philosophy agreed upon by all great civilizations, the divine nature must be perfectly "simple," in the sense of being non-composite and indivisible. To say that God is Three, then, cannot mean that there are three Gods. It must be the One, undivided God who is a Trinity.

In order to explain this paradox of "Triunity," the Church Fathers and later theologians drew a distinction between nature and person. God is not three individual natures or substances; he is three persons. The divine *nature* cannot be divided. It can, however, be *related to itself* in more ways than one—by knowing and loving itself in one simple and eternal act. What is revealed through the Incarnation is the existence in God of "subsisting relationships," which are the divine persons.[10] God *knowing himself* is the relationship of Father to Son, and *loving himself* is the relationship of Son and Father to Holy Spirit. The Spirit is the Love of Father and of Son, their reciprocal and infinite openness and affection—the consummation, in a sense, of the act of knowing that God is. This is the "circle dance," circumincession or *perichoresis* of the Trinity, which is the heavenly model of human love and its ultimate source.

This is implicit in verses such as the following. "All things have been delivered to me by my Father; and no one knows the Son except the Father, and no one knows the Father except the Son and anyone to whom the Son chooses to reveal him" (Matt. 11:27). "'What no eye has seen, nor ear heard, nor the heart of man conceived, what God has prepared for those who love him', God has revealed to us through the Spirit. For the Spirit searches everything, even the depths of God" (1 Cor. 2:9–10). "He who does not love

10. For Aristotle, *relation* belonged among the "accidents," the incidentals or circumstances of being (and in God there are no accidents), whereas substance was the real thing itself. But for Christianity, the "dialogue" in God between the Persons, the *relation* is "an equally primordial form of being" (Ratzinger, *Introduction to Christianity,* 183). Indeed, Adrian Pabst finds already in Boethius the doctrine that "divine substantiality is *constituted by* Trinitarian relations" (*Metaphysics*, 136, my emphasis).

does not know God; for God is love" (1 John 4:8). By way of commentary, a fifth-century Christian writes: "By revealing the Father in the Spirit, Christ has disclosed for us the secret nature of the living God, showing us depths of love in the Trinity. To return to the great affirmations of the Gospel, only the Son knows the Father as the Father knows the Son, and as they are known by the Holy Spirit. In this wonderful unity of the godhead the One is never without the Other. For God is the infinite Unity of Persons, each of whom is a unique way of giving and receiving the divine essence."[11]

The Giving of the Gift

It helps to understand all this in terms of the analogy of "giving"—an idea that is suggested by the phrase "All things have been *delivered to me* by my Father" and emphasized by Diadochus in the above quotation. To "give" means to separate something from myself in order to make it someone else's. I separate it from what belongs to me, I choose it with the recipient in mind, I perhaps wrap it up nicely, and I hand it over. It is no longer mine, as soon as the other has accepted it. At the same time there is another sense in which the gift is never "separated" from me at all, even after it has been handed over. It *carries me with it*, thanks to the spirit of love in which it was offered and accepted. It is a form of *self*-gift. Both aspects are true. I must interiorly detach myself from the gift in order to give it—I must give it without regret, I must not cling to it—and at one and the same time I must put *myself* into the gift.

We can apply this notion of gift first to God, and then to created being. In the case of God, who is self-giving love, we may for example describe Father, Son, and Holy Spirit as respectively the Giver, Receiver,[12] and the Gift (or the Given). But because this is *self*-giving love, and because God is the one divine essence, we know that what is given and received in each person is nothing other than this

11. Diadochus of Photike, cited in Oliver Clément, *The Roots of Christian Mysticism* (London: New City Press, 1993), 59.
12. It should become clear that the Son is not simply "Receiver" without also being a "Giver." It might be more accurate, though it is more cumbersome, to say that the Father is "Giver-Receiver" and the Son is "Receiver-Giver." This will become clearer in the second of the two diagrams shown below.

very essence. He has, in a sense, nothing else to give. Thus we may say that giving and receiving is simply another way of describing the interior relationships that constitute the persons, each distinct from each other though not from the essence—the Son being "from" the Father (generation), and the Spirit "from" both Father and Son as from a single principle (spiration).[13]

The relations can be portrayed diagrammatically in two ways. If A is the Father, B the Son, and C the Holy Spirit, we might show them as related like this:

Thus the Father is the source of Son and Spirit, the Son is begotten by the Father and also has a part in sending the Spirit, and the Spirit is "breathed forth" by the Father and Son. (Naturally there are differences between Eastern and Western Christians here, since the East has traditionally rejected the idea that the Spirit proceeds from the Son as well as the Father—but these differences have now largely been overcome, for example by reference to the traditional Eastern formulation that the Spirit proceeds from the Father *through the Son.*)

Personally, I find much more helpful a diagram I have used before,[14] which uses a straight line to represent the relationship of "begetting" between Father and Son, and a circle to represent "spiration." This gives a more dynamic view, and better conveys the sense that the Holy Spirit is the *unity* of the Father and Son, and the love that unites them.

13. They are not three *individuals*, because that would imply the possibility of lining them up to count, positing an external relation to them that cannot exist.

14. In Stratford Caldecott, *Beauty for Truth's Sake: On the Re-enchantment of Education* (Grand Rapids, MI: Brazos Press, 2009), 79, where it is explained in more detail, along with the *filioque* debate.

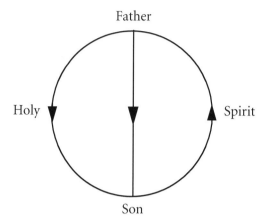

So it is the Father, not the Essence, who gives, but the Father *is* the Essence, or not-other than the Essence, and what is given also *is* the (same) Essence. The Father is the source of the Son and the Spirit, but he also receives, since the love he gives is reciprocated, and if it were not perfectly reciprocated it would not have been perfectly given. The Son receives the Father's love and, as the perfect image (self-knowledge) of the Father, freely gives all that he has received, namely the one and undivided divine Essence, in love to the one from whom he receives it. We might say, with Augustine, that the second Person is so perfect an image of the Father that he gives of himself just as the Father does.[15] Finally the Holy Spirit is also the Essence, one and the same Essence eternally already given and received.

15. In *De Trinitate*, St. Augustine argues that even the procession of the Spirit is "part of what is given by the Father to the Son": see *Augustine: Later Works*, ed. John Burnaby (Philadelphia, PA: Westminster Press, 1955), 158–159. The Father remains the sole principle, because the Son has nothing he has not received from this source. But the Trinity is asymmetrical reciprocity, not a symmetrical hierarchy proceeding from the Father. Its asymmetry is precisely the root of its dynamism as eternal Act, eternal *perichoresis*. The "principle of undiminished giving," of which Neoplatonists sometimes speak, applies here in its highest form. God, being infinite, can give himself completely without diminishing himself at all.

This is no mere passing back and forth of the same gift, which would be an image of sterility. ("Here, have this." "No, you have it." "No, I insist, you have it," and so on for eternity.) The gift is distinct from the giver through being given. It is a total given-awayness that renders the giver (and the receiver) fruitful beyond their own subjectivity because it bears them both within itself, transformed by their communion in one another. This is the archetype of the way a child bears within himself the nature and image of the two parents, making him an (endlessly surprising) gift to each.[16] Purely by virtue of the relationship to Father and Son, the gift which unites them becomes a third Person. Without ever being other than one and the same God, the Holy Spirit is the bond or medium of exchange between Father and Son—completing the Trinitarian process in a "kiss" signifying their mutual delight and their eternal superabundant or "ecstatic" fruition.

As a gift *for and from* the Son, and as gift *from and for* the Father, the Spirit is specifically named "Person-Gift" by Blessed John Paul II:

> It can be said that in the Holy Spirit the intimate life of the Triune God becomes totally gift, an exchange of mutual love between the divine Persons and that through the Holy Spirit God exists in the mode of gift. It is the Holy Spirit who is the personal expression of this self-giving, of this being-love. He is Person-Love. He is Person-Gift. Here we have an inexhaustible treasure of the reality and an inexpressible deepening of the concept of person in God, which only divine Revelation makes known to us.[17]

As Cardinal Ratzinger writes: "Spirit is the unity which God gives himself. In this unity, he himself gives himself. In this unity, the Father and the Son give themselves back to one another."[18]

---

16. The necessary separation of gift from giver in order to be given corresponds in the logic of the Trinity to the Spirit's "otherness" as Person from the Father and the Son—that is, to his being "another Person." The "superabundance" of true gift is rooted in the ever-greater infinity of God's Essence and the otherness within the Essence of the three Persons. This is why Balthasar and Adrienne von Speyr can dare to talk of gratitude and even "surprise" in God—God *surprising* himself.

17. *Dominum et Vivificantem*, 1986, 10.

18. Joseph Ratzinger, "The Holy Spirit as Communio: Concerning the Relationship of Pneumatology and Spirituality in Augustine," *Communio*, Summer 1998, 327.

Of course, the "Gift" is actually not the Holy Spirit but the divine Essence, the substance of God. The Essence itself is the substance of the Gift, one might say. Nevertheless, we are here talking of the Persons in relation to each other rather than of the Essence, and in this context the Spirit is distinguished as Gift, rather than as Giver or Receiver. Similarly, God or the Essence of God can be called "love," and yet the Holy Spirit may be identified as "love" in a particular way. As John Paul says immediately before the quoted passage, "God 'is love,' the essential love shared by the three divine Persons," but still "personal love is the Holy Spirit as the Spirit of the Father and the Son," or "uncreated Love-Gift." And of course we know how often in Holy Scripture we hear of the Spirit being "given."

This theology of gift helps us to see that the subsistent relations in God are the source and archetype of love, which is an eternal act of self-giving and receiving.[19] The Father and Son do not "cling" to their own nature but pour it out in order to beget and to be begotten. But at the same time, as I explained, there is no real separation because the Giver remains *in* the Gift, which is precisely the gift of *self*. It is as Ratzinger says in *Introduction to Christianity*: the Father "*is* the act of begetting, of giving oneself, of streaming forth"[20]— and so in a sense we might do even better to say that the Father is not so much the "Giver" as the *act of giving*, just as the Son is not so

19. It is worth noting that this theology is controversial in Thomist circles, not least because of the notion that there is "receptivity" in God. But as David L. Schindler and Norris Clarke have shown, receptivity here is not an imperfection, and not to be confused with passivity or potentiality. It is in fact a kind of activity. See, e.g., W. Norris Clarke SJ, "Reply to Steven Long," *The Thomist* 61 (1997), 617–24, where he cites the scriptural sources: "All that I have I have received from my Father" (or, "I have from my Father"); "All that the Father has he has given me." By the way, liberation and feminist theologians such as Leonardo Boff and Catherine Mowry LaCugna have also favored a metaphysics of relation rather than substance, but generally carry this to an extreme. To avoid subordinationism or monarchism in the Trinity they abolish the distinctiveness of Persons in total mutuality, or to avoid the subordination of creature to Creator they abolish God's transcendence. See LaCugna, *God For Us* (Harper San Francisco, 1991). But see also the critique of this book in Thomas Weinandy, *The Father's Spirit of Sonship: Re-conceiving the Trinity* (Edinburgh: T&T Clark, 1995).

20. Joseph Ratzinger, *Introduction to Christianity* (San Francisco: Ignatius Press, 2004), 184.

much the "Receiver" as the *act of receiving*, and the Spirit is not so much the "Gift" as the *act of being given*.[21]

Jesus, of course, is not a philosophy professor. He does not expound the doctrine of the Trinity but simply lives it. The doctrine of the Trinity means that, thanks to the Spirit, we are with the Son as he loves and worships the Father. For the Son is the image of the Father, and we know the Father in the Son. By loving the Son, we love the Father. We are not face to face with the three Persons, but face to face with the Father, through the Son, in the Holy Spirit.

Receiving the Gift

Viewed this way, the doctrine of the Trinity (bound up, as it is, with that of the Incarnation) is the revelation that makes Christianity unique, differentiating it from all other religious traditions. From it much else follows. Every religion has a founder, and would hardly exist without a community of disciples or believers (*sangha* or *ummah*). Christianity is certainly no exception; but more can be claimed for it than this. The Church assumes a new aspect in the light of the Trinitarian doctrine. If God's Holy Spirit is Gift, the Church is the human world in the process of being converted into the supreme Receiver for this Gift. In this reality deeper than sociology are found the "marks" of the Church: unity, holiness, catholicity (universality), and apostolicity (or identity with the Church of the Apostles)—celebrated in the Creed ("I believe in one, holy, catholic, and apostolic Church…").

The Church is the work of the Holy Spirit. Beginning with the Blessed Virgin Mary and continuing in the saints, the Church is a sacred vessel, and what she receives is the water and the blood (as Grail), the body of Christ (as Mother, or Pieta), and the Holy Spirit or divine life (from heaven, as Bride). The Spirit, breathed out upon the Cross and yielded up to the Father, withdrawn into heaven and

21. With the same qualification as before: that the act of giving is also an act of receiving back, and the act of receiving is an act of giving in return. I should add after writing the present chapter I discovered a wonderful exposition of the theology of gift by Antonio López FSCB, in Healy and Schindler (eds), *Being Holy in the World: Theology and Culture in the Thought of David L. Schindler* (Grand Rapids, MI: Eerdmans, 2011), 252–80.

then sent down upon the Apostles gathered in prayer around Our Lady at Pentecost, constitutes the Church as community, as communion, as the Body of the Bride. The unity of the Church— despite (and even in a sense *because* of) the diversity of her members—is the Spirit acting as her soul, a life-principle transcending and drawing together the various souls of her members, causing them to coinhere.

The Church's form of life is that of the Trinity, a life of self-giving and self-receiving. It is the Trinity that contains the secret of unity in diversity, of unity in a sense deepened by the diversity it contains, because this is a unity founded in the love of otherness, of that which transcends the self or brings to the self something new. It follows that no individual Christian is alone, turned in upon himself, but all are turned towards others, indeed exist *for* others. To the extent I do turn back to myself, seeking only my private good, to that exact extent I fall away from the unity of the Church and towards oblivion. Of course, the corruption and sins of the Church are all too evident, both historically and at the present moment. The Church is a process, as such not yet completed, continually falling and continually re-emerging spotless from the purification wrought by the sacraments (that is, through contact with Christ). Flowing towards and into the sacrament of reconciliation are all the sins that have brought her members to their knees. In confession, those sins are separated from her members, who arise again in purity. Thus the aphorist Nicolás Gómez Dávila is able to say, accurately if startlingly, "The Church is the sewer of history, the tumultuous flowing of human impurity towards unpolluted oceans."[22]

---

22. Translated by Adrian Walker in private correspondence. The point is made at greater length in Hans Urs von Balthasar's *Explorations in Theology*, especially Volume II, "Spouse of the Word." Roch Kereszty in "The Infallibility of the Church: A Marian Perspective" (*Communio* 38:3, 374–90) summarizes: "The Church has known from the beginning that these terms ["immaculate dove," "without stain or wrinkle," etc.] cannot mean the empirical Church as she appears to believers and unbelievers alike, full of the stain and filth of her members; eventually they realized that she is the immaculately conceived, full of grace mother of God in communion with all the saints, who as the *ecclesia immaculata* is at work in the Church's perfect response to the Son's gift of self" (380).

The Church exists for sinners, and contains a great many of them. As an institution she has numerous limitations and evident flaws. The presence of the Holy Spirit does not ensure the impeccability even of popes (for only the final Church, the Church as she will be at the end of the process of purification, glimpsed even now in heaven, can be without sin). The Spirit interferes and imposes himself to the minimum degree possible, so as to allow the maximum scope for human freedom compatible with the necessary unity of the communion. But that unity nevertheless exists, and the holiness of the saints shines the more brightly against the darkness from which it is constantly struggling to escape. The Church exists at a level deeper than all her obvious imperfections, for the presence of the Spirit makes the Church more than a society, more even than a society of like-minded individuals following the same path or obeying the same laws. The Spirit makes the Church a corporate personality, *Ecclesia*.

The Church also has an authority that derives from the Holy Spirit, for the unity of the Church is precisely a unity *in the truth*— although, again, this extends only as far as that truth which Christ came to reveal; namely, his own reality as Word of the Father and the meaning of the Incarnation for us. Thus, "the Counselor, the Holy Spirit, whom the Father will send in my name, he will teach you all things, and bring to your remembrance all that I have said to you" (John 14:26), and "When the Spirit of truth comes, he will guide you into all the truth; for he will not speak on his own authority, but whatever he hears he will speak. . . . He will take what is mine and declare it to you" (John 16:13–15). The essence of the Church is a unity constituted by receiving the gift of the Holy Spirit, and being led by this gift into the truth at the heart of all things, which is found in the Word of the Father.

The authority of the Church is one of the things that distinguishes Christianity from the "religions" and "traditions," as we find in the context of attempts at the various kinds of dialogue discussed earlier, where no equivalent dialogue partner can be found to engage with the living magisterium of the Church, mediated by the office of Peter and the college of bishops. There is no one who can "speak for" Buddhism as such, or Islam as such, or Hinduism as such, though there are many who are prepared to speak for one tradition or another. But Catholicism, the mainstream of the Christian tradition, is founded on a different conception, namely an act of trust in the presence of the Spirit of unity and truth within the community, sacramentally mediated by those appointed by the Apostles under the living authority of Christ.

The human act of faith in Christ that constitutes the Church, the corollary of which is this act of faith in the Church's teaching authority, is an act made possible only by grace, though the act remains an act not of God but of man. It is only *made possible*, not *performed*, by God. It is often said to be an "intellectual" act, because it involves a judgment of reason, a laying hold of the truth (albeit still in darkness). One might just as well say that it is an act of the will, an act of freedom, and above all an act of the imagination, indeed a *creative* act. To posit and grasp the invisible, bringing it into the realm of the visible by giving it shape and color, is to "create." For this very reason, every man's faith, or rather the form he gives it in living out his call and mission, is as unique as he is.

The significance of all this will become clear later on—the fact that Christian life both begins and ends in creative freedom—but for now we need only note that the gift of the Holy Spirit is an invitation to enter the life of the Trinity by growing in faith, hope, and love. We grow step by step, beginning in darkness with an act of trust in something that can only be grasped imaginatively, and is experienced in fiery, luminous communion.

The Mystery of Islam

I am not intending to produce a systematic overview of the religious traditions in all their variety. These chapters are driven by my particular interests—the things I have found most attractive in those traditions in the course of my own search for truth, and my present attempt to do justice, as a Christian convert, to the truths I have found scattered in many places. Our commitment to truth should logically precede our commitment to any particular faith. We are interested in truth *per se*, and not just "instrumentally"—truths that will help persuade others to our own point of view. We are interested in truth wherever it may lead. If we are Christians, we should be so because we love the truth first of all, and because we believe we have found its fullness in Jesus Christ and in his Church, not because we feel comfortable being Christians, nor because our ancestors were Christian—nor for any other of a million possible lesser reasons.

In the case of the great religions, as distinct from the various heresies within them, we have to take account of the fact that they have not withered after a few generations, or even after many centuries, but have successfully inspired entire civilizations. We recall the counsel of Gamaliel: "[I]f this plan or this undertaking is of men, it will fail; but if it is of God, you will not be able to overthrow them" (Acts 5:38–9). God permits several religions to exist, even though they conflict with each other, and not to die out but to flourish, producing abundant good fruits, as well as evil ones. It is this mystery that we must struggle to understand a bit better. But what hypothesis may be offered for a religion such as Islam, that appears to contradict Christianity on so many points, and whose followers are actively persecuting Christian believers in many parts of the world?[1]

---

1. For details, see Rupert Shortt, *Christianophobia: A Faith Under Attack* (London: Rider, 2012), and news coverage at http://www.acnuk.org/.

Children of Abraham

Islam was born in Arabia in the seventh century. The Arabs trace their ancestry back to Ishmael, the exiled son of Abraham, whose other son, Isaac, was the ancestor of the Jews. Through Abraham, they trace their line back to Shem, the son of Noah, and are therefore known along with the Jews as "Semites." At the heart of Islam is a book written by the Prophet Muhammad over a period of 23 years before his death in the year AD 632. It is not an easily translatable book: the language is Arabic, and we are told that a translation of the Qur'an is not the Qur'an. As a result, although inevitably as it grew and spread it has adapted itself to certain geographical and cultural circumstances, Islam has always tended to imprint its own culture, its own language and patterns of thought, on countries which came under its control.

Islam is the world's fastest-growing religion (the statisticians speak of a growth rate of about 3% per year). Globally speaking, there are at least a billion (thousand million) Muslims in the world at present: that is, as many as there are Catholics—although the number of Christians, if you add together the various denominations, is nearly twice as great. Of course, the Muslim world is not as monolithic as Catholicism, since it has no single authority and is divided between several very different branches (the most famous of these being Shiite and Sunni). In Europe, the overall decline in population predicted in the next fifty years is expected to be partially offset by a rise in the Muslim population (one prediction is for a rise of roughly 3 million per year). In the UK, there were around 620,000 Muslims at the turn of the century, and the number of practicing Muslims is expected to outnumber all churchgoing Christians within 40 years.

Islam is also in many ways the most vigorous and determined opponent of the modern liberal consensus represented by the United Nations and the World Council of Churches. When the Vatican wanted to find allies in the UN against the imposition of birth control policies involving abortion and contraceptive rights, it looked to Islam. There is a large area of overlap between Islamic moral teaching and that of Catholicism. But in other areas, Catholicism is much more accepting of modernity than Islam: the language of human rights and democracy comes more naturally to Christians than it does to Muslims, given the origin of these concepts in the Christian (and post-Christian Enlightenment) civilization.

The Muslim community often has such clarity about its own distinct identity that it tends to thrive where Western churches are drowning in a sea of indifference. Islam seeks to offer a real alternative to Western culture, with more resistance to Americanization than any other major religious group. In his interview with Peter Seewald, Joseph Ratzinger highlighted the difficulty of fitting Islam within a democratic system that assumes the separation of the political from the religious sphere. This separation derives at least in part from Christ's refusal to bring an earthly kingdom, whereas Islam did precisely this:

> Islam has a total organization of life that is completely different from ours; it embraces simply everything. There is a very marked subordination of woman to man; there is a very tightly knit criminal law, indeed, a law regulating all areas of life, that is opposed to our modern ideas about society. One has to have a clear understanding that it is not simply a denomination that can be included in the free realm of a pluralistic society. When one represents the situation in those terms, as often happens today, Islam is defined according to the Christian model and is not seen as it really is in itself. In that sense, the dialogue with Islam is naturally much more complicated than, for example, an internal dialogue among Christians.[2]

It must be remembered despite the predominance in the modern period of an Islamic ideology shaped by a kind of resentment and even hatred of the "West," Islam has a tradition of tolerance and respect for the other "religions of the book" (Judaism, Christianity, Zoroastrianism, and at times even Hinduism) that goes back to the Prophet Muhammad—even if this toleration went along with the exaction of tribute and the relegation of the other religions to a kind of second-class status.

During the Middle Ages, in places like Toledo and Cordoba in the

---

2. Joseph Ratzinger, *Salt of the Earth: The Church at the End of the Millennium*, An Interview with Peter Seewald (San Francisco: Ignatius Press, 1997), 244–5.

golden age (partly mythical, no doubt) of Al Andalus, it is clear that the three religions did learn a great deal from each other in the periods when they weren't actually fighting. During the second half of the first Christian millennium, much of the legacy of Greek civilization that had been largely lost to the West was taken over by the Muslims in their great wave of military expansion. Muslim thinkers then developed certain aspects of this civilization further than the ancients themselves had done, drawing also on the legacy of India, and by the 1100s had begun transmitting to the West through men such as Adelard of Bath and Leonardo Fibonacci the ideas in mathematics, philosophy, and science that were to become the foundations for Gothic cathedral architecture and later the Renaissance.[3]

Regensburg

A major address by Pope Benedict XVI at the University of Regensburg in September 2006 provoked outrage in Muslim circles by its citation of a dialogue written by the medieval emperor of Constantinople during the siege of the city by Muslims around 1400.[4] The Emperor's harsh words concerning Islam were an occasion for Pope Benedict to condemn the spreading of faith by violence as something "unreasonable." The Pope wanted to make the point that "not acting reasonably is contrary to God's nature," and he raised the question of whether this was as true for Muslims as it is for Christians. The Gospel of John tells us "In the beginning was the Word 'Logos,' and the Word was with God, and the Word was God." For Christians, therefore, God is "Logos," which means he must be the very archetype of reasonableness. But Muslims do not *have* John's

3. For a sympathetic, informative, and accessible "textbook" on Islam in all its variety, which at the same time avoids polemic against Christianity, see Seyyed Hossein Nasr, *The Heart of Islam: Enduring Values for Humanity* (San Francisco: Harper, 2004). A good biography of the Prophet is *Muhammad*, by the Muslim convert and Sufi, Martin Lings. See also Christian W. Troll SJ's essay on Islam from the Catholic point of view in Gavin D'Costa, *The Catholic Church and the World Religions: A Theological and Phenomenological Account* (London: T&T Clark International, 2011).

4. The Lecture is available at http://www.vatican.va/, but see also James V. Schall SJ, *The Regensburg Lecture* (South Bend, IN: St Augustine's Press, 2007), for text and commentary.

Gospel. If God is thought to be not Logos but pure Will, is there not a danger we will end up with "a capricious God, who is not even bound to truth and goodness"?

The comments were construed as a criticism of Islam, and Muslims protested that it was an unfair one. There were several incidents of violence against Christians as a result (seeming in the eyes of many to confirm the criticism), but some of the outcomes were more positive. A month after the speech was delivered, thirty-eight Islamic authorities and scholars from around the world joined together to deliver an *Open Letter to the Pope* in the interests of mutual understanding. It was said to be the first time in the modern period that Muslim scholars from every branch of Islam had spoken with a single voice about the teachings of Islam. A year after that letter, a total of 138 Muslim scholars, clerics, and intellectuals from every denomination and school of thought in Islam and every major Islamic country or region in the world issued *A Common Word Between Us and You* addressed to Christians everywhere. In it they affirmed a common ground between the teachings of the Prophet Muhammad and the teachings of Jesus Christ (and the Jewish Scriptures) in the commandments to love God and love one's neighbor. This in turn led to other interfaith initiatives and dialogues aimed at addressing mutual concerns, including a permanent Catholic-Muslim Forum that began work in 2008. The official website of the movement can be found at www.acommonword.com.

One of the key issues addressed in the Pope's lecture was the question of the Qur'an's exhortations to violence. Muhammad was a warrior, after all. The famous *surah* 2:256 which reads "There is no compulsion in religion" is attributed by the Pope to "the early period," when Muhammad was still "powerless and under threat" (so that it could be "abrogated" by later teachings), although the *Open Letter* insists it belongs to the time in Medina when Islam was in the ascendancy, and remains applicable to those who want to force Jewish and Christian conversions to Islam. But the more important point is that the Pope has raised the issue of Qur'anic *interpretation* using the resources of human reason, which is one of the most significant weaknesses of modern Islam. The main schools have remained opposed to *kalam* (the science of debate, theology, or rational exegesis) since the twelfth century, the time of Al Ghazali. (After this time the only relief from the very literalistic and anti-intellectual approach of the Hanbalis and Wahhabis was the more mystical and illuminationist approach of the Sufis and Ismailis.)

Pope Benedict was concerned above all with helping Muslims address the seeds of violence within their own religion, which he saw as linked to the rejection by thinkers such as Ibn Hazm (d.1064) of the *logos* or reasonability of God in favor of extreme voluntarism (with its emphasis on the supremacy of the divine Will): thus he cites one authority as saying "Ibn Hazm went so far as to state that God is not bound even by his own word, and that nothing would oblige him to reveal the truth to us. Were it God's will, we would even have to practice idolatry." In this tradition of thought, in a religion where the revelation of God's will for man takes the form of the Law or *Shariah* (as it does in Judaism, of course, in the form of the *Halakhah*), it became very easy for a purely (and sometimes violently) legalistic mentality to take hold, leading to the fanaticism we see today.[5]

This is a problem within Christianity too, as the Pope points out in his discussion of the decline of scholastic philosophy after Duns Scotus; although voluntarism was never adopted by the mainstream Church. He writes:

> This gives rise [in Christianity] to positions which clearly approach those of Ibn Hazm and might even lead to the image of a capricious God, who is not even bound to truth and goodness. God's transcendence and otherness are so exalted that our reason,

5. For a comparison of the idea of divine law and the role it plays in Judaism, Christianity, and Islam, see Rémi Brague, *The Law of God: The Philosophical History of an Idea* (Chicago University Press, 2007). Brague says that Christianity offered not so much a Law, as a means of fulfilling or following the Law, namely the economy of salvation (sacramental union with Christ): see 260–261. In Judaism and Islam, the need for a "way" to internalize the law and so become united with God was supplied by mysticism. He argues that the very fact that Christians were not "under the law," made possible the modern conception of a purely secular state with no divine foundation.

our sense of the true and good, are no longer an authentic mirror of God, whose deepest possibilities remain eternally unattainable and hidden behind his actual decisions. As opposed to this, the faith of the Church has always insisted that between God and us, between his eternal Creator Spirit and our created reason there exists a real analogy, in which—as the Fourth Lateran Council in 1215 stated—unlikeness remains infinitely greater than likeness, yet not to the point of abolishing analogy and its language. God does not become more divine when we push him away from us in a sheer, impenetrable voluntarism; rather, the truly divine God is the God who has revealed himself as *logos* and, as *logos*, has acted and continues to act lovingly on our behalf. Certainly, love, as Saint Paul says, "transcends" knowledge and is thereby capable of perceiving more than thought alone (cf. Eph. 3:19); nonetheless it continues to be love of the God who is *Logos*.

He concludes by recalling the West, as well as Islam, to a conversation not just between religions, but (and without this interreligious dialogue is impossible) between faith and reason, which means among other things a broadening of the concept of reason itself. The Greek heritage which Islam was so important in mediating to the West has not lost is relevance, but offers a perennially valid reference point for this conversation.[6]

The response of the Open Letter was polite, tactful, and informative. It stressed the importance of freedom of religious belief in Islamic tradition and explored the history and meaning of *jihad* (which means "struggle" rather than "Holy War," and is governed by strict ethical principles). Most importantly, perhaps, the authors, representing the intellectual mainstream of modern Islam, dismissed Ibn Hazm as a "marginal figure" and claimed that the Islamic tradition had "maintained a consonance between the truths of the Qur'anic revelation and the demands of human intelligence, without sacrificing one for the other." This remains a question for debate.

6. David B. Burrell describes the lecture at Regensburg as a *felix culpa*, "ill-advised" for some of its remarks on Islam, but creating an opening for conversation to which his own *Towards a Jewish-Christian-Muslim Theology* also makes a signal contribution.

There is another point, however, that perhaps was left out of the discussion of Islamic voluntarism, and even from some of the Muslim responses to Regensburg. That is the fact that, in the context of Islam as a whole, and often the Islam of the ordinary people (not just the mystics and intellectuals), voluntarism is offset by another strong emphasis, namely the devotional or spiritual dimension of Islam—the tradition of the names of God, and of human virtue. The 99 Names of God (Knowledge, Light, Justice, Majesty, Peace, Beauty, Compassion…) paint a picture of God very different from that of a stark, capricious will that cannot be understood by analogy with anything in the world. In fact the moral or ethical tradition of Islam is profoundly misunderstood if it is seen as a matter simply of obedience to the Law. It is also a question of *how* one obeys the Law, how one conducts oneself. God is beautiful and loves beauty:

> The highest form of beauty in this world is the beauty of the human soul, which is related to *ihsan*, a term that means at once beauty, goodness, and virtue. To possess *ihsan* is to have the virtues of generosity and love and to live at peace in one's Center, where God resides. [Thus] the goal of human life is to beautify the soul through goodness and virtue and to make it worthy of offering to God Who is *the* Beautiful.[7]

Even the militaristic tradition of violence in Islam was softened and to some degree civilized by the ideal of chivalry, in Muhammad as well as in the leaders of the community who followed him, according to this tradition of *ihsan*. As a result the notion of "Holy War" both in medieval Islam and Christendom remained deeply ambiguous—at all times (and on both sides) finding its highest expression in the form of inner warfare, interior *jihad*, against the vices and temptations of the human heart.

A Religion of the Absolute

Of course, many Christians find such arguments pointless and frustrating, in the light of the other major differences between the two

---

7. Nasr, *The Heart of Islam*, 235–6.

faiths.[8] Even Pope John Paul II, in his reflective *Crossing the Threshold of Hope*, and despite his own manifest commitment to dialogue, detects in Islam a movement away from the Christian Revelation: "In Islam all the richness of God's self-revelation, which constitutes the heritage of the Old and New Testaments, has definitely been set aside." Indeed, how can a Christian not feel keenly the loss of all that we most value: the living presence of Christ, the great loving mercy of God revealed on the Cross, the sacraments and "luminous mysteries" of the Kingdom, and the possibility not only of reconciliation with each other and with God, but of a Vision of God that answers the impossible demand of the human heart?

Consequently many Christian writers (including the pugnacious Hilaire Belloc) have argued strenuously that Islam is nothing but a Christian heresy grown rampant. Vladimir Solovyov, in his 1889 book *Russia and the Universal Church*, pointed out that it arose at the moment when the Eastern Emperor Heraclius corrupted large parts of Christendom with the heresy of Monothelitism—the idea that there was no human will in Christ, only the divine will; which Solovyov calls "the disguised denial of human freedom and energy." In Byzantinism, "which was hostile in principle to Christian progress and which aimed at reducing the whole of religion to a fact of past history, a dogmatic formula, and a liturgical ceremonial," he saw an "anti-Christianity concealed beneath the mask of orthodoxy" which was "bound to collapse in moral impotence before the open and sincere anti-Christianity of Islam." Islam, in Solovyov's view, is a synthesis of the Monothelite and Iconoclastic heresies. Byzantium had attempted to close a theological debate with a political compromise, and paid the penalty.

A more irenic approach would begin by establishing that Islam and Christianity may in fact be doctrinally closer than is frequently assumed by both Muslims and Christians. The statements of the Qur'an which contradict Christian doctrine may be mitigated to some extent by noticing that they seem to be directed against

8. The very real and complex divergences between the Bible and the Qur'an are analyzed in detail in Michael Lodahl in *Claiming Abraham: Reading the Bible and the Qur'an Side by Side* (Grand Rapids, MI: Brazos Press, 2010).

misunderstandings that were indeed prevalent at the time of Muhammad, particularly in the Jewish and heretical Christian communities with which he may have had most direct contact—thus giving a very different reading of the same historical facts to that offered by Solovyov. Louis Bouyer argued along these lines some years ago in his book *The Invisible Father*: for Bouyer, Islam is intelligible partly as a protest movement directed against a Christian tendency towards idolatry and tritheism. The "truth, the original and lasting authenticity of the prophetic element" in this protest is attested by "the quality of the mysticism Islam has nourished" ever since. Bouyer therefore looks forward to the time when the "Wedding of the Lamb . . . will consummate the truth of the prophetic protest of Israel and of Islam, and do this within the pure confession of a Christianity which will have overcome every historical temptation."

Let us see how this "doctrinal closeness" might be maintained in the face of the widespread opinion that Muslims and Christians worship "different Gods," because "our God is a Trinity," whereas the doctrine of the Trinity is explicitly denied by Islam. If we look at the denial more closely, we find that the Qur'an alleges that Christians believe that there are three Gods (4:171–2). In reality, Christians want to uphold the Unity of God as strongly as Muslims do. The threeness of the Trinity is not intended as a numerical threeness, like that of three apples, or three oranges: it is "meta-mathematical" threeness. As the Athanasian Creed states, God is "not three eternals but one eternal." As we have seen, there are not three Gods, but three Persons in one God—it would be more accurate, though still slightly misleading, to say there are three aspects (faces) of one God, or three ways of being the One God. So here, although the Qur'an is plainly wrong in its attribution of tritheism to Christianity, it can be plausibly read as not denying the Trinity *as Christians understand it* at all, provided, of course, that it is not claiming that Christian Trinitarianism leads inevitably to tritheism.

Islam further rejects the idea that God could "beget" a Son (6:95–101), on the grounds that God has no wife; it even rejects the idea that he might "adopt" a Son (19:88–98), on the grounds that all creatures can be nothing but servants of God. But once more

Islam's intention in these two instances is positive: to emphasize and safeguard the Unity, Transcendence, and Absoluteness of God against those who would "associate" others with him. Christian theology uses terms like "begets" and "Son" analogously, and therefore does not ascribe biological generation to the divinity, though it does see biological generation as a distant image of intra-divine engendering. And it could well be argued that you need the whole context of Christian theology to make sense of such statements. On the other hand, it is intriguing that when Muhammad's followers were destroying the idols in the Kaaba, he protected with his own hands, along with a painting of Abraham that was found there, an icon of the Madonna and Child. And the Qur'an accepts the Virgin Birth, stating: "we made the son of Mary and his mother a sign" (23:50).

In order to concentrate on the transcendence of God, Islam had to disentangle God from history. On this basis it was able to accept Christ only in diminished form, as a prophet rather than a divine Incarnation. From a Christian point of view, of course, much more has been lost than gained by this. In Islam the identity of God as Love remains hidden, or esoteric. To the ordinary Muslim, *God is God*: there can be no Trinity, no Hypostatic Union, no divinization of man. God cannot have died on the Cross for us. Instead, the gulf between man and God is overcome politically, by attempting to establish a theocratic state (as was done also in Islam's half-brother and rival, Judaism).

One of the most serious points of disagreement between Islam and Christianity is the former's denial that Jesus died on the Cross, although this rests on a rather ambiguous text (4:157–9). In one translation the passage reads:

> [T]hey said (in boast): "We killed Christ Jesus the son of Mary, the Messenger of Allah." But they killed him not, nor crucified him, but so it was made to appear to them, and those who differ therein are full of doubts, with no (certain) knowledge, but only conjecture to follow, for of a surety they killed him not. Nay, Allah raised him up unto himself; and Allah is exalted in power, wise. And there is none of the people of the book (Jews and Christians) but must believe in him [Jesus] before his death; and on the Day of Judgment he will be a witness against them.

Here the Qur'an seems mainly concerned to refute the enemies of Christ who wrongly claimed to have put an end to him. It is less concerned with the Cross than with the fact that Jesus is still alive. Without adverting to the Resurrection at all, it states vaguely that God "raised him unto himself," and gave him victory over his enemies. The best that can be said of this, from a Christian point of view, is that the text at least intends to vindicate Jesus rather than to attack Christianity; though, of course, it misses the whole importance of the divine sacrifice.

If we look for the *positive* religious content of Islam, instead of always comparing it with Christianity to see how it falls short, or dwelling on the violence of its modern extremists, we find that one important function that Islam has performed has been to preserve Abrahamic monotheism into the post-Christian era, alongside the Judaism that has rejected Christ, while transforming that faith into a universal creed open to all people, even the most unsophisticated. The creed of Islam lays special emphasis on the divine Unity: *There is no God but God, and Muhammad is his Prophet.* The first part of this statement is the most important, concerning God. The reference to the Prophet is in a sense secondary. Muhammad is of course not regarded by Islam as the *only* Prophet of God, although he is the "Seal of Prophets" and the last before the return of the Messiah. At the heart of Islam is a kind of "contemplative asceticism" focused on the Absolute as such. The God of Islam is the same God as that of Christianity, albeit not here revealing himself as a Trinity, but rather contemplated in his Unity by a people who worship him under that attribute. As we will see in a moment, this people stands at a mysterious point of intersection between Old Testament expectation and the "last of days."[9]

A Providential Role for Islam?

If we accept for the moment that many doctrinal differences between Islam and Christianity might be downplayed, and the violence associated with Islam, if not excused or mitigated, at least

9. On all this see Roch Kereszty O.Cist., "The Word of God: A Catholic Perspective in Dialogue with Judaism and Islam," *Communio*, Fall 2001, 568–580.

understood in its context (remembering that Christians have been guilty of similar crimes), what is a Christian to make of this religion that claims to have been inspired by God and yet differs so profoundly from his own? Things would be so much easier if we could dismiss it as "the work of the devil."

Muslims believe that the Qur'an was dictated by the Angel Gabriel. A Christian will understandably find that hard to accept. It is easier to account for the elements of revealed truth in the Qur'an by the influence of Jewish and Christian writings or oral traditions that derived from the earlier revelations.[10]

The more interesting question is perhaps that of the theological role played by Islam in human history, which I raised at the beginning of this chapter. Why does God permit Islam to survive and flourish? Here I think the previous chapter may help us. If God is essentially self-gift (love, Trinity), then his nature is to communicate, to give himself, to make himself known, and he will do so by every means possible. If at the same time he is working with nature rather than overpowering it, and allowing freedom instead of suppressing it, he will no doubt make the best use he can even of broken or incomplete or imperfect human structures. A religious structure such as Islam may be imperfect, as far as Christianity is concerned, but God can still work through it. In that sense, an incomplete religion may still have a share in goodness, truth, and beauty; it may still have a providential role in the self-revelation of God.[11]

---

10. Fr. Roch Kereszty points out that the Church has distinguished between personal inspiration and an inspired text. A saint may be inspired in many ways without the divine action extending to whatever the saint writes. Thus for a Christian "the Qur'an may be the work of an inspired person, but its text itself is not the inspired Word of God. God did not protect Muhammad and the Qur'an from making what Christians believe are erroneous statements contrary to the Judeo-Christian revelation" (ibid., 579). Even among texts, no doubt, there are different degrees and types of inspiration.

11. The Catholic scholar of Islam Louis Massignon (d. 1962) would argue strongly for the presence of divine inspiration among the devotees of Islam. He himself was an admirer of the martyred Al-Hallaj, whom he wished to see canonized by the Catholic Church. The close friend of two popes, especially Paul VI, Massignon's influence helped to shape the document *Nostra Aetate*.

Let us pursue this line of thought a little further, to see if we can flesh out this idea of a "providential role" for Islam. Muhammad was born after Christ, yet in many ways he seems to belong to an earlier world, a world no later than that of the Psalms, for example—a time prior to the full revelation of the Trinity. Perhaps from the point of view of Christianity he does indeed belong to a time before the Incarnation, rather than after it.[12] Along with Judaism, this would make Islam part of the "unfinished business" of the Old Testament—the "mystery of Islam" being an echo of the continuing mystery of the Jews. And yet as I hinted earlier, insofar as they describe Muhammad as the Seal of the Prophets, Muslims declare themselves to be a people of the end times, a prolongation of the religion of Abraham in the direction of the *eschaton.*

The key to the whole mystery might then be the fact that Christianity failed to convert the People of God themselves: that the Jew Christ was ultimately opposed, betrayed, and handed over to be crucified by those he came to save. For Jesus of Nazareth was indeed the Messiah of the Jews, but he was not yet (or not yet explicitly) the glorified Messiah that had been foretold. Paradoxically, it was only after he had been rejected and put to death that Jesus appeared in glory, even though the universally visible and permanent manifestation of that glory remains reserved for his second coming.

The failure to recognize Jesus as the Messiah is connected with the "scandal" of the Cross. Not only did this Messiah not restore the earthly Kingdom of his ancestor David, but he was executed like a criminal and died in humiliation. Christianity began by reinterpreting the whole notion of divine glory as it had been understood up to that time in the light of Isaiah's prophecy of the Suffering Servant. The Cross became a Throne, the thorns a Crown. The rejection of

---

12. I should add that I am trying to tread a delicate line here. The distinguished ecumenist George C. Anawati OP was critical of the Christian "maximalists" who distinguish between chronological and "paralectical" time. I am not claiming anything more than a psychological reality for this "time before"—just as a convert to Christianity may blame himself for not earlier having caught up with the existence and reality of Christ, and living in a state of (perhaps at that time in his life) "invincible ignorance."

the Messiah was therefore connected with the incomprehensibility of the Cross as an instrument of salvation for the whole world. In fact God used this very incomprehensibility—and the rejection by the Jews partly out of faithfulness to Moses—as a means of bringing about the glorification of the Messiah in blood and torment, for the redemption of the whole world.

We might go further and speculate that if Judaism had been entirely absorbed by Christianity, the Second Coming would have been combined with the First. But that Judaism was *not* absorbed in this way by Christianity means that there must be a divine providence in the non-conversion of the Jewish people (as St. Paul implies). As St. Paul clearly indicates in his Letter to the Romans (11:25–36), the Jews remain the Chosen People. In the words of *Nostra Aetate*, God "does not repent of the gifts he makes or of the calls he issues." God's call, once made, is irrevocable.[13]

Could we say that the mysterious providential role for the continuance of the Jewish people after the coming of Christ extends, in some equally mysterious way, to the appearance of Islam? Certainly, if the Christian fulfillment of the Covenant had enfolded the whole world, there would have been no space either for Judaism or for Islam. But if this space has some theological meaning, what might that meaning be in the case of Islam?

Certainly, if Christians had fully understood the doctrine of the Unity of God, without losing hold on the truth of the Trinity, there would have been no "need" for this revival of strict monotheism. One Christian writer who took a similar line was the German Protestant mystic, Jacob Boehme, whom we shall meet again later. In *Mysterium Magnum* (1623) he points out in relation to Matthew

---

13. By treating Judaism and Jewish religious leaders with great respect, as well as in their official teachings about the value of Judaism as such, the Second Vatican Council and the post-conciliar popes have succeeded in overturning a great deal of the anti-semitism that at various times has marred Christian attitudes and history. The attitude that "it was the Jews who killed Jesus" has given way before the realization that it was a small clique of Jewish leaders together with the Romans who actually had him killed. Jesus himself *was* Jewish, along with all his closest disciples, and Christianity is inextricably and eternally bound up with the religion of Moses.

12:32 that "the Turks do not blaspheme the Holy Spirit, who manifested himself in the humanity, but they reproach the humanity, and say a creature cannot be God. But that God hath wrought, and done wonders in Christ, that they confess, and blaspheme not the Spirit which hath wrought in Christ, viz. in the humanity. Blindness is happened unto them, so that they walk under a veil." And the reason God has obscured for them the truth of the Incarnation is not their fault, but due to the sins of Christendom and the Arian heresy, wherein "the holy name of God, which had manifested itself in the humanity, was abused." They are put back into their mother's womb—that is, Hagar, who represents for Boehme the world of nature—so that they will not be guilty of taking the Lord's name in vain. But "the angel of great counsel, viz. the holy voice of Christ, is not departed from them, eternally to forget them, so little as a mother can forget her child, that she should not have pity upon the son of her womb, albeit he were disobedient to her."

He goes on to say that just as the angel went to Hagar to console her in the desert, and just as God promised to make Ishmael a great nation, so the Turks (i.e. Muslims) have become powerful by God's grace in the world of nature, but in the end will come back like the prodigal son "with great joy, and with great humility, to Abraham, viz. to Christ." But the prophetic denunciation of Christendom, which he sees as the occasion for God's grace towards the Ishmaelites, is scathing:

> Christendom is full of strife and contention about Christ's deity, and humanity; and abominably profaneth the holy name in his humanity; and uses it only for a form of custom to swear [and covenant by] also to idolatry [and hypocrisy], and is gone from the sword of the Holy Spirit, unto a bloodthirsty confounding sword, wherein is nothing but contending, and contemning one another; and the whole titular Christendom is turned into mere sects and orders, where one sect doth despise and brand another for unrighteous. And thus they have made of Christendom a mere murdering den, full of blasphemies about Christ's person; and have bound the spirit of Christ (in which a Christian should live in deepest humility) to the forms and orders of disputation; and have

set foolish reason to be a master of the understanding above Christ's kingdom.[14]

It would be insufficient, however, to reduce the mystery of Islam to a sort of divine "scourge" of Christian infidelity. The spread of Islam seems to mirror the opening out of the Covenant in Christ to include the "gentiles." This mirroring could be interpreted as an attempt to co-opt the Christological fulfillment of Israel for an alien purpose, and there is surely something to this interpretation. On the other hand, it also seems plausible to read Islam—against its mainstream self-interpretations—less as a substitute for faith in Christ than as a divinely permitted cleansing of it in view of his second coming. From this point of view, Islam would be an extension of Old Testament expectation to the gentiles, an extension that presupposes, but does not necessarily seek to replace, the fulfillment of that expectation in Jesus.

What we can be sure of is that Christians are enjoined to go out into the whole world and proclaim the Gospel. At the same time we are given no guarantee that all men will be found capable of welcoming that Gospel, nor any guarantee that God will not allow that work to be hindered, either for the sake of purification or for other, more mysterious reasons. Islam itself seems to be marked by a tension or pull in two directions—either towards humble service of Christ's second coming without denial of the fullness of his first, or towards aggressive replacement of full faith in his first coming and, therefore, in his second. It seems to me that, in this life, we can never fully disentangle these two opposite strands.

Even this inextricability, however, may have a theological meaning, and the uneasy kinship between Christians and Muslims may be divinely willed. Perhaps the best way to make this point is to recall that Islam, too, represents a divine Promise, if not a Covenant. *Islam is the religion of Ishmael rather than Isaac.* Ishmael was born to Abraham before the visit of the Three Strangers in whom Christianity sees a symbol of the Trinity. Isaac, who is born after this visit, is linked to the revelation of the Trinity in the very con-

14. Jacob Boehme, *Mysterium Magnum: An Exposition of the First Book of Moses Called Genesis* (London: John M. Watkins, 1965), 369.

crete sense that Christ is to be born of his line, as a Jew among Jews. Ishmael is rather a prolongation of the earlier dispensation of God, and the people he represents exist outside the Covenant in which God establishes a family relationship with men. Nevertheless God says of him, "I will make of him a great nation." (On all this, see Genesis 16–18, especially 16:7–13 and 17:20.)

The Jesus of Ibn Arabi

The mystery of Islam is not something we can hope fully to understand in this life, but a personal friendship with Muslims combined with a study of their culture and writings may enable us to glimpse the human "face" of this religion. In certain great figures representative of Islam we sense the presence of the mystery we have been discussing. The spiritual successes of Islam are real enough, despite the ignorance of them among Christians, who cannot be expected to have studied the literature of an alien (and often hostile) religion with much care. We are mostly aware of the spiritual failures, the bigotry, the acts of cruelty and aggression, which to some extent have blighted Christian history too.

The ideology of radical Islam (or "Islamism") is best seen as a modern phenomenon, the distortion of a tradition. Islam has always been militaristic, but from its earliest days it was also capable of chivalry. The heart and soul of Islam have been ripped out by the fanatics; today we are seeing only a caricature of the religion. It is as though Christianity were to be judged on the basis of some extreme fundamentalist sect holed up in the American Midwest. Unfortunately this is a sect that has taken over half the world, owns most of the oil, and is on the verge of acquiring a nuclear arsenal. If modernity is marked by conflict or tension between faith and reason, you could say that while in the West "reason" came out on top, at the expense of faith, the Islamic world took the other path. Both traditions now manifest the worst results of their choice. In the West we have rationalism opposed to faith, leading to enclosure within a materialistic society, in the Islamic world we have an anti-rational fideism that ends in the persecution of religious minorities and a terrorist war of attrition. Both of these tendencies lead to forms of totalitarian state, both feed each other.

The missing "heart and soul" of Islam can still be found, however. People have asked whether Islam is capable of reforming itself and developing a more nuanced, rational, and humane interpretation of the Qur'an. It is mainly the Sufis who offer that possibility.[15] In fact, despite a long and distinguished history within the Islamic world, Sufism is so different from the Islam we see in the headlines that many have (rather patronizingly) argued it is not a natural part of Islam at all, but evidence of an early Christian influence. And, of course, there are not a few Muslims who are eager to agree with them, in order to dismiss it as a heresy and suppress its influence.

In the writings and devotions of the Sufis we almost glimpse the possibility of a Christian interpretation of the Qur'an. Muhiyddin Ibn Arabi (1165–1240), known by Sufis as the Greatest Shaikh and almost certainly the most influential, in his chapter on Jesus in his book on the Prophets (the *Fusus al-Hikam* or *Bezels of Wisdom*), draws our attention to the Qur'anic verse at 4:171 that describes Jesus as God's "word deposited with Mary, and a spirit from Himself." Ibn Arabi comments that "Gabriel was, in fact, transmitting God's word to Mary, just as an apostle transmits His word to his community.[16] He also says in the opening of the chapter:

> God purified him [Jesus] in body and made him transcendent
> In the Spirit, making him like Himself in creating.[17]

An alternative translation by Reza Shah-Kazemi reads: "God purified him in body and exalted him in spirit, / And made of him a symbol of engendering."[18] This translation is intriguing because "a

---

15. To be more precise, I am talking not just about Sufism, which is found largely among the Sunnis, but of Islamic mysticism in general, including Shiite *Irfan* (*gnosis*), characterized by its devotion to the twelve Imams. Anyone who doubts the possibility of a serious engagement with Christian theology from the Muslim side should read, for example, Samuel Zinner, *Christianity and Islam: Essays on Ontology and Archetype* (London: Matheson Trust, 2010).

16. Ibn Al-'Arabi, *Ibn Al 'Arabi: The Bezels of Wisdom*, transl. R.W.J. Austin (New York: Paulist Press, 1980), 175.

17. Ibid.

18. Reza Shah-Kazemi, at http://www.ibnarabisociety.org/rezashah.html: "Jesus in the Qur'an: An Akbari Perspective." For another interesting study of Ibn Arabi's

symbol of engendering" could be even taken as a coded reference to the name "Son," which is a symbol of the relation of begetting.

Of course, Ibn Arabi also cites the statement of the Qur'an, "*They are concealers [unbelievers] who say that God is the Messiah, son of Mary.*"[19] But then, a Christian too can agree with that statement: for in our terms the Son of Mary is not God (i.e., the Trinity, or the Father); he is specifically God the Son (the Second Person). Jesus is not the Incarnation of "God," then, but specifically of God's Self-knowledge. This in turn means that by loving Jesus we human creatures may enter into that relationship God has with himself, in himself, through the Holy Spirit that unites the Persons in God. Similarly, when Islam insists that "*He, God, is One, God the Self-Subsistent. He neither begets, nor is He begotten,*" Christianity can in a sense agree, since it is the *Father* who begets, not God as such. I realize that this can be dismissed as mere wordplay, but I think it helps to bring out a theological point that lies at the root of much misunderstanding.

Intriguingly, Ibn Arabi distinguishes those Christians who confuse divinity with the human form (son of Mary) from those others—of whom he appears to approve—who assert that the divine identity is rather "*the subject in* the human form" [my emphasis]. "Thus he is [at once] the Word of God, the Spirit of God, and the slave of God, and such a [triple] manifestation in sensible form belongs to no other." He describes Jesus as the Seal of Sanctity, just as Muhammad is the Seal of Prophecy.

He continues:

> Every other man is attributed to his formal father, not to the one who blows His Spirit into human form.... All creatures are indeed words of God, which are inexhaustible, stemming as they do from [the command] *Be,* which is the Word of God. Now, can the Word be attributed to God as He is in Himself, so that its nature may never be known, or can God descend to the form of him who says *Be* [i.e., the form of a human being], so that the

views on Jesus see Saoud Hakim, "The Spirit and the Son of the Spirit" online at http://www.ibnarabisociety.org/articles/spirit.html.

19. Ibn Al-'Arabi, *Ibn Al 'Arabi*, 177.

word *Be* may be said to be the reality of the form to which He descends and in which He is manifest [i.e. can the Word of God be identified with the human being Jesus of Nazareth]?

He concludes: "This matter is one that can be known only by direct experience."[20] I am not suggesting that Ibn Arabi was secretly a Christian (though his opponents alleged as much, and he himself did claim to have been taught directly by Jesus).[21] I am simply noting that the contortions he goes through in this chapter seem to indicate that he is wrestling with the problem of the uniqueness of Jesus Christ, a uniqueness expressed not just in Sufi commentaries but in the Qur'an itself by references to the virgin birth and the miracle of raising the dead.[22]

---

20. Ibid., 178. The interpretations in square brackets are my own.

21. The closest he comes to speaking of the Trinity is when he describes the Absolute as Oneness above all relations, even the concept of number, distinguishing this from the "singleness" of the Absolute which contains an active *triplicity* of Essence, Word, and Will mirrored by a receptive triplicity on the part of the things to be created (thingness, hearing, and obeying). See Toshihiko Izutsu, *Sufism and Taoism: A Comparative Study of Key Philosophical Concepts* (Los Angeles: University of California Press, 1983), 198–9. Interestingly, since Ibn Arabi's key doctrine is said to be the "unity of being" (*wujud*) and he is accused of a kind of monism in which all diversity and distinction in creation is destined to be extinguished in the divine Face, he nevertheless teaches that "the annihilation of self that is experienced by perfect human beings is not absolute" (William C. Chittick, *Imaginal Worlds: Ibn al-'Arabi and the Problem of Religious Diversity* [State University of New York Press, 1994], 61). As we shall see, Meister Eckhart is similarly liable to misinterpretation.

22. Ibn Arabi describes this as a "divine prerogative" only on rare occasions shared with the saints. "Jesus came forth raising the dead because he was a divine spirit. In this the quickening was of God, while the blowing itself came from Jesus, just as the blowing [of the spirit into Mary] was from Gabriel, while the Word was of God" (176). R.W.J. Austin comments that according to Ibn Arabi, the prophecy of Jesus, or his being "informed" by the divine Word, unlike that of other prophets, "was not only verbal but also vital, in that the spiritual 'blowing' of which he was a channel transmits the divine Command in all its modes. Thus by virtue of the direct means of his being begotten, Jesus was able to communicate the divine Spirit not only verbally, but also vitally, since the Spirit enlivens at every level" (174). To pursue this further one would also need to explore Ibn Arabi's chapter on Adam, where his ontological analysis of the prophet who is the archetype and father of humanity appears to be as relevant to the "Second Adam" as it is to the First.

Conclusion

Dominus Iesus (section 14) invites us to explore the question "whether and in what way the historical figures and positive elements of [other] religions may fall within the divine plan of salvation," thus suggesting that not only Moses (obviously) but even Muhammad may have a providential role to play in salvation history. So we come back to the question: what might this role be? Louis Bouyer, a bit like Boehme, saw Islam as in part a prophetic protest against the "degradation of popular Christian piety into polytheism and a real, if not theoretical, idolatry." The passages in the Old Testament where God uses the pagan kings to rebuke Israel and to bring about his purposes in history are there to confirm this possibility.

I find it hard to believe that, with enormous cultural and spiritual achievements to its credit, Islam can be founded on pure malice. At the very least it has been permitted to flourish by God for a reason. Muslims believe that it is Jesus, rather than Muhammad, who will come back at the end of the world to institute the reign of God. Islam no doubt requires its own purification before the End, and of that I am not qualified to speak. Nevertheless, when Jesus *does* return, the Muslims, unlike our Western atheists, will at least have been taught to expect his arrival. Christians may yet learn to see Islam as a message akin in some ways to that of John the Baptist, sent "in the spirit of Elias" to prepare the way for the arrival of the Son of Man on the clouds of glory at the end of time.

An image comes to mind: a kind of triptych, like the ones that used to be painted for church altars. The central panel shows Jesus on the Cross. Above him the Father's hand is depicted, sending down the Holy Spirit. Perhaps the picture would include a small representation of the Nativity in the background on one side and the Resurrection or Ascension of Christ on the other. On the left-hand panel of the triptych is an image of Moses receiving the Commandments on Mount Sinai—an image representing the Old Covenant. On the right is a panel echoing it, but this one portrays the Prophet Muhammad receiving the Qur'an. This is not an image that would please the Muslims, to put it mildly, since apart from anything else they would not want the Prophet depicted at all. Nor would it please Christians or Jews. But it is not intended as an image for veneration in churches. Rather this is an imaginative depiction of the historical process: first Judaism, then Christianity, then Islam mirroring Judaism; three panels destined one day to be folded together.

God is indeed the Compassionate, the Merciful, the Source of Peace, the Majestic, the Creator, the Opener, the All-Seeing, the Forbearing, the Watchful, the Glorious. These names or attributes of God have inspired Muslim mystics and poets for centuries. God is One, and there is no other beside him. Yet as Christians know, he is also Father, Son and Holy Spirit, and these are Names that define his very substance. This revealed truth is bound up with the message of salvation, as Christians understand it. It is tragic that our words, and our lives, all too often fail to communicate this Gospel to others. Without ceasing to be one Nature, God is three Persons. These three Names reveal what it truly means for Him to be *Al-Wadud*, the Loving.

Aspects of Buddhism

As it developed, Christian theology incorporated elements from the Greek and Roman (not to mention Jewish and later Islamic) thought-worlds that surrounded it. Other elements were rejected, sometimes violently, and yet others tailored by the Church Fathers to fit the new religious perspective. This process of dialogue, critique, reaction, and creative incorporation was exceedingly complex, and has been well documented. Catholic believers regard it as no haphazard adventure through time, but rather as providentially ordered by the Holy Spirit to enable the *gestalt* of Christian truth— the face of Christ—to emerge ever more clearly into view. An adventure, perhaps, then, but hardly "haphazard," because the *sensus fidelium*, like a homing instinct or sense of balance, enables the diversions and distractions of the journey to be integrated with the essential center of things, as revealed to the eyes of faith. The Christian man of letters and amateur theologian G. K. Chesterton famously put it this way in his book *Orthodoxy*:

> It is always simple to fall; there are an infinity of angles at which one falls, only one at which one stands. To have fallen into any one of the fads from Gnosticism to Christian Science would indeed have been obvious and tame. But to have avoided them all has been one whirling adventure; and in my vision the heavenly chariot flies thundering through the ages, the dull heresies sprawling and prostrate, the wild truth reeling but erect.

In our day Christians face a similar challenge, being in close contact not just with the ancient Classical civilizations of the Mediterranean basin and Middle East, but with every religious or philosophical tradition from Japan to Australia and all points between. To keep our balance in this maelstrom of concepts and images and practices, while integrating what is of value within orthodox Christianity, calls for a renewed sense of the *gestalt* and much careful, intelligent discernment. The challenge is not merely an academic or intellectual one. Religious experience involves more than the appreciation of concepts, and the discernment I have in mind must involve an attempt to penetrate to the heart of that experience. In this chapter and the next I am trying to do justice to what I perceive of the Asian religious experience.

The Great Perfection

In his biography of Jesus Christ, the great Christian writer Romano Guardini said of the Buddha:

> There is only one whom we might be inclined to compare with Jesus: Buddha. This man is a great mystery. He lived in an awful, almost superhuman freedom, yet his kindness was powerful as a cosmic force. Perhaps Buddha will be the last religious genius to be explained by Christianity. As yet no one has uncovered his Christian significance. Perhaps Christ had not only one precursor, John, last of the prophets, but three: John the Baptist for the Chosen People, Socrates from the heart of antiquity, and Buddha, who spoke the ultimate word in Eastern religious cognition. Buddha is free; but his freedom is not that of Christ. Possibly Buddha's freedom is only the ultimate and supremely liberating knowledge of the vanity of this fallen world.[1]

When asked who he was, the Buddha (Siddhartha Gautama), who lived around A D 400, did not reply, "I am God" or "I am a messenger of God" or even "I am one who knows the truth." He replied: "I am Awake." (The word *Buddha* in fact means "the Awakened One.")[2] He also named himself *Tathagata*, the one who has *thus-come* and *thus-gone*. He did not teach that there was a God or that there was not a God: this seemed irrelevant—as did the question of the world's origin, since the Buddha was concerned only with the very practical question of how to bring an end to suffering.

Buddhism as a religious system and a civilization sprang from this experience of enlightenment and the "Middle Way" between extreme asceticism and worldly indulgence Gautama taught to the

---

1. Romano Guardini, *The Lord* (Chicago: Regnery Gateway, 1954), 305.
2. This exchange is reminiscent of Moses at the Burning Bush, asking the same question and receiving a different but similarly syntax-bending answer.

disciples who gathered around him. His teaching, or Dharma, was enshrined in "Four Noble Truths": the truth of universal suffering (what a Christian would call the world's state of fallenness); the truth that suffering originates in "craving" (what a Christian would term concupiscence); the truth that the cessation of suffering— liberation, *nirvana*—can be brought about by destroying the igno- rance at its root;[3] and the truth that the way to achieve this *nirvana* is by the "Eightfold Path"—appropriate views, intentions, speech, action, livelihood, effort, mindfulness, and concentration.

Buddhism was primarily a monastic religion, because to practice it fully you had to renounce the world and live a form of moderate asceticism that included at least temporary celibacy. The order of monks and nuns, the *Sangha* or Community, has always been at the heart of the religion, and the role of the laity is to support and learn from them—though laypeople, too, can achieve enlightenment. The main branches of Buddhism as it spread were divided by schisms over the monastic rule itself. The Theravada tradition pre- serves its scriptures in the ancient Pali language, along with the emphasis on individual enlightenment. The Mahayana tradition was more flexible and universal and, being more capable of "incul- turation," spread further: the emphasis here was not just on ending one's own suffering, but liberating all sentient beings through the life of compassion. Furthermore the Buddha was regarded as still around (in a place or state called the "Pure Land"), still available as teacher.[4] Tibetan Buddhism and Japanese Zen—the two forms of Buddhism most familiar in the West—are both part of the Mahay- ana tradition.

---

3. Buddhagosha describes *Nirvana* (*Nibbana* in Pali) in extremely positive terms, as "Truth transcendental, difficult to be seen, without decay, eternal, inde- structible, immortal, happy, peaceful, wonderful, holy, pure and an island of ref- uge." An interesting case could therefore be made for identifying the Buddhist concept of *Nirvana* not with "nihilism," since in Buddhist writings this state is often described as a plenitude rather than a cessation of consciousness, but with the unfashionable Christian notion of *Limbo*—a state of perfect natural happiness but without the Beatific Vision.

4. I am basing myself on the excellent summary by Paul Williams in D'Costa (ed.), *The Catholic Church and the World Religions*, 141–77.

My own limited experience of this tradition, apart from reading translations of the Buddhist Scriptures (the *sutras*, the Dhammapada, etc.) from an early age, comes from the fact that for a short time I once studied with Namkhai Norbu Rinpoche, a Tibetan master of Dzogchen. A Buddhist tradition whose name means "Great Perfection," Dzogchen is regarded by Tibetans as the purest form of both Buddhism and Bon (the native shamanic religion); it is said, however, to transcend both these religious forms, and indeed all religious forms, being found in thirteen solar systems apart from our own (13).[5]

Later I turned away from Buddhism towards Christianity, but I never felt that I was rejecting a religious path that was simply wrong and evil. On the contrary, I had the impression that what was of value and true in Dzogchen was in some sense compatible with my new faith. Now, after more than 30 years as a Catholic, perhaps near the end of my life, I find myself needing to return to that impression, to look at it more closely in the light of my Christian experience.

Self-Perfection

The teachings of Dzogchen are summarized in the "Six Vajra Verses" (xv):

> *Although apparent phenomena manifest as diversity,*
> *yet this diversity is non-dual,*
> *and of all the multiplicity of individual things that exist*
> *none can be confined in a limited concept.*
> *Staying free from the trap of any attempt to say "it's like this," or*
> *"like that,"*
> *it becomes clear that all manifested forms are aspects of the infinite*
> *formless,*
> *and, indivisible from it, are self-perfected.*
> *Seeing that everything is self-perfected from the very beginning,*
> *the disease of striving for any achievement is surrendered,*
> *and, just remaining in the natural state as it is,*

---

5. This and the next few page references are to the book by my teacher, Namkhai Norbu, *The Crystal and the Way of Light* (London: Routledge & Kegan Paul, 1986).

*the presence of non-dual contemplation continuously spontane-
ously arises.*

It would appear at first sight that this runs completely counter to
Christianity. It seems to deny creation and the Fall, for example, and
be aimed at inducing a state of passivity or quietism. If everything is
perfect why bother to do anything? If all things are aspects of the
Formless and their diversity merely "apparent," then "I" and my
neighbor must simply disappear. What then becomes of the Christian injunction to "love my neighbor as myself"? A Christian critique of Buddhism along these lines is easy and tempting to make,
and has been made on many occasions—one of the most interesting
and sophisticated being by Henri de Lubac SJ (*Aspects of Buddhism*).

G.K. Chesterton, reviewing a book by an English Buddhist,
writes that for Buddhism it appears that "Existence is simply a
destructive cataract of perpetually disappearing thoughts and feelings, at no moment of which can anybody be said to possess anything, least of all a personality."[6] And in his book *Orthodoxy* he
assimilates Buddhism (rather unfairly) to the Theosophy of Mrs.
Besant:

> According to Mrs. Besant . . . there are no real walls of individual-
> ity between man and man. If I may put it so, she does not tell us to
> love our neighbors; she tells us to be our neighbors. That is Mrs.
> Besant's thoughtful and suggestive description of the religion in
> which all men must find themselves in agreement. And I never
> heard of any suggestion in my life with which I more violently dis-
> agree. I want to love my neighbor not because he is I, but precisely
> because he is not I. I want to adore the world, not as one likes a
> looking-glass, because it is one's self, but as one loves a woman,
> because she is entirely different. If souls are separate love is possi-
> ble. If souls are united love is obviously impossible. A man may be
> said loosely to love himself, but he can hardly fall in love with
> himself, or, if he does, it must be a monotonous courtship. If the
> world is full of real selves, they can be really unselfish selves. But
> upon Mrs. Besant's principle the whole cosmos is only one enor-

6. From a collection of his essays called *Generally Speaking* (London: Methuen,
1928), 94–9.

mously selfish person. It is just here that Buddhism is on the side of modern pantheism and immanence. And it is just here that Christianity is on the side of humanity and liberty and love. Love desires personality; therefore love desires division.[7]

But things are more complicated than they may appear. Notice that the existence of things is not actually denied in the Six Verses, although they are said to be merely "aspects of the infinite formless." Nor is the phrase "self-perfection" intended to refer to some kind of *moral* state. (In fact the moral teachings of Dzogchen are almost non-existent, based as they are on the refusal to make judgments such as good or bad, beautiful or ugly, as we shall see in a moment.) The use of the word "self" here also needs careful analysis, since Dzogchen teaches that there is in reality no real "self" or "ego" (33). Possibly the phrase has been badly translated. Finally, when the Six Verses talk of "the disease of striving" we are not meant to conclude from this that we should give up any aspiration to understand our condition—which is, after all, the motivation for engaging in the practice.

Dzogchen does, however, distinguish itself from Buddhist traditions for which the goal of human existence is the *cessation* of thought and suffering. Instead, the goal is to understand thought and suffering for what they are, and to arrive at a state of contemplation that transcends them. The practitioner does not withdraw from society or from the full range of normal behavior, since one of the main characteristics of Dzogchen is that daily life continues much as before.

So what is this state of "non-dual contemplation"? I believe that it is simply the realization that *all things in the field of our awareness are manifestations of consciousness.* That may appear to be a truism, but the important word here is "realization." We may easily *agree* with a truism, but to *realize* it is something different. Our normal state is said in Dzogchen to be "dualistic" because we are continually separating ourselves from the objects of our awareness. In fact, it is hard to conceive how we might do otherwise, since our conscious-

7. G.K. Chesterton, *The Collected Works*, vol. 1 (San Francisco: Ignatius Press, 1986), 336–7.

ness of things as things is a product of our identification of them as "this" or "that" distinct from ourselves. We look "through" the experience of a thing, to reach the thing itself. Bound up with this process of separation/identification is our desire for some things and rejection of others, along with the whole complex of judgments we make about them that defines who we are and how we live our lives.

Non-dual contemplation is an attempt to detach ourselves from this process of judgment and descend into pure awareness. The goal is not to destroy these judgments, but to become aware of the process of making them. The practice of Dzogchen is therefore not to quieten the mind by suppressing or repressing its contents, but to allow those to arise and depart naturally without engaging with or "following" them mentally or emotionally (77–8). Mentally we remain in one place—that is, in what Dzogchen calls the "primordial state" or "base" of consciousness.

To achieve this state is desirable because it dissolves the passions that cause evil and suffering. There is no selfishness, no self-centered passion, possible to one who is truly detached from the process of identification. The "infinite formless" can act through the person, instead of some limited, self-generated ego. That, at least, is the theory.

Buddhism and Christianity

As I already suspected when I became a Christian, similar teachings are present within the Christian tradition. The most helpful parallels I have found are those in Dumitru Staniloae's account of the passions as understood by the Orthodox tradition.[8] Echoing Blondel as well as Dostoevsky, he speaks first of man's "thirst for the infinite." He goes on to argue that it is the passions which define the objects of our consciousness, and they do so in order to have something to control and consume, as a substitute for the Infinite which is the true object of natural desire. The root of the passions is egotism. "Instead of quenching his thirst for the infinite, he sought to gather everything around himself, as around a center. But because man

8. Dmitru Staniloae, *Orthodox Spirituality* (South Canaan, PA: St Thikhon's Seminary Press, 2002). Again, page references are given in the main text.

isn't a true center in himself, this nature of his took revenge; it made him in reality run after things, even enslaving him to them" (79).

Compare the following passage from a Dzogchen text:

> Once the idea of "I" and "mine" has arisen, the entire mechanism of sense objects and consciousness, or subject and object, proceeds in order to gratify the acquisitiveness of this imagined "I" through concrete sensory experiences. The imagined "I" tries to make itself feel real by creating and pursuing sensory experiences. This is a brief description of how grasping consciousness and grasped-at objects arise, producing and perpetuating *samsara*.[9]

By contrast, what is natural to man (or, as Christians might say, what was natural before the Fall) is a continual "sharing in the infinite," in the sense of a conscious reception of one's own existence from a Source that remains ever transcendent. "Being in a state of grace" is the Christian version of what the Buddhist calls the primordial state or "essence of mind." It is not passive in the sense of being merely inert, but *actively receptive* to whatever comes from the Infinite.

Staniloae himself is concerned with distinguishing Christian dispassion from Buddhist *nirvana* (188–9). The concern of the Buddhist, he says, is only with his own "egotistic tranquility," whereas the Christian's dispassion will manifest itself in the form of love. This first point does not seem entirely fair, since a concern for one's own tranquility is one of the things supposed to be eliminated on the Buddhist's path. Such a subtle form of egotism may, however, be the form most easily taken by an imperfect form of Buddhism, just as do-gooding moralism or self-righteousness may be the natural form of an imperfect Christianity. Both types of imperfection are, as we know, only too common.

But perhaps there is a deeper and more valid contrast between the two religions, suggested by Staniloae's reference to "love." Henri de Lubac, in his essay "Buddhist Charity,"[10] explores the meaning of

---

9. Long-chen-pa, et al., *The Four-Themed Precious Garland: An Introduction to Dzog Ch'en*, The Library of Tibetan Works and Archives of His Holiness the Dalai Lama (Dharamsala, 1979), 42.

10. Henri de Lubac, *Aspects of Buddhism* (London: Sheed & Ward, 1953), 15–52.

the references throughout Buddhist teachings to "love," "compassion," and "altruism," and concluded that these words receive a very different meaning depending on the assumptions about the self in both religions. For Buddhism man is "nothing but a mass of component parts, with no inner unity, therefore there is nothing in the human being that can call for, or make possible, any ultimate love. Altruism of any kind, whatever its tinge, and however ardent it may be, can only be a procedure for getting rid of desire" (41).

Buddhism cannot speak of finding the true self, but only losing the false one. Furthermore, it assumes the "self" is ultimately *consciousness*. Christianity revolves around the notion of the *person*, which derives from the doctrine of the Trinity. The "person" is that in us which calls for love. It is not consciousness but the possessor of consciousness. It is the inner unity that transcends the flux into which Buddhism would dissolve us—a flux of physical and psychical elements, of individual moments in time generated one after another by *karma*. But it is a paradoxical unity, thanks to the Trinitarian image in man. Staniloae points out that "man isn't a true center in himself." The attempt to establish such a center, as we have seen, merely manufactures an ego with its various passions. In that sense Dzogchen is right, as far as it goes. Our unity as persons is extrinsic; it only exists in relationship with others, and therefore outside of the ego. It cannot be found by introspection, which is the main "method" of Buddhism.

Non-Dual Meditation

And yet Dzogchen (like many forms of Buddhism) claims to be a technique of meditation that transcends religious forms. Can this actual technique be of any help to Christians? It is a question fraught with difficulty, and I don't regard my own conclusions as definitive.

Dzogchen teaches the attainment of non-dual awareness. Why would the Christian *not* find this helpful in dissolving the root of the passions, namely the ego or false self that we create by clustering our conceptions of things around a false center? For Dzogchen is surely correct in pointing out that our idea of ourselves—composed as it is of the manifold images of what we need, desire, love, and hate, what we have done and intend to do, the way we think others see us, and so on—is literally an imaginative construction. Not only is it not to be identified with our true self, but once established, this construction cannot be destroyed by violence. Extreme ascetic practices such as flagellation and fasting, which weaken the body, tend to strengthen the egotistic will to dominate the body and perfect the self. (This is why the Buddha in the end, under the Bodhi tree, abandoned extreme asceticism and achieved enlightenment by the Middle Way of moderation.) What is needed is a change of consciousness, in which the mind ceases to use the objects of its awareness to build the ego. The contemplative state is "non-dual" not because subject and object cease to exist, but because *our experiences of both* are perceived as aspects of the same thing, namely consciousness itself.

The things that come and go in our consciousness are perhaps described in the Six Verses as "self-perfected" because we do not need to "do" anything to them. This does not imply a value judgment but more accurately a refusal to judge, since judgment is exercised by the ego and to judge them is to play into the ego's hands. If I see or feel something and immediately categorize it as "good" or "bad," I am reinforcing the image I have made of myself as the measure of all things. This does not mean that I am rejecting the distinction between moral good and evil. What is being rejected here is the habitual tendency to judge things *from the point of view of the ego*. Instead we allow Being, "that which is," to speak to us, to reveal itself. In Christian terms we allow God to be the judge in place of ourselves. The distinction is a bit like that between "eating from the tree of the knowledge of good and evil" and being given to eat from the "tree of life."

There is a sense in which the Christian must first "die," in order to let Christ live his life. For our only true self is the self that exists in Christ, not a self that exists in itself (we are not "self-subsistent"). The process of "dying" is described very well in Dzogchen. What is *not* described is the process of being born again. How could it be? If God has not been revealed in Christ as Christians believe, then we do not have any basis for such a description. The symbol of Dzogchen is a round mirror, representing the field of consciousness underlying all experience. We may juxtapose this with one of the symbols of Christianity, which superficially looks a bit similar: the

Eucharist displayed in a monstrance—a small white disk surrounded by golden rays. In the Catholic teaching, that disk enshrines the real presence of the incarnate God. When a Catholic kneels before the Blessed Sacrament displayed in this fashion, the receptivity of the "mirror" is perfected by the active Presence that fills it. The ego is forgotten, and the true self begins to take its place.

The Sacrifice

Let us approach this point from a slightly different angle. Buddhism and Christianity obviously have very different attitudes to suffering. The ostensible goal of Buddhism is to abolish suffering by destroying its causes, and Dzogchen is framed within this tradition, even if it adopts the gentle approach of dissolving the causes in non-dual awareness rather than directly confronting and attempting to uproot them. Christianity, by contrast, treats suffering as a kind of sacrament. Paul Claudel once said, "Christ did not come to abolish suffering but to fill it with his presence." Our suffering (and this includes the mental sufferings of humiliation and failure as much as physical pain) becomes a way of uniting ourselves to Christ, the sacrificial victim who died to open a way for us into eternal life, into the bosom of the Trinity. Thus Catholics are often told to "offer up" these sufferings in order to make them spiritually fruitful. At the back of this idea lies the doctrine of the Trinity, the ultimate source of being, in which everything exists only in so far as it is given and received, and of the person as a relational entity distinct from consciousness.

But it is a false understanding of Christianity that insists on *unnecessary* suffering, despite the fact that some saints have been able to use self-imposed suffering as a technique of sanctification (what Buddhism calls an *upaya* or "skillful means"). Normally, it would be the suffering that comes to us inevitably, in the ordinary course of life, that is offered up—and it can be offered up precisely because it is understood as having been given to us. For a gift that is recognized as having been given is never merely taken for granted. It is welcomed, and the giver is thanked. The gift then becomes ours to employ and to use. It is not, however, *myself*. In other words, to be able truly to receive it is also to be able to be detached from it.

Here lies a possible link between Dzogchen and Christian spirituality. In order truly to appreciate that which comes to us—whether we would call it good or bad—as a gift from outside ourselves, it helps to achieve a state of non-dual contemplation in which our awareness is calmed down to the purest mirror-like receptivity. All that comes into this consciousness is then able to be recognized as other than myself. The ego has become a receptive *nothing*—the mirror-mind. Everything that comes into that mirror is gift, to be welcomed but not clung to. It flows. What we long for, what it is legitimate still to desire, is the Source of all these gifts, the invisible transcendent Principle, the loving Father from whom the Son receives his nature, and from whom we receive the "secret name" that defines our eternal personhood (Rev. 2:17).

The sacrament of confession or reconciliation comes into play partly as a method of objectifying—and thus distancing ourselves from—those actions and states of mind that have obstructed the flow of grace in us. As long as I cannot "confess" out loud, I am too closely identified with my sin. But the point about *sacramental* confession is that it is more than this, because Christ is present. It is no longer just about me detaching myself, but of my putting myself at the disposal of the Healer and allowing him to take an active role within my psyche. *Only say the Word, and my soul shall be healed.* It is again a case not just of receptivity, but of what that receptivity enables to come. It allows us to be refashioned, to be born not to the same kind of life in time, but an eternal life in the Spirit.

Conclusion

As a Christian, to "offer up" is an expression that puzzled me for a long time. How do I separate myself from the thing that has come to me or been done to me, and what precisely am I supposed to do with it? In the light of what I have just been saying, it appears that the act of sacrifice has two parts. The first part is to separate myself from what has come, descending to that level in myself that exists before all gifts have been received except bare existence itself. This part is the one too often neglected by Christians, for we try to offer the sacrifice while the ego is still clinging to its imaginary identity. Here Dzogchen may be a great help. But the second part of the act is more mysterious. It is something I am not capable of performing, and that is why Dzogchen remains silent about it. For only *Christ in me* can perform the second part of the sacrifice.

Perhaps the mistake we Christians make is to try too actively to imitate Christ instead of simply letting ourselves be joined to him by the Holy Spirit. To imitate him often becomes a contorted exercise in the manufacture of another (pious) ego, continually veering between the extremes of humility and self-righteousness. But the Church teaches that, since the Fall, mankind has been incapable of doing a single purely good deed. For a "good deed" is one in which our will is entirely united with that of God. That is precisely why God became man, in order to perform the good deed for us and to make it possible, through the Church, for it to be *done in us*.

All good deeds are ultimately summed up in one (just as all sins are summed up in one). Every action of Christ throughout his life was summed up on the Cross in his act of dying, which was an act of giving himself back to his Father and, at the same time, giving himself for us. That act of ego-less self-sacrifice was itself a pure expression of the one Act that God performs in all eternity, namely the Trinitarian *kenosis*, the self-giving of each divine Person to the others which constitutes them as one God. (This will be the subject of a later chapter.)

Once all this has been revealed, and has been accepted in an act of faith, the non-dual contemplation of Dzogchen seems to find its place, not as an alternative to Christian spirituality but as a support or helpful preparation for it. Something like this is essential, not to enable us to be saved (for no mere technique can save us), but for us to make real progress during life in the war with the passions—the war, that is, with the ego.

> You must give up your old way of life; you must put aside your old self, which gets corrupted by following illusory desires. Your mind must be renewed by a spiritual revolution so that you can put on the new self that has been created in God's way, in the goodness and holiness of the truth. (Eph. 4:22–4)

Non-Dualism

Dzogchen, of course, is one tradition among many, and quite a small one at that. It has played quite a large role in my life, and I find it both attractive and interesting. Of course, for that reason alone it might not seem worth including. But it may serve as a good example of the type of religious experience that does often draw Westerners away from Christianity. In the present chapter I want to broaden the focus again, to look at the whole context of non-dualistic philosophy, especially as it is found in the rich religious traditions of the Indian subcontinent and the Far East. The focus in the present chapter will be specifically on Advaita Vedanta, a non-dualist interpretation of the Upanishads (the primary philosophical texts of Vedic India)[1] by the eighth-century Hindu sage Shankara—quite close, in some ways, to the Buddhism we have just been discussing.

As far as Shankara's actual teaching is concerned, I am as usual dependent on translations and Western commentaries, but my prime concern is to address the interpretation offered by a number of scholars working in the West, who claim to recognize a similar or even identical doctrine in the writings of the Sufis of Islam (especially Muhyiddin Ibn Arabi with his doctrine of the Unity of Being) and the Christian preacher, Meister Eckhart. This school of thought—known as "perennialism"—is increasingly influential, and it deserves some close attention from anyone who is interested in the direction of inter-religious dialogue today.

1. Brahamanism or "Hinduism" is based on scriptures that include the four liturgical Vedas, the Brahmanas or explanations of the ritual, and the Upanishads, which explain the doctrine behind the liturgy. These date from before 500 BC. The Brahma Sutra (a condensation of the Upanishads) and the Bhagavad Gita (a popular exposition in mythological form) date from a few centuries later. For a translation of the Vedas with commentary see Raimundo Panikkar, *The Vedic Experience Mantramanjari: An Anthology of the Vedas for Modern Man and Contemporary Celebration* (London: DLT, 1977).

Perennialism in the sense I have given it was founded by Boston-based Indologist and art historian Ananda K. Coomaraswamy (d. 1947), along with two Western converts to Islamic Sufism, René Guénon (who died in Cairo in 1951) and Frithjof Schuon (d. 1998).[2] Christian admirers of this group included Eric Gill, T.S. Eliot, Philip Sherrard, and Thomas Merton (although not all of them would have agreed with the founders of the school in every respect), and its best-known living exponent at the time of writing is the Muslim scholar, Seyyed Hossein Nasr, whose writings on Islamic science in particular have won wide respect. It has influenced a growing school of exponents within the academy, as well as well-known popularizers and sympathizers such as Huston Smith and Karen Armstrong.

As expounded by Guénon and Schuon, perennialism claims to be an expression of the perennial wisdom (*Sophia Perennis* or *Sanathana Dharma*) always potentially accessible to the human spirit, and present as the "kernel" within all valid religious systems. It is in fact in many respects an exceptionally powerful and flexible tool for the interpretation of religious forms—philosophies, theologies, mythologies, and symbolism in general. Schuon, whose seminal book on the subject was called *The Transcendental Unity of Religions*, summarizes its basic principles as follows:

> In metaphysics, it is necessary to start from the idea that the Supreme Reality is absolute, and that being absolute it is infinite. That is absolute which allows of no augmentation or diminution, or of no repetition or division; it is therefore that which is at once solely itself and totally itself.... The Infinite is so to speak the intrinsic dimension of plenitude proper to the Absolute, the one being inconceivable without the other.... The distinction between

2. It should be mentioned that Aldous Huxley's *The Perennial Philosophy* (1945) was also an attempt to summarize the *Sanathana Dharma*, but though influential it was less intellectually rigorous and rather more eclectic than the work of the thinkers I am primarily concerned with here. I have tried to situate these modern religious movements in a broader context in an essay on the New Age movement in D'Costa (ed.), *The Catholic Church and the World Religions*, 178–215. This book also contains an excellent survey of Hinduism—making the important point that it is far from being a monolithic religious system—by Martin Ganeri OP (106–40).

the Absolute and the Infinite expresses the two fundamental aspects of the Real, that of essentiality and that of potentiality; this is the highest principial prefiguration of the masculine and feminine poles. Universal Radiation, thus *Maya* both divine and cosmic, springs from the second aspect, the Infinite, which coincides with All-Possibility. . . .[3] In reality, the creation to which we belong is but one cycle of universal manifestation, this manifestation being composed of an indefinite number of cycles that are "necessary" as regards their existence but "free" as regards their particularity. The Universe is a fabric woven of necessity and freedom, of mathematical rigor and musical play; every phenomenon participates in these two principles.[4] The first distinction to be made in a complete doctrine is between the Absolute and the relative, or between the Infinite and the finite; between *Atma* and *Maya*. The first term expresses *a priori* the single Essence, the Eckhartian "Godhead" (*Gottheit*), Beyond-Being; the "personal God" already pertains to *Maya*, of which He is the "relatively absolute" summit; He encompasses the entire domain of relativity down to the extreme limit of the cosmogonic projection.[5]

Schuon goes on to add other distinctions,[6] but what concerns us here is primarily that between the Absolute, which he calls the "Godhead" Beyond-Being (*Para Brahman*), and the Relative, which he elsewhere designates as Being (*Apara Brahman*). This primary

3. Maya he defines elsewhere as Relativity, Illusion, comprising everything except the supreme Absolute; that is, Para Brahman or Atma, as we see below. It includes the divine in the sense of the Creator and indeed the Logos, as celestial archetype and center of the World.

4. According to Schuon, the Infinite proceeds necessarily into all-possibility, like an inexhaustible fountain that does not in any way deplete its eternal source or add anything to it. The procession is by way of knowledge rather than will; the knowledge not of an Other but of the One Self and all it contains. The non-existence of the world is therefore literally inconceivable (except in the sense of a rhythmic cycle of manifestation and return to non-manifestation, implicit in the ordered unfolding of possibility).

5. Frithjof Schuon, *Survey of Metaphysics and Esoterism* (Bloomington: World Wisdom Books, 1986), 15–19.

6. Such as that between God, also called "the Principle" (comprising both Absolute and Relative Absolute), and the World or Manifestation, which includes the Logos as the central reflection of the Principle. Another distinction is between Heaven and Earth, in which Heaven comprises the Principle plus the Logos.

distinction, derived directly from Advaita Vedanta, requires the Absolute to be unconditioned by and unrelated to anything other than itself; that is, it excludes any relationality from its own proper nature. Basing himself on this exclusion of relativity from the bosom of the Absolute, Schuon describes Christianity as just one among many "exoteric" vehicles for a universal and non-dualistic "esotericism."[7] The Trinity, insofar as it implies relationality, belongs to the Relative, or the "relatively Absolute," and hence to the exoteric domain rather than the esoteric realm of pure, non-dual unity. For Schuon the alternative is strictly absurd: "that the Trinitarian relationships belong, not to this relative absoluteness [of Being] but to the pure and intrinsic Absolute, or to the absoluteness of the Essence, amounts to asking us to accept that two and two make five or that an effect has no cause, which no religious message can do and the Christian message has certainly never done."[8] A non-dualism based solely on the distinctions drawn by Schuon in the quoted passage fits easily into the dialectic of modernity: but it does so by collapsing the Many into the One, and only a better grasp of the Christian doctrine of the Trinity can prevent it from doing so. At any rate, it should be clear that Schuon's "first distinction" marks a very clear departure from Christian orthodoxy, for in orthodox Christian thought the doctrine of the Trinity pertains not merely to the realm of *maya*, but to the very essence of God—the Godhead itself. (As we shall see shortly, the Advaita school preferred by the perennialists is not the only orthodox school of interpretation of the Vedas, and Catholic Christians would find the writings

7. The distinction, introduced by Guénon, is developed by Schuon in his first book, *The Transcendent Unity of Religions*. The notion of Christian "esotericism" has been subjected to a searching critique in Jean Borella, *Guénonian Esoterism and Christian Mystery* (Hillsdale, NY: Sophia Perennis, 2004).

8. Frithjof Schuon, "Evidence and Mystery" in *The Fullness of God: Frithjof Schuon on Christianity,* ed. James S. Cutsinger (Bloomington: World Wisdom Books, 2004), 126. Cf. his treatment of the Trinity in "Transcendence is Not Contrary to Sense," in *From the Divine to the Human* (Bloomington: World Wisdom Books, 1982), 19–32. The Catholic writer Timothy A. Mahoney has effectively refuted Schuon's position in his essay "Christian Metaphysics: Trinity, Incarnation and Creation," *Sophia: The Journal of Traditional Studies* 8, no. 1 (Summer 2002): 79–102 (also online at http://www.secondspring.co.uk/ under "Articles").

of Ramanuja much closer to their own position. For the Vishishtad-vaita school of Ramanuja, God may be without duality—"One"—but he is not without relations. He is the personal creator God of a really existing world of creatures.)

Some perennialists seem to regard Eastern Orthodoxy as a more authentic form of Christianity than Catholicism, perhaps because of the distinction drawn by St. Gregory Palamas between the unknowable Essence and the knowable Energies of God, which recall the Advaitic distinction between Para and Apara Brahman. However, one of the most telling critiques of the subordination of Revelation to monadic logic ending in the complete suppression of the personal can be found in a book of essays by the Greek Ortho-dox writer Philip Sherrard.[9] Sherrard is a strong defender, in other respects, of the perennialists, but in this connection he writes, for example, that for the Orthodox, "each Person of the Trinity, although distinct from the other Persons, is as real and as absolute as each of the other Persons, and the reality and absoluteness and infinitude possessed by each Person are those of Reality itself, and the Absolute and Infinite Itself, in the fullest sense of the words" (83). Another Greek Orthodox theologian, Metropolitan John Ziz-ioulas, draws this doctrine out of the writings of Maximus the Con-fessor and Cappadocian fathers, where "the three persons of the Trinity do not share a pre-existing or logically prior to them divine nature, but coincide with it." As he points out, "the philosophical scandal of the Trinity can be resolved or accepted only if substance gives way to personhood as the causing principle or *arche* in ontol-ogy." Thus the (logical) origin of the Trinity is not an abstracted divine nature or Essence, but the Father, who is of course only "Father" in relation to the Son and the Spirit.[10] Zizioulas explores the anthropological consequences of this insight in terms of the divine image in man, who is fully human only insofar as he tran-scends his own nature in personhood; that is, in "the identity cre-

9. Philip Sherrard, *Christianity: Lineaments of a Sacred Tradition* (Brookline, MA: Holy Cross Orthodox Press, 1998), 76–113.

10. John Zizioulas, *Communion and Otherness: Further Studies in Personhood and the Church* (London: T&T Clark, 2006), 159, 162–63.

ated freely by love and not by the necessity of its self-existence"
(167).

The Real World

Two of the teachings that are most closely associated with the Asian
traditions, whether Buddhist or Hindu, in the popular mind are the
teaching on reincarnation, and the teaching that the world is an
illusion (*maya*). In their context, both teachings are more complex
than they appear to Westerners raised on crude simplifications. In
the case of reincarnation, the sagacious Coomaraswamy asserts
forthrightly that:

> [N]o doctrine of reincarnation, according to which the being and
> person of a man who has once lived on earth and is now deceased
> will be reborn of another terrestrial mother, has ever been taught
> in India, even in Buddhism—or for that matter in the Neoplatonic
> or any other orthodox tradition.[11]

He adds, of course, a slight qualification. Reincarnation may
indeed be found in the popular *misinterpretations* of symbolic texts
and in folklore. But formal Hindu and Buddhist teaching excludes
it. Those who depart this life do so forever; nothing of what we are
accustomed to call the "human personality" survives death.[12]
"Theosophical" theories of reincarnation, so prevalent in New Age
circles, are not authentically oriental but a construct based on
applying the modern Western idea of evolution to the idea of a spiritual self.[13]

According to Coomaraswamy, the genuine Hindu teaching on

---

11. A.K. Coomaraswamy, *Coomaraswamy 2: Selected Papers, Metaphysics*, ed. by
Roger Lipsey, Bollingen Series LXXXIX (Princeton University Press, 1977), 15.

12. There are, however, aspects of the person that may be "passed on," ranging
from what we would call genetic characteristics to more spiritual ones, as Jesus
indicated when he described John the Baptist as Elijah—meaning that the spirit or
mission or role of Elijah was present in John. If Coomaraswamy is right, this is
what lies behind the traditional Tibetan search for the next reincarnation of the
Dalai Lama, rather than any belief that the personal essence of the previous one had
been reborn from another womb.

13. In a later chapter of this book you will find a footnote on the notion of reincarnation proposed in *Meditations on the Tarot*.

life after death might be better termed "transmigration," and it refers to that "consciousness of being" achieved by some before death—a state of "living in the spirit" that transcends the earthly personality. This implies a continued life, not in this world or this temporal universe, but in some other state of being, which in turn may lead through another death to another state, until all the states are exhausted and the spirit comes face to face with its own Source and End.

Coomaraswamy quotes Shankara: "Verily, there is no other trans-migrant than the Lord."[14] It is, in fact, no individual personality that continues after death, but a "ray," as it were, of that supernal Sun that is the Spirit, Atman, the inner life of all. The terminology of Buddhism is slightly different, but only slightly. Since for the Buddha there is no continuing "self" in anything, each moment of our existence is not "ours" but simply one more projection of the unmanifested Truth Body or Dharmakaya, the ground of existence, with which the Buddha himself is identified. It is in this sense that Coomaraswamy would interpret also the saying of Christ that "no man hath ascended up to heaven, but he that came down from heaven, even the Son of Man which is in heaven" (John 3:13). And of course St. Paul's mystical teaching may be read in this connection: "I live, yet not I, but Christ in me" (Gal. 2:20), and many other passages of Scripture besides.[15]

Coomaraswamy points out that much harm has been done by translators and commentators unfamiliar with the key terms of the other tradition, or lacking any metaphysical sense of their own. Many of them have been trained in linguistics or anthropology rather than the medieval or ancient philosophy, especially the phi-losophy of Thomas Aquinas, that would give them a more precise vocabulary into which to translate these oriental texts. At least with Coomaraswamy one feels on firm ground, even if one has to resist the temptation to be swept away by a flood of citations. But it is just as possible for a Christian to offer insights that clarify the meaning

14. Ibid., 66.
15. Ibid., 84. The Christian interpretation of such phrases will be discussed later in the book.

of a Hindu text as it is for a Hindu to explain the true meaning of a Christian one, as we shall see.

The teaching on *maya* ("divine power") is a case in point. Coomaraswamy insists that *maya* is not "illusion," but rather the maternal measure and means essential to the manifestation of a quantitative, and in this sense "material," world of appearances, by which we may either be enlightened or deluded according to the degree of our own maturity."[16] Shankara speaks of a rope that is mistaken for a snake; pointing out that though the snake does not exist, *something* does, namely the rope, which he identifies with Absolute Being. However, the origin of our delusion that anything exists other than Being is not really explained in either Hinduism or Buddhism. This is an opening where Christianity has something to offer the East (if only a refinement of terminology). For we agree that the world is normally taken for much more than it really is, and to that extent is illusory; that is to say, it is something, but not what it seems when we look at it, as we almost inevitably tend to do, as "standing alongside" or being "separate" from God.[17] This double affirmation—that the world is both something and nothing, depending on one's perspective, is the point of St. Thomas's account of created *esse* as complete and simple, but not subsistent, and of his doctrine of the divine knowledge of creatures.[18] The origin of our delusion is, of course, explained by the doctrine of the Fall.

---

16. A.K. Coomaraswamy, *Hinduism and Buddhism* (New Delhi: Munshiram Manoharlal, 1975), 3. *Maya* comes from a word meaning to impose "measure" or order, which connects it profoundly with ancient Western notions of creation, for example in the Book of Genesis. Some claim that *maya* is related to the origin of the term "magic," but this is disputed.

17. If we view things *as they are in God*, rather than separate from him, then they are indeed real, but to what extent are they then *other than God*? I want to affirm that it is the (Trinitarian) unity of God that makes the distinctness of the creature real without its being "other," just as the Father is the unoriginate origin of the Son and Spirit without ever being anything other than one and the same Essence. See the next chapter.

18. If we are thinking of the Essence, God has only one "Idea" for all things, but if we are thinking of the many ways individual creatures imitate that Essence and fall short of it, there is a plurality of divine ideas. Thus God understands himself, but he also understands the relations things have to his Essence (the ideas). But in

Advaita and Catholicism

Schuon and Guénon were both converts to Islam, and Coomaraswamy remained a Hindu, but Christians who find themselves drawn to Advaita have to wrestle harder to reconcile their faith and their metaphysics. One such attempt to combine the perennialist approach with Catholic orthodoxy is *Christianity and the Doctrine of Non-Dualism*, written anonymously by "a Monk of the West."[19] The Monk writes not as an academic but as a man of prayer and Christian faith who has meditated deeply on his religious experience.

The two points of view that the Monk hopes to bring into accord appear on the surface completely contradictory. On the one hand, we have the Christian doctrines of the creation of the world by God, with the (unique) hypostatic union of divine and human natures in Christ. On the other we have the "Supreme Identity" (*tat tvam asi* or "That are Thou") of the Upanishads—roughly speaking, the identity of the Self (Atman) with God (Brahman). The Monk claims that "since they do not pertain to the same order of Reality, hypostatic union and Supreme Identity do not in themselves exclude one another, or stated otherwise, they are not metaphysically incompatible" (116). However, he also speculates that it is the former (the unique Incarnation of God in Christ) that alone permits the realization of the identity of Atman and Brahman in those who eventually transcend the point of view of creation (by the grace of divinization), giving this precise sense to the following sentence

God both are one undivided act of understanding. Sara Grant RSCJ, in a book that argues for a Christian interpretation of Advaita, sees a convergence between Shankara and St. Thomas Aquinas: "A systematic study of Sankara's use of relational terms made it quite clear to me that he agrees with St. Thomas Aquinas in regarding the relation between creation and the ultimate Source of all being as a *non-reciprocal dependence relation*, i.e., a relation in which a subsistent effect or 'relative absolute' is dependent on its cause for its very existence as a subsistent entity, whereas the cause is in no way dependent on the effect for its subsistence, though there is a necessary logical relation between cause and effect, i.e. a relation which is perceived by the mind when it reflects on the implications of the existence of the cosmos" (*Toward an Alternative Theology*, 40)

19. According to the Preface by Alvin Moore, Jr., the author's actual name was Alphonse Levée. Having studied Vedanta under the influence of René Guénon, he became a monk of La Trappe in 1951.

of John Paul II, "[Man] must, so to speak, enter into Christ with all his being, he must 'appropriate' to himself and assimilate all the reality of the Incarnation and Redemption *in order to find himself*" (117).[20] More precisely, he proposes that while Christ's realization of the Supreme Identity depends simply on the hypostatic union of his human and divine natures in the Person of the Son, our own realization of the Supreme Identity is dependent upon our incorporation in Christ. This proposal is probably equally offensive to both sides in the dialogue. Orthodox Christians will most likely protest against the claim that "to find himself" must ultimately mean for man to dissolve himself into the supreme (non-dual) identity. Christianity is surely the religion of creation *ex nihilo* and of the human person loved forever by a God who is different from himself. Advaitins or perennialist non-dualists, for their part, will find it hard to comprehend how the attainment of supreme realization might be made to depend on the incarnation of God at one particular point in history. As the author himself points out, the Supreme Identity is "not an event or a fact, but the permanent and immutable Truth (and so *uncreated*), of all that exists" (116). If it is true that "I am *that*," it will be true at any time and under any historical conditions whatsoever. Christ's birth in time makes no difference to this, just as it makes no difference to the truth of the Bhagavad Gita whether Krishna was an historical or an entirely mythological figure. That said, the Monk is surely on to something. His position is at least in one important respect different from that of the typical perennialist. He believes that while the Upanishads are fundamentally correct about the supreme identity, nevertheless our *realization* of this immutable truth is entirely dependent on a relationship with the historical Incarnation of the Son of God (whether we know this or not). In other words, he proposes a Christological re-reading of the supreme identity—though unfortunately he leaves the proposal undeveloped at the conclusion of his book.

20. John Paul II, *Redemptor Hominis* (1978), 10. The emphasis here is the Monk's. He quotes a larger portion of this passage at 35–36.

Jesus *Purusha*?

Another Catholic writer—not in this case a perennialist—Ian Davie, author of a remarkable book called *Jesus Purusha*, begins where the Monk leaves off. He writes:

> What Christianity claims to be uniquely true of Jesus, Hinduism claims to be universally true of mankind: if the Hindu claim thereby places divinity within the definition of man, Christianity, *qua* fulfillment of Hinduism, must hold that Jesus instantiates the universal truth of this claim. The primary question for theology, however, is not whether the identity of Atman and Brahman is personally realized in Jesus—since it is personally realized in any-one—but whether it is uniquely dependent on Jesus for its realization anywhere. And that, I shall argue, can only be so if Jesus is *Purusha* and *Atman*, His very Self; or if, as the Gospel according to Hinduism avers, Jesus is God's *Self-in-Person.*"[21]

This is indeed the question. Davie thinks that the Hindu metaphysics may prove even more suitable as a vehicle for expressing and exploring the meaning of Christianity than the Greek metaphysics we have used up to now—or at least that the Hindu is certainly suited to helping reveal a fuller understanding of the Incarnation, being a sophisticated intellectual reflection on a "revealed religion which is complementary to Judaism."[22] He is aware of the complexity of Hindu tradition, and unlike the perennialists does not prioritize the Advaitins but writes:

> My conclusion is that for Hindu theology to be fully assimilated by Western theology, three principle sources have to be drawn upon: the school of Sankara (Advaitin), the school of Ramanuja (Visishtadvaitin), and the Samkhya school's metaphysics of Purusha-Prakriti. These three schools, however incommensurable their teachings may be when taken in isolation from each other, com-

21. Ian Davie, *Jesus Purusha: A Vedanta-Based Doctrine of* Jesus (New York: Inner Traditions/ Lindisfarne Press, 1985), 12–13.

22. Ibid., 76. He is not by any means the only Western admirer of Hinduism to make that claim or suggestion, but others, to my mind, including in the end Henri le Saux or Abhishiktananda whose earlier writings were so promising, and the theologian Raimundo Panikkar, author of *The Unknown Christ of Hinduism*, have compromised something essential about Christianity in a way that Davie does not.

bine to produce a distinctive and coherent Hindu Jesuology, and one which is, moreover, capable of invigorating and transforming Western theology.[23]

In other words, he claims to show that it is Christian doctrine that alone can give a convincing explanation of the frequently heard Hindu claim that these three rival schools of Vedantic interpretation are complementary and not mutually exclusive. In this way Christianity can both gain from Hinduism and assist Hinduism in better understanding its own scriptural tradition.

So who or what is "*Purusha*," and why does Davie think it so important? Purusha is the primal Person, the Personhood of God, "the Person at the heart of the cosmos in whom the identity of Atman with Brahman is realized,"[24] for make no mistake, argues Davie, "the identity of Brahman and Atman could not be affirmed without there being a *locus* for its realization," in respect of which A is judged identical with B.[25] Thus Davie ends up identifying the Christian Trinity not with any of the conventional Hindu Triads, such as Brahma-Vishnu-Shiva, or even Sat-Chit-Ananda, but with Brahman-Purusha-Atman,[26] which he calls the "I," "Thou," and "We" of God's relationship with himself—the "Utterer," the "Uttered," and the "Uttering."[27] As he puts it, the most coherent

23. Ibid., 155.

24. Ibid., 60.

25. Ibid., 63.

26. The identification of Atman with the Holy Spirit is suggested also by the etymology—both come from a word meaning "breath." See Coomaraswamy, *Hinduism and Buddhism*, 34, and the same author's *The Vedas: Essays in Translation and Exegesis* (Beckenham: Prologos Books, 1976) for a detailed commentary on selected Vedic materials.

27. Davie, *Jesus Purusha*, 61. Panikkar sees the related Hindu term Isvara (Supreme Person or Lord) as the most suitable to apply to Christ, but does not explore and probably is not aware of the particular Trinitarian interpretation offered by Davie. Another term, Prajapati (the Creator God of early Vedic commentary) might be more suitably applied to the first Person of the Christian Trinity: Davie draws attention to the parallel to the Prologue of John's Gospel in the *Tandya Maha Brahmana* (xx.14.2): "In the beginning there was only Prajapati. His word was with him. This word was his double" (*Jesus Purusha*, 3). (Another Hindu term, *Vac*, sometimes translated "Word," seems to correspond more closely to the Biblical Sophia, or Wisdom.)

interpretation of Hinduism is achieved by equating the Atman, the inner "I," with the source of intelligibility, Brahman, "so that the intelligibility of the world (*vacakatva*) is seen to be consequent upon Brahman's being its source (*Sabda*), Atman its vehicle (*sambandhah*), and Purusha its content (*artha*)."[28]

This is the key which opens the possibility of going beyond the perennialist approach and seeing in Hinduism a doctrine corresponding to the Christian Trinity. It enables us to resolve the various "contradictions" between major Hindu schools of thought by seeing them in the light of the Gospel, particularly, of course, the Gospel of John with its explicit Logos-Christology. In fact Davie sees the complementarity of the Shankaran and Ramanujan schools of thought as parallel to that of Hinduism and Judaism within the Christian scheme of redemption.[29] "For Shankara, Atman and Brahman are ultimately identical as the One Universal Self, the sole Reality, while Ramanuja recognizes the existence of a plurality of differentiated Atmans."[30] This is because for Ramanuja unity can express itself (and even become deeper) through differentiation. Davie quotes John Braisted Carman as saying that for Ramanuja, God "includes all finite beings with their infinite variety of distinctive natures within His own Infinite Being. He can do this because He is the Inner Self, both of the universe collectively and of each individual being within it."[31]

Having established compatibility between the two traditions, Davie goes on to develop a Christology (in which Jesus is aware of his own divinity and mission) using Hindu terminology. The crucial

---

28. Ibid., 63–4.

29. Ibid., 148.

30. Ibid., 153. Davie distinguishes two (complementary) philosophical senses of unity: unity "of which" (Sankara) and unity "in which" (Ramanuja). "For Jesus to be deiform, the Atman-Brahman relation which is realized in him must be one of *identity* as to form *of-which*, but for him to be *this* Person (whose body lets him be Jesus), the Atman-Brahman relation must also express individual difference as to form *in-which*" (*Jesus Purusha*, 154).

31. Ibid., 153fn. From a Christian point of view, the Trinity allows us to distinguish between *otherness*, by which one finite thing differs from another according to its essence, and *distinction*, which, in the Trinity, is a difference of a higher kind

point is that he asserts an *identity* between the eternal procession of Purusha and the temporal Incarnation of Christ; between the eternal self-giving, self-receiving of the Word *in God* and the Passion of Christ *in time* that brings about the Redemption. They are the same thing, expressed on what he calls a "vertical" and a "horizontal" axis.

This brings Davie close to the famous insight of C.S. Lewis that marked his conversion to Christianity in 1930—the realization that while many ancient legends speak of a dying and rising God, we cannot dismiss Christianity as one more fairytale, because this universal replication and anticipation of the "greatest story ever told" is exactly what would be expected if Christianity were true. Lewis came to believe that "the story of Christ is simply a true myth," and that "the Pagan stories are God expressing Himself through the minds of poets...while Christianity is God expressing Himself through what we call 'real things.'" If we substitute the word "Vedas" for the expression "Pagan stories" the application to Hinduism becomes obvious.[32]

In fact, Davie has an interesting section where he talks about the nature of mythological and poetic writing—which is the genre of the Vedas and other early Hindu scriptures on which the later, more philosophical commentaries were based. Having distinguished the vertical (ontological) dimension from the horizontal (historical, empirical), he explains that the "vertical" is always best expressed in poetry and myth. This leads him to deplore the "demythologization" of religion. In a theological context, he says, the word "mythology" means "the horizontal (i.e., spatio-temporal) representation of a

that does not involve finite, quidditative otherness. And the point is that, while creatures in God—the divine ideas—are not other than God in a dualistic sense, they are distinct from him in a higher sense by participation in the Trinitarian relations. It is here, in the Trinity, that we must look for a way in which things can be distinctly themselves in God *non-dualistically*. More on this later.

32. Sara Grant puts a similar insight thus: "The Hindu gods, then, are not historical figures, but *projections of the Hindu psyche* under the impact of a profound religious experience of that supreme Mystery which illumines everyone born into this world, of which the historically conditioned humanity of Jesus of Nazareth is the authentic and tangible Self-communication" (*Toward an Alternative Theology*, 75).

vertical (i.e., eternal) truth: when there is no vertical dimension, I would want to say we are dealing, not with theological myth, but with theological fable."[33]

> The theological method . . . is neither one nor the other; neither mythological nor historical, but a combination of both. Thus it uses history as a critique of myth, and myth as a critique of history; for the whole theological purport of myth is to indicate the limits of history, to elicit from the mythological language (which it necessarily uses in speaking of events which are transhistorical, in the exact sense that they are *limits* of history) a sense of what lies beyond history, the "beyond" of all time.[34]

It is this identification of the eternal with the temporal—symbolized by the junction of the two axes of the Cross—that enables Davie to claim that Christ is the *unique instantiation of Purusha*, through participation in whom others become divinized by grace. It is a much more satisfactory solution, because grounded in the Trinity, than that of the perennialists which leads them to dismiss the Christian Trinity in the name of Supreme Unity.

Exponents of the "transcendental unity of religions" are normally content to show that each revelation from heaven possesses its own claim to uniqueness, its own relative "absoluteness"—while remaining only one manifestation among many of the Primordial Tradition which remains (archetypally) transcendent to them. Yet surely "a theology that cannot imagine a unique, unsurpassable self-manifestation of God in history cannot do justice to the true absoluteness of God."[35] Certainly the absoluteness of the Principle is reflected in a multitude of prophetic revelations, each of which is absolute for those who accept it in faith. But Christians believe there must also be one Revelation (based on Hypostatic Union) that is absolute even in relation to this multitude, in order fittingly to express the uniqueness of God.

33. Ibid., 117.
34. Ibid., 117–18.
35. Michael Schulz, in Massimo Serretti (ed.), *The Uniqueness and Universality of Jesus Christ*, 124.

Divine Knowledge

The teachings of the medieval Dominican preacher Meister Eckhart (1260–1327) are often taken as a "Trojan horse" for Sankaran or perennialist monism or non-dualism within the Christian citadel.[1] His vernacular sermons (radiating a strong and vibrant personality of deep faith) certainly strive to express things that often might have been easier and safer to leave unspoken. He is a Christian mystic beloved by non-Christians and Christians alike. Nevertheless, his fundamental insights were Christian, Trinitarian, and orthodox, as I hope to show. If I can do so, it will help to strengthen the points made in the previous chapter, and take us deeper into an appreciation of the doctrine of the Trinity—in such a way that we can see its relevance to inter-religious dialogue (as more than just a conversation-stopper).

Eckhart's Orthodoxy

Notoriously, Eckhart does speak of a *deitas* or Godhead beyond the Trinity: "the silent desert into which no distinction ever peeped, of Father, Son or Holy Ghost" (Sermon 60).[2] In other places he appears to erode the distinction between Christ and the soul: "Between the only-begotten Son and the soul there is no difference" (Sermon 66). And again, he appears at times to imply the pantheistic doctrine that the world is God: "for he who has God and all things with God has no more than one who has God alone" (Sermon 10).

There is an extensive literature discussing the relationship of such statements to Christian orthodoxy, and the works of Bernard

---

1. Advaita and Perennialism being monistic in the way they are often understood, even if they are not so simple to dismiss in themselves.

2. Eckhart's sermons will be quoted mainly from the English translation by M. O'C. Walshe (Watkins Publishing, 1979, reprinted Element Books, 1987).

McGinn are especially helpful in this regard. The papal bull *In Agro Dominico* (1329) of John XXII, promulgated after Eckhart's death, did not formally brand him a heretic, but as far as the discussion of his ideas was concerned it raised the stakes among his contemporaries, for whom even the suspicion of heresy was a deeply serious matter. Nevertheless, his works continued to be circulated and studied throughout Europe. His direct influence flowed through disciples such as Tauler, Suso, and Cardinal Nicholas of Cusa, and his indirect influence was of course incalculable. During life Eckhart had replied to his critics robustly, denying any heretical intention whatever. He had no intention of founding a new school or sect, but remained a faithful Dominican to the very end. Indeed he often stands closer to Aquinas, and to a wider community of Dominican contemporaries, than one might think from reading isolated quotations out of context.

How then are we to read the kinds of statements already quoted, which seem to have shocked many of his readers? The passage already quoted concerning the "silent desert" may be read as saying little more than that the Trinity *does not divide the Unity of God*: a doctrinal proposition familiar from the very earliest centuries of Christianity.[3] Eckhart himself may be cited in support of this

3. The passage from Sermon 60 is an important one, and admittedly difficult to interpret. In it Eckhart refers to the uncreated "spark" in the soul, to be discussed in a later chapter ("God in Man, Man in God"): "It is this Light that discloses God unveiled and unmanifested as he is in himself; indeed, it discloses him in his act of Self-affirmation. Thus I can most truly say that this Light is indeed one with God rather than one with my soul-powers, which are nonetheless one with it in its isness. . . . I swear that it is not enough for the Light to disclose even the unity of the processions of the divine nature. Indeed I will say more, and this may sound surprising: I say by eternal truth that it is not enough for this Light to disclose the impartible, immutable divine Being, which neither gives nor takes; it will rather disclose that from which this Being comes; it will penetrate directly into its unconditioned Principle, into the silent desert, in which no distinction ever enters, neither Father, nor Son, nor Holy Spirit. Only there in the Innermost, where no individualized one (or other) abides, is the Light fulfilled." This "silent desert" lies beyond the Trinity only in the sense that it is the interior or primal "moment" of the trinitarian act; not the Trinity apprehended, but the Trinity apprehending—God caught "in the act of begetting," as Eckhart also says. It is the *esse* of which "Being" is an affirmation, but which transcends Being when the latter is taken as a mere concept.

interpretation: "I said that the distinction in the Trinity comes from the unity. The unity is the distinction, and the distinction *is* the unity. The greater the distinction, the greater the unity, for that is distinction without distinction" (Sermon 66).[4]

In the second passage (the one that appeared to identify Christ and the soul) Eckhart is again intending nothing unorthodox. He is speaking of *theosis* or divinization—the patristic doctrine that God became man so that man could become God. In the Incarnation of Christ, God took on human nature (not abstractly, but concretely in the man Jesus), so that we may find him in the ground of our soul. "And if His substance, His being and His nature are mine, then I am the Son of God" (Sermon 7). Yet he adds immediately that in order to enter into this nature, we must become "nothing." Whatever he intends this to mean, it is not that the soul, beloved by God, is an illusion, or even that it is destined to be dissolved in God. For he also states categorically: "God is in the soul with His nature, with His being and with His Godhead, and yet He is not the soul" (Sermon 56). "Then the soul loses her name and her power, but not her will and her existence" (Sermon 94). He speaks, in other words, of the birth of God in the soul, not of the soul becoming God. He speaks of Christ assuming human nature, not of his assuming the individuality of each human being. Not even in *theosis* are we to be "absorbed" into God. "The unity is the distinction, and the distinction *is* the unity."[5]

---

4. Bernard McGinn draws attention to this passage in his "Theological Summary" of Eckhart in *Meister Eckhart: The Essential Sermons, Commentaries, Treatises, and Defense*, trans. Edmund College OSA and Bernard McGinn (New York: Paulist Press, 1981), 36–37, as an example of the texts that hint at "a dialectical relation between the indistinct divine ground and the relational distinctions of the Persons." This relation is not fully developed by Eckhart himself, but was clearly a part of his understanding of what he was saying about the Trinity. It is a mistake to read his other statements, which appear to suggest that the divine ground lies "behind" the Persons, as though this were not the case.

5. Once again, other passages of Eckhart might be cited that seem at first sight to prove the opposite. In Sermon 5 he writes: "Where two are to become one, one of them must lose its being. So it is: and if God and your soul are to become one, your soul must lose her being and her life.... Now the Holy Ghost says: 'Let them be one as we are one.' 'I pray Thee, make them one in us.'" Thus, Eckhart continues,

Knowing God in God

The impression of heterodoxy in Eckhart's writings, and particularly in his vernacular sermons, is largely created by the free, rhetor-
ical, and dynamic manner in which he liked to express himself.
Louis Bouyer views Eckhart as "at once one of perhaps the most
paradoxical and the most coherent Christian theologians, and to
quote him in isolation or to base one's interpretations on a few
propositions abstracted from the full cycle of his thought is inevitably to travesty him."[6] Hans Urs von Balthasar, though more critical
than Bouyer, judges Eckhart's experience to be "authentically Christian, even in its most daring conceptions," adding: "we have to
divest Eckhart's wholly limpid and shadowless experience of God of
its conceptual and verbal attire."[7]

For Balthasar, Eckhart opens up the possibility of dialogue with

---

"there is no need to think of Henry or Conrad." Notice, however, that he is speaking of the two becoming one "as we are one." If Eckhart does not deny the existence
of the Son as distinct from that of the Father, no more can he deny the existence of
Henry or Conrad. It is the existence of the human individual as understood in the
world, through images and names, that he wishes to deny. God does not know
himself through any image (Eckhart writes in Sermon 1). The "disappearance" of
Henry and Conrad is due to their being wholly absorbed into the participation in
God's life. But absorption is the assumption of all that pertains to the individual
"ego" by personality. It is thus also an expansion of individuality beyond all worldly
limits in the infinity of the divine Essence. In this sense, it is analogous to the way in
which the divine Persons have always been "relations," not individuals; in the end,
God's likeness in us will be perfected in this respect also. Then it will be truly "no
longer I who live, but Christ who lives in me" (Gal 2:20). I must die as Henry or
Conrad, in order to receive "a new name" (Rev 2:17).

6. Louis Bouyer, *The Invisible Father: Approaches to the Mystery of the Divinity*
(Edinburgh: T&T Clark, 1999), 271. Similarly, Leo Scheffczyk, in his *Creation and
Providence* (London: Burns & Oates, 1970), 167, concludes: "Eckhart, therefore, did
not wreck the Scholastic synthesis, he gave it a mystical interpretation. Into the
relationship between God and the world he instilled a new dynamism which burst
out of the static categories of Scholasticism"—a dynamism, it must be admitted,
with mixed consequences.

7. Balthasar, *The Glory of the Lord*, V, 30. Here and in *Theo-Drama*, especially
vol. v, 433–462, he situates Eckhart in the school of Rhenish-Flemish mysticism
(Tauler, Suso, Ruysbroeck), which draws upon the same experience but expresses it
with more care, correcting the excesses and omissions of the Meister. I am trying to
read Eckhart as these other mystics did: in the light of the tradition to which he
believed himself faithful. A summary of Balthasar's negative assessment of Eckhart

"Asian metaphysical ways of redemption."[8] As mentioned, Eckhart is often cited in discussions with other religious traditions. But if he is to be truly helpful in our contemporary interfaith dialogue we need to clear away the common misunderstandings of his doctrine. And at the root of most of these is Eckhart's attempt to express, not our own knowledge as individual creatures (our theological knowledge as creatures *in via*), but the divine knowledge itself, meaning God's knowledge.

This he does by basing himself in the ground of the soul. God's Trinitarian Essence, which is his unlimited Act of knowing, can never be for us an "object" to be grasped by our minds, as though we could stand outside it. It can be known only if the divine knowledge itself becomes our knowledge, as Scripture itself hints that it will (John 3:13; 1 Cor. 13:12; 1 John 3:2). As Eckhart says, "only in the ground of the soul is God known as he is," for there "the intellect knows as it were *within the Trinity* and without otherness."[9]

C. F. Kelley's *Meister Eckhart on Divine Knowledge* is a masterly study of exactly this point. But, as Kelley explains, "A genuine understanding of the principial mode, which is constituted as it were within Godhead, is an understanding of truth that is beyond the potentiality of human cognition, restricted as that cognition is to individuality."[10] Man would therefore have no possibility of knowing God "as God knows God"—and, furthermore, knowing

---

may be found in Raymond Gawronski SJ, *Word and Silence: Hans Urs von Balthasar and the Spiritual Encounter between East and West* (Edinburgh and Grand Rapids: T&T Clark and Eerdmans, 1995), 63–7. In his article, "Balthasar and Eckhart: Theological Principles and Catholicity," *The Thomist* 60 (1996), Cyril O'Regan examines Balthasar's negative and positive assessments of Eckhart (which he calls "conflicted" and "bifocal") as exemplifying an overall strategy of inclusiveness. Balthasar is reluctant to exclude any thinker from the Catholic symphony, even one as disrespectful of analogy and as "christologically underdetermined" as Eckhart. To pursue this strategy, Balthasar must to some extent turn a blind eye to Eckhart's deficiencies, drawing on the insights of a Thomas or a Maximus to compensate. My own strategy here is an extension of Balthasar's, despite the obvious danger of misreading Eckhart in historical terms.

8. Balthasar, *The Glory of the Lord*, V, 52.

9. Kelley, *Meister Eckhart on Divine Knowledge*, 128.

10. Ibid., 115.

the world in God as God knows it—if it were not for the self-revelation of the Word "in the ground of the intellective soul," a revelation which is inseparably linked to the Incarnation of Christ.[11] Eckhart makes it clear that the birth of Mary's Son and the birth of God in the soul are two sides of the same coin, and their common archetype is found in eternity, where God is born from God, Son from Father, in the divine Trinity. Thus, "The Father gives birth to the Son in the soul in the very same way as he gives birth to him in eternity, and no differently" (Sermon 65). As for Ian Davie (who is an admirer of Kelley's book), it is the hypostatic union of divine and human natures that opens for us a way into the bosom of the Trinity.

Kelley (somewhat disingenuously perhaps) cites St. Thomas Aquinas in support of Eckhart's position. "Now the intellect which, by God's grace, is united to the divine essence understands all things as from God's understanding."[12] Aquinas draws a distinction between God's knowledge of things "from the point of view of the knower" (in which they are one with him) and his knowledge "from the point of view of the thing known" (in which they are distinguished from him).[13] However, for Aquinas we normally cannot know from the point of view of the divine knower unless our mind is bathed in the Light of Glory, and so is not "in this life" any more, but has arrived at final beatitude. Even when divine omnipotence brings it about that the human mind is united to the divine Essence in the present life *without* being bathed in glory, St. Thomas adds, this creates a state of "rapture" which separates it from that which naturally belongs to it (i.e. the activity of the senses).[14] St. Paul's experience, alluded to in 2 Corinthians (12:2–4) is the usual example Thomas gives of such a rapture.

The difference between Thomas Aquinas and Eckhart, then, seems to lie partly in Eckhart's claim that by situating ourselves in the Word made flesh, we may "think" metaphysically from the

11. Ibid, 114.

12. Ibid., 38. Kelley gives as source *Perihermenias*, 1, 14.

13. Aquinas, *Truth*, q. 2, art. 3, 2.

14. Aquinas, *Truth*, q. 10, art. 11. Also see the whole of q. 13 on "Rapture." In q.18, where he denies that Adam saw God through his Essence, St. Thomas writes that "It is proper to Christ alone to be wayfarer and possessor at the same time."

standpoint of the divine Essence *without being in a state of rapture*. This may be judged presumptuous, but it need not be heretical. Eckhart—who discusses Paul's rapture in his first two Sermons—is not speaking of attaining the Beatific Vision in this life, even as an exceptional experience or "passing impression" (as St. Thomas calls it). While we are still in this life, full intellectual realization remains "virtual" not "actual" in us.[15] Even now, however, the "ground of the soul" is necessarily outside time, because even though our lives unfold in time, their unity is not simply the result of our temporal action, but enfolds all of that action from above. It is there, in that ground, which from the point of view of eternity must already "exist," that we may understand all things "without otherness." This is the "highest peak of the soul which stands above time and knows nothing of time or of the body" (Sermon 11).

The Creation in God

Eckhart's discussion of knowing God in God is not simply a matter of theological method. It is itself meant to be a reflexive unfolding or anticipation of the process of deification. Understanding this is crucial to grasping the point of Eckhart's presentation of the God-world relation. For in Eckhart's vision the beginning is understood only in the light of the end. Both are immediately present to God, of course, and to the uncreated intellect. Yet they cannot simply be juxtaposed in this static fashion, for between them lies the whole drama of *exitus* and *reditus*, which in Christian perspective is a drama of divine and human freedom. For Eckhart these two cannot be separated. Eckhart thinks the beginning in the light of the end, creation in terms of deification. God creates in his eternity, where

---

However, in his commentary on the "Divine Names" of Dionysius, he writes of "that most divine knowledge of God, which is attained by unknowing in a union that transcends the mind, when the mind recedes from all things and then leaves even itself, and is united to the super-resplendent rays, being illumined in them and from them by the unsearchable depth of wisdom" (cited from *Thomas Aquinas: Selected Writings*, ed. M.C. D'Arcy, 187). This sounds closer to Eckhart, perhaps because it is closer to Dionysius. But again St. Thomas may have in mind the state of rapture.

15. Kelley, *Meister Eckhart on Divine Knowledge*, 210.

he already sees the intellectual creature as it "will be" when it has arrived at deifying union with himself. Each moment of the intellectual creature's actual journey to God is thus at once a new event and a deeper realization of what has always already been true.

The paradox of creation and return—that they are one, precisely in their abiding difference—explains much of Eckhart's insistence on the unity between God and the creature, which, if read apart from this paradox, can be misleading. As already suggested, it helps us to understand his notion of the uncreated intellect, since if *one day* I will be united with God in the divine Essence, that "one day" already exists in eternity, which may therefore be regarded as another level of my present existence, even if it still remains for me to do the work of integrating my present with God's eternity.

Eckhart was quoted as saying that "all things added to God are not more than God alone." Now is this statement pantheistic or monistic? To answer the question we have to be able to say something about the difference between "all things" and the "God alone" who creates them. According to St. Thomas (and before him to Ibn Sina/Avicenna), God is utterly One because he is the sole reality whose Existence and Essence are one and the same. Consequently we can say that God just "is," without putting any limitation or restriction on that Act of existing. Any limitation, any definition of God's nature, would make God a thing comparable to any other, and therefore in need of a cause for being *that* thing rather than some other. Thus for Thomas, the word "being" cannot be predicated univocally of God and any other thing whatever.

This implies that the difference between God and things in general is *infinite*. In other words, weighed in the scales next to God, every (created) reality is strictly "nothing." So it seems that Eckhart is merely expounding St. Thomas (albeit rather boldly) when he says, "People think that they have more if they have things together with God, than if they had God without the things. But this is wrong, for all things added to God are not more than God alone."[16]

---

16. Eckhart, *Meister Eckhart: Selected Treatises and Sermons*, trans. James M. Clark and John V. Skinner (London: Faber & Faber, 1958), 56, from "Sermon for St. Dominic's Day." So confident is Eckhart of the orthodoxy of this teaching that in

In fact, as McGinn points out, Aquinas had said the very same thing in the *Summa*: "Each created thing, in that it does not have existence save from another, taken in itself is nothing."[17]

This is quite a common theme in mystical literature of the most orthodox sort, as we saw when we were considering the relation of Christianity to Vedanta. One more example will suffice. Cardinal Journet writes of God: "He exists in a way other than everything else. All things *have* being; He alone *is* Being. The word here assumes a meaning absolutely unique, vivid and thunderous like none other." He continues by citing the *Dialogue* of St Catherine:

> "Know, my daughter, what thou art and what I am.... Thou art what is not, and I am He Who is...." Yes, I am he who is not. All these things about me: the sweetness of the air, the scent of roses, all these things that I love; and the anguish and the grief, so many lovely things, so many sad things, all these ravished lives and homelands, so many crimes, so many blasphemies, so many horrors—these things are not nothing; they are real; and yet there is always one point of view from which it is true to say that they all are *not*. It is rigorously true to say that, in the manner in which God *is,* they are not. The peace that the understanding of this gives is inexpressible. And this knowledge measures the abyss which separates the level on which the problem of evil binds us, from the infinite height whence it is seen to be resolved.[18]

There is, nevertheless, a difference in perspective between Eckhart and Aquinas. St. Thomas lays great emphasis on the analogy of being. Created being has a certain claim to reality. It is made *ex nihilo*; it is not *nihil.* Secondary causes really are causes. There are, consequently, analogies between the things in the world and the Uncreated. Eckhart would not deny this, but he prefers a more dialectical approach, emphasizing the contrast between God and the

---

his "Defense" against accusations of error in 1326 he turned the tables on his accusers: "to say that the world is not nothing in itself and from itself, but is some slight bit of existence is open blasphemy" (*Meister Eckhart: The Essential Sermons,* 75).

17. Cited in McGinn, *The Mystical Thought of Meister Eckhart: The Man From Whom God Hid Nothing* (New York: Crossroad, 2001), 105.

18. Charles Journet, *The Dark Knowledge of God* (London: Sheed & Ward, 1948), 7.

world.[19] The reason for this is not far to seek: Eckhart's "inverted" perspective on the world, which he views as if from the perspective of God. Theological analogies work only in one direction: from the world to God. God does not compare the world to himself, in order to see similarities between them. He knows the world in the unity of his own Essence, as a participation in himself.[20] That is to say, he knows it, not as something else beside himself, but yet as other than himself.

"God with His uncreatedness upholds her Nothingness and preserves her in His Something" (Sermon 6). In this paradoxical sentence Eckhart neatly captures the relationship between the existence and the non-existence of the world. He reminds us that created being is always hovering on the edge of non-existence ("Everything is perishing except His Face," as the Qur'an puts it). Things eternally flow from him without diminishing his being, and return to him again. Things are not their own self-sufficient sources, and so Eckhart can describe them as being "insubstantial." What this really means, though, is that their existence is nothing but gift, and that they are always in the process of receiving their being. The immutable essences of all things are clothed in sensible appearances in order to praise and glorify their creator. It is this state of radical dependency or fluidity, this state of continual creation, which characterizes all worldly substance, in Eckhart's view. What Eckhart is saying is not that created things are not substantial at all, but that their very substantiality has no self-given existence apart from God. The relative truth of Aristotelianism is enfolded within, and grounded by, the more encompassing truth of creation out of nothing.

We have to distinguish two motions here however, not one. Not only does creation continually flow from the Creator, but it also returns to God. That is why we find Eckhart saying that "the first beginning is for the sake of the last end. Yes, God never takes rest

19. See Bernard McGinn, *The Mystical Thought of Meister Eckhart*. See also the article already referred to by Cyril O'Regan. In fact Eckhart is not rejecting analogy, but emphasizing the "greater dissimilarity" that it conceals.

20. See Kelley, "Inverse Analogy," in *Meister Eckhart on Divine Knowledge*, 167–172.

there where he is the first beginning; he takes rest there where he is
an end and a repose of all being, *not that this being should perish*, but
rather it is there perfected in its last end according to its highest perfection."[21]

Breaking Through

It is this eternal circular motion that Eckhart also seems to be struggling to express in one of his most confusing sermons, a sermon in
which he asks God to make him "free of 'God' if we take 'God' to be
the beginning of created things." He is speaking of the return to
God (which he calls "breaking through"), compared to the flowing
out from God in the beginning. The crucial passage begins:

> A great authority says that his breaking through is nobler than his
> flowing out; and that is true. When I flowed out from God, all
> things said: "God is." And this cannot make me blessed, for with
> this I acknowledge that I am a creature. But in the breaking-
> through, when I come to be free of will of myself and of God's will
> and of all his works and of God himself, then I am above all cre-
> ated things, and I am neither God nor creature, but I am what I
> was and what I shall remain, now and eternally.[22]

To "break through," to become "deified," is in Eckhart's terms to
be "neither God nor creature" but to enter a third category. I am not
God, because only God is God. Yet I am not simply a creature, if by
"simply a creature" is meant a sort of "pure nature" existing on its
own apart from God. There is no such thing, as Thomas himself
teaches, though his doctrine on this point was obscured for a long
time by many of his Scholastic commentators. Indeed, through
God's grace I have become divine. And since "God" is that from
which all creatures flow, I am "free of God," since I have entered the
repose of the divine Essence in which there is no flowing forth any
more: the Son rests in the Father and the Spirit, and the Father rests
in the Son, and the creature is there in its deepest ground.

The most difficult thing to understand in Eckhart is probably this

21. *Meister Eckhart: The Essential Sermons*, 196. My emphasis.
22. Ibid., 203. The "great authority" is possibly Eckhart's joking reference to
himself.

relationship between God (Trinity) and Godhead, between the flowing of the Persons and their repose in each other, which so often leads readers to assume that he is elevating an impersonal Absolute above the Trinitarian God. (In that case the human person could not be deified by participation, but only dissolved into final nothingness as the Persons give way to That which transcends them.) It is here that Balthasar makes his strongest criticisms of Eckhart, writing at one point that his thinking omits the analogy of being and thus "what is missing is the Marian principle.... Unfortunately, the whole trinitarian process is clearly undermined in favor of a (Neoplatonic) trend toward absolute unity...."[23] If this were the whole tendency of Eckhart's thought, it would signify a significant betrayal of the Christian revelation. Here Adrian Walker assists me with a formulation I find extremely convincing:

> When Eckhart talks about the utterly simple ground, he is actually talking about the Father's innascibility; and when he talks about our oneness with this ground, he is actually talking about our participation in it, insofar as we give birth to the Son in our souls: not only like Mary, but *in* Mary. We receive this participation by grace, but it is also our return into the ground of our souls.[24]

Others have accused Eckhart of falling into what Louis Bouyer calls "the standing temptation of Latin Trinitarianism: putting prior to the Persons, or over and above them, an essence from which they in turn proceed and which, as is clear from Cajetan, is the equivalent of what we mean by person—a being subsisting in and by itself." But Bouyer does not believe Eckhart did this:

---

23. Balthasar, *Theo-Drama*, V, 441–3. In general one might say that Balthasar draws a distinction within Neoplatonism between Proclus and Plotinus, regarding the influence of the latter as more benign.

24. Private correspondence. Thus the Word "came to his own home, and his own people received him not. But to all who received him, who believed in his name, he gave power to become children of God; who were born, not of blood nor of the will of the flesh nor of the will of man, but of God" (John 1:11–13); while in John 19:26–7, John takes Mary into his home as his Mother, at the very moment when Christ is making our rebirth possible through his exaltation/sending of the Holy Spirit.

What he did do, in our view, was something quite different. His deity, with its sublime unity, consists in the dynamism, communication, communion which is simply identical with that "pure being" which is the one being of God. Indeed, following the formula which was perhaps Eckhart's greatest stroke of genius, God is being at its poorest, i.e., he who only possesses himself by giving himself.[25]

The word "giving" contains the clue to how we might elucidate (or expand) Eckhart's Trinitarian thought. Bouyer is right in drawing attention to it, for it captures the dynamic quality of Eckhart's God, and at the same time explains how he was able to slip into sounding, at times, as though he were leaving the Persons behind. One of the puzzles in Eckhart is that he sometimes describes the Father as the "One," the supreme unity or even ground of the divine nature, and at others refers to the Father himself as emerging from or being born from the womb of the One, which appears therefore to transcend the Trinity. The point here is that each Person in himself (and the Father, of course, pre-eminently) is indistinguishable from the Godhead as such. But what does it mean to be indistinguishable from the Godhead as such? It means, in Trinitarian terms, that each Person is centered or grounded not in himself but in the other. To be indistinguishable from the Godhead means to be the Infinite Act that consists in infinite self-outpouring. The "Godhead beyond God" turns out to be (ecstatic) love.[26]

Thus we may speak of the Persons continually appearing and disappearing into each other, or even "boiling" (*bullitio*), as Eckhart puts it. This vivid image reminds us that with God we are using human words based on the things we see in the world. When

---

25. Bouyer, *The Invisible Father*, 270.
26. Eckhart: "the Father gave His only-begotten Son all that He has to offer, all His Godhead, all His bliss, holding nothing back. . . . In fact I declare: He utters the root of the Godhead completely in the Son" (Sermon 12). And "Each and every form of production cannot be understood without the mutual pleasure and love that is the bond of the producer and the thing produced and is of the same nature with them" (*Meister Eckhart: Teacher and Preacher*, 185). Eckhart's Trinitarian teaching is displayed most fully in, for example, his Commentary on John, part of which is translated in *Meister Eckhart: Teacher and Preacher*, 182–193.

we speak of one Person "flowing" from another, "giving" himself to the other, "proceeding from" or "being generated by" the Father, such expressions are metaphors—sanctioned by Revelation and tradition, but still metaphors. Furthermore, they are metaphors of *process*. God himself, however, is not in time and is not in "process."

The "repose" of God is a metaphor too. Eckhart introduces it in order to correct or complete or balance the metaphors of process. Effectively, he reminds us that in God all action is eternally-already complete, just as truly as it is also always beginning afresh. The circumincession of the Father and the Son will never come to an "end," and yet we may speak of the completion that it promises as lying in some sense "beyond" it in a non-temporal, non-spatial direction. That, it seems to me, is the real function of Eckhart's talk about the Godhead lying beyond the Trinity. It does not mean that there will come a day when the Trinity will stop circumincessing and sit still.

In fact, it is the Holy Spirit, the unity and the bliss of the Trinity, who is the repose of the Son in the Father and of the Father in the Son. The Spirit brings the circumincession to an "end," not by stopping it, but by allowing it to be the infinite fullness it is. He is not beyond the circumincession, but is the *beyond of the circumincession*; he is its completeness, its infinite superabundance.

I have said that the act of being is an act of giving, an act of knowing, an act of love. It is Trinitarian. The same cluster of metaphors illuminates the nature of created being, the dynamic relationship to God which is intrinsic to all existing things. Giftedness is the signature of God upon creation. But our being is not simply a gift to us; it is God's gift to himself. Created human nature is a gift that the Father gives to the Son, along with his divine nature. And it is a gift that the Son gives the Father, by being born as Man, dying on the Cross, and rising to new life. Creation is therefore gift both in relation to God, and in relation specifically to each of the Persons. Filled with the Holy Spirit in order to be given to the Father by the Son, it is transformed into the Son's Eucharist or "thanksgiving." The world indwelt by the Spirit is therefore now infinitely more than it was when it was created. It speaks not only with its own voice, but with the voice of the Son, who gives glory to his Father with this transformed creation.[27]

Eckhart's strange talk of "breaking through" seems to be a way of referring to the state of things "after" this return to the Father, *after* divinization. And he describes it as a state of rest or perfection, in which no words, no distinctions, any more apply—even those of Father, Son, and Spirit. He does not mean that the Trinity ceases to exist, or that we cease to exist in the Trinity. On the contrary, "In the same being of God where God is above being and above distinction, there I myself was, there I willed myself and committed myself to create this man."[28] That is not non-existence, but it is a state of existence that bursts the limits of human speech. In the ground of the Godhead, everything is one, not because distinctions collapse, but because they are revealed finally as what they truly are: not barriers to infinite self-outpouring, but internal modes of it.

Eckhart can say that there is no distinction and therefore no creature and no Trinity—but that is because what he means is that we are here situated *within* the creature and *within* the Trinity, indeed within God's own (Trinitarian) knowledge of himself. That knowledge is not a grasping from without, but a simple Act of love, the eternal begetting of the Son from the Father, the knowing of the Father in the Son.

After all, the divine consciousness, knowledge, and will are each identical with the divine Essence and are the same in each person. These three ways of being God (not three Gods!) are so utterly and completely different from each other that no worldly difference

---

27. In at least one translation of his extended sermon "The Nobleman," Eckhart writes that "God gives being to every creature [in his mind as prototypes or ideas] and afterwards in time [as created beings in the visible universe], and even beyond time and beyond everything that pertains to it" (*Meister Eckhart: Selected Treatises*, 154–5). On these three modes of participation in God, see Stratford Caldecott, "Creation as a Call to Holiness," *Communio* 30, no. 1 (Spring 2003). The creature is in God as the Son is present in the Father: as Logos or Idea. It is in God as the Father is present in the Son: as *esse* received, i.e., as existence. It is in God as the Spirit is present in Father and Son: as *esse* given, i.e., as existence transformed by grace.

28. Eckhart, *Meister Eckhart: The Essential Sermons*, 202.

between things can be greater. Yet the difference lies entirely in being other, in being a relationally distinct pole of the total self-out-pouring that is of the very essence of Deity; it does not imply that the divine consciousness of the Father is different in its content from that of Son or Spirit, for this would compromise the divine simplicity and make each Person less than fully God. As we saw in the last chapter, each Person is other than the other Persons, but not other than the divine Essence. Thus utter unity coexists with utter difference.

Hans Urs von Balthasar asks, at the very end of his *Theo-Drama*, "What Does God Gain from the World?" The question is answered in one way by Eckhart's "all things added to God are not more than God alone," and by his repeated insistence that God is "without a Why." The divine nature, being already infinite, cannot be increased by any gift, however sublime. The creation is not added to the divine nature, but rather brought within the super-dynamic relationship of the Trinity as an expression of the Son's inexhaustible love for the Father.

Applying this to ourselves, and reconciling it with Balthasar's own answer to the question he has posed, it means that in God's eternity *we are already what we will become in time and at the end of time.* For "In reaching it we are only reaching something that has already been reached; becoming coincides with being."[29] The original divine knowledge of myself, which is my "idea" in God's essence, by which he knows me and creates me in the beginning, is also (from God's point of view, of course, not mine as a creature still *in*

---

29. Balthasar, *Theo-Drama*, V, 512, quoting Adrienne von Speyr. Balthasar finds a similar understanding in Maximus: see *Cosmic Liturgy*, 134. But if becoming ultimately coincides with being, being also coincides with becoming: the creature in God must not be thought of as confined to a static state, for "within the divine fruitfulness there is a kind of eternal 'ever-more,' 'everything that lives in heaven seems to be growing'; but this takes place 'beyond time and space' in the mode of being of eternal Love. And since God's freedom and love require something like 'super-times' and 'super-space' so that his love can expand infinitely, we too shall experience, beyond our transitory nature, a kind of 'elasticity' of duration in which there will be a coincidence of the 'eternal here' and the 'eternal now'" (*Theo-Drama*, V, 400–401).

via) the deified self that comes to be through the indwelling of the Holy Spirit.[30]

Conclusion

Eckhart's position is summed up by Kelley as follows:

> This self, which the human knower is, is born in time. But insofar as the self is now wholly absorbed in intellection, it is not born in time. "It proceeds from eternity." It necessarily is prior *in* that transcendent, ultimate, and "divine selfhood" in whom there is no temporality or individuality.[31]

All things—and human knowers in particular—are in God not in their own selves but as God, as the divine Essence known by the divine Essence (in the Son).[32] They have overcome their own "selves," meaning the inevitable limitations of an ego centered upon (and therefore closed upon) itself. The self, once opened up, by being centered on the Other, and in a sense "drowned" in the Other, becomes more substantially, more really, a Self than it could ever have been otherwise. In that sense, I am not God, but my "truest I" is God, and Eckhart does not tire of saying it.

In so doing, of course, he does sound very like Sankara (and also like the Sufi martyr Al-Hallaj, crying out "I am the Real"). These resemblances are intriguing, although problematic if we use them to short-circuit the discussion of important differences between diverse religious perspectives. Eckhart's conclusion arises out of a

---

30. For the Latin tradition, as we shall discuss later, created nature is deified by participating in the intra-trinitarian act of love/knowledge made possible by the assumption of created nature in the Son and the pouring out of the Spirit, in eternity and on the Cross. Thus the Scholastics speak of the divinized saints as seeing (and seeing by) God's Essence, yet not in such a way that they comprehend it completely (ST I, q. 12, a. 7 ad 3). Knowledge of God is poured out on the creature, but can only be received according to its own limited capacity.

31. Kelley, *Meister Eckhart on Divine Knowledge*, 66.

32. According to St. Thomas, God knows all things as possibilities of existing which he wills to exist. He knows his essence as capable of imitation by a creature, and thus knows the "idea" of that creature in knowing himself (ST I, q. 15, a. 2). The creature as known by God is an idea contained within the divine Essence, and it therefore has existence in God more truly than it has in itself (Truth, q. 4, a. 6).

Trinitarian experience of God, and an intimate union with the Son of God made man. In the Sermon 70, commenting on the text "God is love, and he who dwells in love dwells in God, and God in him" (1 John 4:16), Eckhart writes of the "highest perfection of the spirit to which man can attain spiritually in this life," which is as we have seen to grasp God "as in the ground, where He is above all being." But he continues: "Yet this is not the highest perfection: that which we shall possess forever with body and soul. Then the outer man will be entirely maintained through the supportive possession of eternal being, just as humanity and divinity are one personal being in the person of Christ."

It is sometimes said that Eckhart only ever preached one sermon. If so, it might have been based upon Luke 9:24. "For whoever would save his life will lose it; and whoever loses his life for my sake, he will save it." To save one's life, according to Eckhart, is to find it again in God. There is only a "place" for one's life in God, however, because beyond all the multiplicity of this world there is the diversity-in-unity of the Trinity, in which everything is given and everything received.

> Out of the ground the rod grows, which is the soul in her purest and highest. It shoots out of this primal ground at the breaking forth of the Son from the Father. Upon the rod there opens a flower, the flower is the Holy Ghost who will rest and repose there. Let us now pray to our dear Lord that we may so rest in Him, and He is us, as will redound to His praise and glory." (Sermon 61)

Creator

> I repent me of the ignorance wherein I ever said that
> God made men out of nothing: there is no nothing out
> of which to make anything; God is all in all, and he made
> us out of himself. He who is parted from God has no
> original nothingness with which to take refuge.
> (George MacDonald, *Weighed and Wanting*)[1]

The doctrine of "creation" and God as Creator—the world as created *ex nihilo*—is a distinctive theme in the Christian and Judeo-Islamic traditions. I have written about it elsewhere,[2] touched upon it in the chapters on scientific cosmology, and in the present chapter am struggling to understand it more deeply in theological and metaphysical terms.

A search for truth in the religions of the world led me to focus on the doctrine at the heart of Christianity that seems to offer a home for every truth I have encountered elsewhere. The *Trinity* is for me the key that opens every lock, including the doctrine of creation, since it allows for the value of diversity and difference, as well as unity. That is why I think it is so important to defend it against the monists who prefer to absorb everything prematurely into one Supreme Identity—gaining the whole world but losing their soul in a strange way: losing it by drowning in light. These monists can be found in every religion, because in the end it is easier to believe in one thing than in many. But also, in every religion can be found more subtle thinkers whose understanding, I believe, is more convergent with Christianity.

We have seen that Eckhart's doctrine has certain similarities with

---

1. Cited in George MacDonald, *The Wind from the Stars* (London: Harper Collins, 1992), 5.

2. Stratford Caldecott, *All Things Made New: The Mysteries of the World in Christ* (San Rafael, CA: Angelico Press/ Sophia Perennis, 2011), 20–36.

Advaita.[3] It may be that by understanding Eckhart aright, we will come to see that Advaita itself is not mere "monism," but that something more profound is going on there. There is indeed a sense in which the multiplicity and complexity of creation has no existence in itself; that is, outside the unity of the divine Essence. But Eckhart preserves this truth by grounding it in the Trinity. Thanks to the Trinity, the plurality of creatures does have existence *within* the unity of the divine Essence, through loving self-gift—although, when we see this fact from God's point of view, as we will do in the next life, it will surely look quite different. The Trinity is creation's eternal home, for the universe is "produced in the Son."[4] And just as the oneness of the Trinitarian Persons with and in the divine Essence presumes their mutual distinctness as Persons, so when we say that *creatures* pre-exist in God as God we are indeed denying that they lie alongside God as one finite thing does another, but we are not denying their distinctness from God but actually establishing it, for like Aquinas in *De Trinitate*, Eckhart insists that distinction, rather than otherness, is the principle of plurality, as I have already noted: "the distinction in the Trinity comes from the unity. The unity is the distinction, and the distinction *is* the unity. The greater the distinction the greater the unity."[5]

The Fourfold Distinction

It was St. Thomas, building on the achievements of Arabian philosophy, who gave the clearest philosophical expression to the idea of God as creative principle. Created things only exist because the God in whom they participate is Existence (the *actus essendi*) and deliberately communicates existence to them.

Hans Urs von Balthasar regards the so-called "real distinction" of Thomas between essence and existence in all that is not God as the very center and touchstone of an authentically Christian worldview.

---

3. Possibly, to be fair, Ibn Arabi's teaching does too, if correctly understood.

4. See Eckhart's commentary on John's Prologue in *Meister Eckhart: The Essential Sermons, Commentaries, Treatises, and Defense*, 143.

5. Sermon 66, in *Meister Eckhart: Sermons and Treatises*, vol. 2, trans. M. O'C. Walshe (Boston: Element Books, 1989), 145.

Lacking this distinction, Aristotle had taught the eternity of the world; with it, Aquinas was able to make sense of the doctrine of God as Creator. (Balthasar finds the distinction implicitly even in an earlier thinker, Denys the Areopagite.)[6]

After St. Thomas the world is conceived as having a reality which is more than simply that of the "ideas" in the mind of God, even if *what* it is remains entirely the expression of those ideas. For its reality, its deepest substance, the energy of its existence, its "to be" (*esse*), is continually received from God: its nature is that of a freely given gift. It receives from God even its capacity to receive. (And yet it does truly *receive*. It is not simply a mode of God's knowledge of himself, but a nature in its own right, albeit one which exists perpetually in dependence upon God.)

Hans Urs von Balthasar writes:

> The metaphysics of Thomas is thus the philosophical reflection of the free glory of the living God of the Bible and in this way is the interior completion of ancient (and thus human) philosophy. It is a celebration of the reality of the real, of that all-embracing mystery of being which surpasses the powers of human thought, a mystery in which creatures have access to participation in the reality of God, a mystery which in its nothingness and non-subsistence is shot through with the light of the freedom of the creative principle, of unfathomable love.[7]

Balthasar believes, however, that in the end the full majesty of Being and the gift-nature of creation is revealed fully and can be preserved *only in a religion that possesses the doctrine of the Trinity.* His "fourfold distinction" is a way of affirming the fundamental dualism in reality that is grounded in the Trinity. It is elaborated in the final part of *The Glory of the Lord*, V, and is widely regarded as the heart of his contribution to metaphysics.[8]

---

6. Balthasar, *The Glory of the Lord*, II, 186–9. A similar point is made concerning Nicholas of Cusa in vol. v, 235. Even Plotinus as read by Balthasar seems closer to Aquinas than to Plato: *The Glory of the Lord*, IV, 301.

7. Ibid., IV, 406–7.

8. Again I am grateful to Adrian Walker for helping me to improve the following exposition.

(1) The *first distinction* is the polarity I discover between "self" and "other" as I become aware of my own existence in relationship to other human beings, such as my mother leaning over me in the cradle. This is the discovery of the self and the other as mutual gift.

(2) This matures into an awareness of a distinction between the multitude of existents (myself and all others) and the inexhaustible Unity we all belong to, on which we are dependent, which could be called Being. This is the *second distinction*, the distinction of existents (*essentia*) from Being (*esse*). It is the discovery of Being as gift.

(3) But if we stayed at this second level, we might conclude that all things are a sort of inevitable unfolding or mechanical self-expression of Being or Spirit (monism, pantheism, idealism). That still leaves actuality itself, along with our sense of Being as gift, unaccounted for. Neither Being (*esse*) nor existents (*essentia*) are absolutely prior with respect to the other: existents need Being in order to be, but Being also needs existents to receive it. This is the *third distinction*, by which we recognize not only that existents depend upon Being, but also that Being depends on existents (polarity, co-dependency).

(4) Since Being and existents both differ from and depend upon each other, together they point beyond themselves to something higher or deeper. We find we have to distinguish between the "Being of the world" and the pure Act that makes things exist. Worldly existence (the dual unity of *esse* and *essentia*) must be grounded in a necessarily existent Act, pure "is-ness" whose essence is "to be" and which therefore cannot not be. Thus the fourth distinction is between worldly existence and God (also named variously "subsistent *esse*," "Beyond-Being," *actus purus,* or "the Good").[9]

But doing justice to this fourth distinction requires, even philosophically, a notion of creation as distinct from mere emanation.

---

9. For Plato and Plotinus it seems the first principle is the Good or the One, whereas the Thomistic tradition tends to identify the first principle as Being. The Good is sometimes referred to as "Beyond-Being." David C. Schindler reconciles these different ways of speaking in *Hans Urs von Balthasar and the Dramatic Structure of Truth: A Philosophical Investigation* (New York: Fordham University Press, 2004), 414–15, where he argues that "there is a certain sense in which being itself is

The ground of everything is pure freedom. Thus the distinction is really between God as creator and the World as created—the discovery of the Giver of the gift. Indeed, in the light of revelation, Christ manifests this unconditioned existence of pure Act as gratuitous, self-giving love (Trinity).

Commenting on the fourth distinction, Balthasar writes: "This mystery of the streaming self-illumination of Being, which was glimpsed by Plato and Plotinus and which alone explains the possibility of a world (that is, the paradoxical existence 'alongside' Infinite Being which fills all things and which stands in need of none), attains its transparency only when, from the sphere of the biblical revelation, absolute freedom (as the spirituality and personality of God) shines in" (*The Glory of the Lord,* V, 626). He goes on:

> God is the Wholly Other only as the *Non-Aliud,* the Not-Other (Nicolas of Cusa): as he who covers all finite entities with the one mantle of his indivisible Being in so far as they are able to participate in his reality at an infinite remove—as "entities," which are not him, but which owe their possibility to his power, and their wealth (to grasp him as the One who is actual and to shelter in him) to his creative freedom.

Metaphysics in Our Time

A Vatican document states: "the Trinitarian mystery of love and communion is the eminent model for human relations and the foundation of dialogue."[10] By *preparing* ourselves for dialogue, even if none takes place, we deepen our contemplation of the truth that it has been granted us to know. And if the dialogue is genuine (not

---

'beyond being,' that is, because transcendence is the inner meaning of being." We might add that transcendence is implied in the definition of God as that whose essence is "to be." Being thus takes the place of the One, the Good, not as "containing all beings" (Plotinus) but as the source of all that participates in existence. This only becomes luminously clear in the light of the revelation of the Trinitarian nature of the One. The move from the contemplation of Being to the contemplation of the Good (as Trinity) is described in St. Bonaventure, *The Mind's Journey to God,* chs. 5–6.

10. The Pontifical Council for Inter-religious Dialogue, *Letter to Presidents of Bishops' Conferences on the Spirituality of Dialogue* (Vatican, 1999).

merely a disguised attempt to convert), it will be a search for those truths we ourselves do not yet possess or fully understand, and which turn up in the most unexpected places. Dialogue is possible, and it does not require us first to agree on the doctrine of the Trinity. The perennialist, Reza Shah-Kazemi, writes—not on the basis of a Trinitarian doctrine but on the grounds of the infinity of the One—that

> the other in its very otherness, in all its particularities, in all its irreducible difference, is respected not simply out of a sentiment of religious tolerance, but on the basis of a perception that the other is an expression of the One. The One reveals itself in diversity and infinite differentiation; it does not deny or abolish differences on the plane of its infinite unfolding. The difference between oneself and the other is therefore simultaneously upheld and transcended: upheld on the plane of irreducible form, and transcended only on the supra-phenomenal plane of the divine Principle itself in which all differences are embraced and unified.[11]

No doubt Christians must part company with this statement and affirm that differences are upheld by the Principle itself, within the Trinity, but this divergence does not affect the agreement to accept diversity and appreciate difference, which is essential to dialogue. Thus Shah-Kazemi asks explicitly, "if nothing but God is real, and there is no 'otherness,' in reality, what is the meaning of dialogue with the other?" and then answers as follows:

> [T]he oneness of reality, far from excluding multiplicity, implies it, embraces it and integrates it—the "many" belong to the One, are projected by it into relativity, and return to It, this process manifesting to the One its own infinite richness: this, in essence, is the "dialogue" constituted by existence itself, and which might be regarded as the ultimate "prototype" or enlivening sap of all dialogues at the human level.[12]

Both perspectives give a basis for dialogue, and more than that— for collaboration, not least in the recovery of metaphysics and the

---

11. Reza Shah-Kazemi, *The Other in the Light of the One: The Universality of the Qur'an and Interfaith Dialogue* (Cambridge: Islamic Texts Society, 2006), xxv.

12. Ibid., 75.

sense of the sacred in our time. Pope John Paul II, in his 1998 encyclical letter on *Faith and Reason* addressed to the bishops of the Catholic Church, called for a renewal of metaphysics, "because I am convinced that it is the path to be taken in order to move beyond the crisis pervading large sectors of philosophy at the moment, and thus to correct certain mistaken modes of behavior now widespread in our society." In that renewal the perennialists have an important part to play.

But there is a spiritual danger, a "final temptation," that lies in wait for anyone who separates metaphysics too self-confidently from theology, and that is to dispense with the humble submission to revealed truth, which is proper to the creature as such. It should be remembered that Lucifer—that purest and highest of created intellectual substances—was, and knew himself to be, an Angel of light.[13] Humble faith, on the other hand, is a sure path that leads through hope to love, and in love to the most complete and active participation in divine knowledge, through the indwelling grace of the Holy Spirit. In this way theology, or at least authentic theology—an expression of what Balthasar calls the "esotericism of the saints"—will always overtake metaphysics.

Perhaps Chesterton was right when he remarked (in his book on Aquinas) that metaphysics should be banned because they are too exciting. The next section launches us again into deep waters.

The Freedom of God

How free is God? Is he free not to be a creator? Did he have to create the world? What exactly does the word "create" (in the Hebrew

---

13. "As St. Thomas points out so clearly, the fallen spirits have lost none of their intellectual privileges; there is not the slightest obscurity in their mind.... The incorruptibility of mind of the fallen angels is absolute, and to such an extent is this true, according to St. Thomas, that neither God not the good Angels have ceased to communicate to them those lights which belong to the angelic nature. God still enlightens their intellects in all matters that belong to the natural state of the spirit. The only things about which they are kept in ignorance are the mysteries of divine grace. Those mysteries are communicated to the good Angels; their brightness is such that the bad spirits may be said to be in darkness." This is from Dom Anscar Vonier, *The Collected Works* III (London: Burns Oates, 1953), 181–3.

Bible, the rare word *bara*) mean? It was one of the most important achievements of St. Thomas to defend the freedom of God in the face of the predominant (Islamic, Neo-Platonist) philosophies that seemed to assume or demonstrate the opposite. In doing so he was defending the notion of the universe as created. The renowned Thomist, Anton C. Pegis, makes this very clear in his Marquette Aquinas Lecture:

> A God who must produce the universe is for St. Thomas not a creator. A God who must do what he does and cannot choose to do this or that without violating his goodness is again not a creator. A divine goodness which in order to be good must produce necessarily is not the goodness of a God who is the creator of the universe.... And finally, the universe which exists necessarily, which must be as it is, which exhausts all the possibilities of divine causality, is not a created universe.[14]

The God of Christianity differs from the "One" of Plato in being Creator. The bridge was perhaps Plato's mythopoetic notion of the Demiurge or Craftsman of the universe, introduced into the creation account in the *Timaeus* and influential on Christian thinkers throughout the Middle Ages, because it seemed to mesh so well with the account in Genesis. The Craftsman fashions the world out of primordial chaos by endowing it with order and beauty, to make it as similar as possible to himself (*Tim.* 29c–30b).

God was "free" in his act of creation, it is implied here, but what does that freedom actually mean? Does it mean anything more than that he created out of no pre-existing material (if we can identify the primordial chaos of *Timaeus* with the Dyad of the Unwritten Philosophy), and thus that he was not "constrained" by his materials? Aquinas inherited from Avicenna a crucial distinction between *essence* or "being something" and *existing* or the "act of being," but gave it a final twist of his own by elevating God, whose essence is to exist, above all possible created things that merely participate in his act of being. In this way it became clear that all depended on God while God depended on no one and nothing else, and so the cre-

---

14. Anton C. Pegis, *St. Thomas and the Greeks* (Marquette University Press, 1980), 70–71.

ation was a completely free act, whether or not it had a beginning in time.[15]

Arthur Lovejoy (strongly criticized by Pegis in his lecture) gave the name "principle of plenitude" to the theory that God must create everything, or every type of thing, that can exist, in order to communicate his goodness to the maximum extent. There must be no "gaps" in the created order, he argues. St. Thomas himself seems to accept the principle of plenitude when he states (in SCG 1, 75–6) that in willing himself God wills all things which participate in his own goodness and beauty, and that he wills himself and them "by one act of will." For "in willing Himself God wills all that is in Him. But all things in a certain manner pre-exist in Him through their proper models." But God does not will all these other things in a "necessary" way, he adds (SCG 1, 81), because their existence is not necessary to one who is already perfect: "For the divine goodness neither depends on the perfection of the universe nor is anything added to it from this perfection" (SCG 1, 86, 6). Nor, according to Thomas, does *everything* that might participate in God's goodness *actually* exist, although his argument here—to the effect that the creation is not infinite—seems a bit weak (SCG 1, 81, 4).

Thomas also tries to safeguard the freedom of God by making several important distinctions, not least between different conceptions of "freedom." He argues that God cannot be said to act simply by "natural necessity" since he acts intelligently, by decision, according to his own wisdom, and therefore moves himself to act (SCG 2, 23–30). Another distinction Thomas makes is between necessity and *convenientia* (convenience or "fittingness"). He writes of the human will that "[w]hen it is inclined to something as absolutely necessary to the end, it is moved to it with a certain necessity; but when it tends to something only because of a certain befittingness, it tends to it without necessity. Hence, neither does the divine

---

15. David B. Burrell CSC explores the twists and turns of this story in his book *Towards a Jewish-Christian-Muslim Theology* (Oxford: Wiley-Blackwell, 2011), 9–25, and earlier in *Knowing the Unknowable God: Ibn-Sina, Maimonides, Aquinas* (South Bend, IN: University of Notre Dame Press, 1986).

will tend to its effects in a necessary way" (SCG 1, 82, 8). According to Thomas, therefore, God creates whatever exists because it is *fitting*, not because it is *necessary* to him, nor because he is *constrained* by something outside himself. The end or goal of things is in God, whereas God's end is not in them but in himself.[16]

Thus (*pace* Anton C. Pegis) St. Thomas does end up with a "principle of plenitude," albeit in a modified form. He has taken the Greek philosophical legacy and integrated it with his Christian worldview—reason and faith working together. It was not necessary but *fitting* that God should create all things as an image of divine Wisdom, and God will always do what is fitting, though he is not constrained to do so. If we deny this, we are implying that his acts are merely arbitrary or whimsical. No, things are beautiful, and they are created in order to reflect and participate in the beauty of God.[17]

16. Aquinas: "Hence, if natural things, in so far as they are perfect, communicate their good to others, much more does it appertain to the divine will to communicate by likeness its own good to others as much as possible. Thus, then, he wills both himself to be, and other things to be; but himself as the end, and other things as ordained to that end; inasmuch as it befits the divine goodness that other things should be partakers therein" (*ST* I, q. 19, a. 2).

17. Robert Bolton, in his important but neglected work *The Order of the Ages*, explores the polemical battles between pagan and Christian writers that led to a rather simplistic Christian view of the non-eternity of the world, beginning with Philoponus against Proclus in the 6th century, whose arguments based on an inadequate conception of infinity continued to be repeated until the 14th century and the development of proofs of the existence of actual infinities such as the natural and irrational number series, for example. The essential Christian truth of creation can be preserved by insisting on the direct dependence of all things on the Creator, regardless of their temporal "position" in a causal sequence. The apparent automatism of a Platonistic emanation *via* the Forms to their (inevitable) instantiations in matter is overcome by recalling this same ontological dependence, which establishes a direct link between God and each individual—making possible a higher order of divine Providence over the whole pattern that includes such things as the answers to prayer and the production of miracles. These ideas are further explored in Bolton's subsequent books, *Keys of Gnosis* and *Self and Spirit*. Questions concerning God's freedom are given a more technical treatment by Lawrence Dewan OP, in "St Thomas, Norman Kretzmann, and Divine Freedom in Creating," *Nova et Vetera*, English Edition, 4, no. 3 (2006), 495–514.

The Nature of Freedom

It seems to me that in Pegis's argument against a God who "must do what he does" there is a failure to understand the deepest nature of freedom, and an opening to the "voluntarism" that took root in Western thought after Duns Scotus and William of Ockham, a voluntarism that defines the Good as that which God happens to will, and not that to which God (by his nature) must conform.

The same tension existed in Islamic and Jewish thought. It is a legacy of the idea of a divine creation ex nihilo. It raises a familiar difficulty about the reality of human freedom, for if God creates everything, including the very acts of human beings, how can we do otherwise than we have done? God has created even our choices. The great thinkers of all three traditions devoted themselves to this question. In Jewish thought, the notion of the tsimtsum or "withdrawal" of God to give the world (and human action) some "space" in which to flourish was one solution. In Islam, the Mu'tazilites proposed separate arenas for human and divine agency, and even Ghazali did not entirely escape the dilemma philosophically, though he did so spiritually. As David B. Burrell explains, the problem could only be solved as Aquinas solved it, by noting the complete incommensurability of human and divine action: we are not "agents" in the same sense. Divine providence "works through intermediaries," and the abundance of God's goodness imparts to creatures too the dignity of causing, so that its own decision becomes an essential part of the sufficient cause of certain events.[18]

According to Burrell, the real problem is caused by the mistake ("initiated by Scotus and elaborated by Kant") of separating the will from the intellect, making will alone the principle of freedom. There is a freedom that pertains to means and one that pertains to ends. Means and ends are related, but free choice is more applicable to means, whereas our freedom with regard to ends is expressed in the form of discernment. Our ends are, ultimately, determined by our nature: we all desire the good. The question is, first, discerning the good, and, second, choosing how best to attain it. There is of

18. See Burrell, *Towards a Jewish-Christian-Muslim Theology*, 25–49, and esp. 41–42.

course, especially in the latter case, plenty of scope for making mistakes.

> Aquinas's understanding of our very existence as a gift from God as well as the source of all that I might do, for action follows upon being, delineates how the activity of sorting our goals and pursuing them roots human freedom more in discernment than choice, more in contemplation or vision than in "deciding."[19]

As for God, who is his own end, freedom and necessity coincide, for both represent a type of perfection. A God who must conform to the Good, which is himself, is perfectly free. The freedom to create or not create a particular world, or any world, is an expression of that very freedom. Another way of putting it is that whatever world God creates is an expression of his infinite goodness and wisdom, as well as being completely dependent upon his will that causes it to exist. God himself exists necessarily and without dependence or contingency of any kind, including any constraint to choose between any or all of a set of alternative or possible worlds, or preexisting possibilities. He creates the very possibility of a creature in the act of creating the creature.

In fact the idea of freedom goes even deeper than this, under the influence of Christian revelation, and will lead us to approach the "creation" from another direction (the unity of will and intellect). The key difference between Classical thought and Christianity is less the idea of *creatio ex nihilo* than that of God as Trinity. It is the doctrine of the Trinity that enables us to understand something more of the freedom of God in the act of creation. This is because every natural inclination of the Good to diffuse itself, to share itself, and to give itself away, is completely and fully satisfied within the Trinity. Aquinas himself writes:

> [T]he knowledge of the divine persons was necessary . . . for the right idea of creation. The fact of saying that God made all things by his Word excludes the error of those who say that God produced things by necessity. When we say that in him there is a procession of love, we show that God produced creatures not because

---

19. Burrell, ibid., 44.

he needed them, nor because of any other extrinsic reason, but on account of the love of his own goodness. [20]

Similarly, of course, the Father is not "free" not to love the Son, or the Son not to love the Father. God is not free not to be God, not to *be love*. Love is the perfection of freedom, and freedom is the power to be fully oneself, not merely the power to choose between alternatives.

For Christianity, the natural tendency of the Good to communicate itself is completely fulfilled in the Trinity itself, without any need to go beyond the divine nature. There is no "reason," then, for God to create. Or rather, as we shall see, the reason is love.[21]

20. *ST* I, q. 32, a. 1, ad 3.
21. For Hans Urs von Balthasar, the creation which the Son presents to the Father is indeed an addition, an enrichment, to God's life, and the cause of rejoicing—nevertheless, because God is beyond time one has to also be able to see that the "addition" was always already received, and therefore cannot "change" God (the fullness of Being, or Beyond-being). Both statements are true.

PART III

SOPHIA

We behold something which is glorious that can know no end, something which is sublime, lofty, boundless, that is more ancient than heaven and chaos.[1]

---

1. Hymn for the First Vespers of the feast of the Transfiguration, as cited by Emile Mersch SJ, *The Theology of the Mystical Body* (St Louis: Herder, 1951), 477.

Nature and Grace

The truth is that only in the mystery of the incarnate Word does the mystery of man take on light. For Adam, the first man, was a figure of him who was to come, namely Christ the Lord. Christ, the final Adam, by the revelation of the mystery of the Father and His love, fully reveals man to man himself and makes his supreme calling clear. (*Gaudium et Spes*, n. 22)

G. K. Chesterton once said that we are made like arrows for hitting the mark of beatitude. In this remark is implied the entire *nouvelle théologie*. An arrow can hit many things, but this arrow is made for only one target, and it is not anything in the natural world. "Beatitude" is not any merely natural happiness, but the Beatific Vision itself, in which we are made one with God. Human beings are made, Chesterton suggests, to be content with nothing less.

To extend this metaphor: the bow is perhaps the circumstances of our lives, and the string is our human will. God bends the bow and stretches the string to maximum before he lets us fly. But it is our will that sends us to the target. The image tries to capture the intimate relationship between the human and divine will. We are dependent upon God, not only for our existence, and for our identity, but for our very strength. Nevertheless, what he gives us becomes ours, and it is with this strength that we reach out to him, and with this same strength that we love each other.

The great Thomist writer, Anscar Vonier, Abbot of Buckfast between the wars, put it this way:

There is only one end for man, and that end is not to be found within himself. Man's end, man's purpose is God, something outside himself which is greater than himself. It would be false Christian spirituality to say that the end of man is his own perfection. That is not the end of man. Man's perfection is not in himself, nor

can it ever be in himself. Man's perfection is in God, in incorporation in Christ, and, through Christ, in God. All your virtues and
all your piety, so to speak, would remain unfinished and incomplete if you were not raised above yourself to God.[1]

One of the biggest, most important, but at the same time most
obscure quarrels in modern theology is the one that rages around
the correct interpretation of the "natural desire for God" and the
question of nature's relation to the supernatural—the battle for the
correct interpretation of St. Augustine's famous expression *our
hearts are restless till they rest in Thee*. In fact St. Thomas taught that
all our desires, even for limited ends such as wealth or sexual pleasure or fame, can only be perfectly fulfilled in God and so imply a
desire for him. Certainly our desire to know is insatiable. But this
means that by nature we desire a happiness, an end, that we can't
give ourselves by nature, because the Essence of God is infinitely
beyond our natural grasp as finite creatures. The further problem is
that, once he has created us this way, God might seem "obliged" to
offer us a way of reaching this (otherwise impossible) fulfillment.

As St. Thomas writes in *Summa Contra Gentiles* (*SCG*), III, ch.
25, "to understand God is the end [*telos*, goal] of every intellectual
substance [mind]," for "all creatures, even those devoid of understanding, are ordered to God as to an ultimate end," and intellectual
creatures like ourselves or the angels can only achieve it "through
their proper operation of understanding," i.e., by *understanding*
God—not merely *that* he is, but *what* he is (his substance or
Essence). In chapters 51-53 he explains that because we have a natural desire to understand the divine substance, it must be possible for
this desire to be fulfilled; that is, for God's Essence to be seen intellectually (just as the presence of thirst implies the existence of
water). But this can only happen if the divine Essence becomes
"both *what* is seen and *that whereby* it is seen," i.e., if the Essence is
"joined as an intelligible form to the intellect" so that we can see
God *through* God and not through anything less than him (such as
our own limited ideas). Only God can see God, so if we are to see

1. Cited in *Magnificat* (International English Edition), 13:12, February 2012, 142.

him it must be by *participating in his knowledge of himself.* The created intellect is made able to receive this Essence as intelligible form by divine assistance in the guise of the "light of glory" promised in Psalm 35:10, "In thy light we shall see light."

But does this (some theologians worry) give us a "right" to grace and thus deprive God's gift of its freedom, since he is under an obligation to give it to us? Hardly, since it was his decision to create intellectual creatures that have this need. In any case, as we have seen, the divine freedom is perfect, and so coincides with necessity. For the highest freedom is not freedom of choice but self-possession; or, one might say, the complete "ownership" of every decision or act of will. Free choice between various options is a kind of second best: it is simply what freedom looks like when transposed into the realm of ignorance. If a good person *knew* what was the right thing to do, he would simply do it, without bothering about alternatives. God does what he wills, and he wills according to his wisdom and justice and goodness—i.e., according to his love.

This was the position advanced and defended by Henri de Lubac SJ in the early twentieth century, against a Neo-Scholastic tradition that saw man as having been created with a *natural* end (that is, a possibility of natural happiness in this world), and then gratuitously called by God to a supernatural fulfillment through grace. The difference may seem very slight, but its implications are huge. The latter position implies secularism. Or at least it leads to the separation of theology from every other discipline concerned with this world, since it implies that the world is intelligible without theology. (It represents a retreat to a kind of pseudo- or quasi-Aristotelian position, in which philosophy can satisfy our curiosity by arriving at the Prime Mover and so explaining the world, while theology adds on top of this the revealed doctrine of the Trinity and Incarnation which we have to accept on faith.)

Theology, in the separationist view, concerns a supernatural call that is not intrinsically related to the structures and tendencies of this world. Persons without faith, or sciences that prescind from faith, can therefore proceed about their business without any reference to God or to theology, which can be treated as superfluous. De Lubac's position, on the contrary, implies that every science has some intrinsic relation to theology, and that human nature cannot be finally understood except in the light of Revelation.

A Tripartite Nature

Let us turn now to the Trinitarian structure of the individual person, a structure that forms the basis for the intimate, paradoxical relationship between nature and grace in the constitution of man.

> Far more glorious than the body is the soul,
> and more glorious still than the soul is the spirit,
> but more hidden than the spirit is the Godhead.
> At the end, the body will put on the beauty of the soul,
> the soul will put on that of the spirit,
> while the spirit shall put on the very likeness of God's majesty.
> For bodies shall be raised to the level of souls,
> and the soul to that of the spirit,
> while the spirit shall put on
> the very likeness of God's majesty.[2]

We are created to share in the life of God, but we are not *compelled* to do so: we can attain that life only through the exercise of freedom. If we are called towards union with God, this fact must imply something about the structure, the nature, of the human person. To be apt for such a union, as other creatures are not, there must be something special about us, some factor in us to allow that union. All things, all creatures have some degree of interiority that corresponds to their *being created* as the kinds of creature they are. In the case of animals, this interiority takes the form of the soul—indeed the soul in scholastic terms is the "form" that animates from within. In the case of man, even this interiority has an interiority.[3]

---

2. St. Ephrem the Syrian, from Hymn 9, verses 20–21, of his *Hymns on Paradise,* transl. Sebastian Brock (Crestwood, NY: St Vladimir's Seminary Press, 1990), 143.

3. In fact the human ordination to grace is only a special case of what we have seen as the mark of the Trinity on all things. Everything that exists—all of "nature"—has an intrinsic or constitutive relationship to its supernatural origin and end, its Creator. We must move beyond the notion of simple identity (X = X) to one of relational identity in which X is not X except in relation to not-X. On this

From the very beginning of the Christian tradition, the "something special" about human beings, the "interior of the soul" or "soul of the soul," has been called the human "spirit" (*pneuma*) or "intellect" (*nous*). This is not the same as the Holy Spirit and yet is the place where the human and divine spirits can touch—it is the place in us where we receive the kiss of life from our Creator (Gen. 2:7), where his breath enters us, and where God makes his throne in the saints. God created the human spirit in each of us as a "nest" for the Holy Spirit. In other words the "spirit" indicates the existence in us of a natural openness to God, capable of welcoming the supernatural gift as fulfilling the normal desire of our hearts.[4]

Hans Urs von Balthasar explain that in the writings of St. Irenaeus, who makes much of this distinction between body, soul, and spirit,

> Spirit is the thing in man that is essentially more than man, something which does not "rise from below" but "comes down from above." Like all the Fathers, Irenaeus is thinking of just the concrete (supernatural) order of the world; the call to grace and the life of grace belong to the concrete integrity of man. The doctrine of these three elements in man ('trichotomism') is, therefore, to be regarded as a first attempt, admittedly not a full worked-out one, at understanding the relationship of nature and grace.[5]

It is also important in the early Christological controversies; that is, in the early attempts to work out the relationship between Christ's humanity and his divinity. If Jesus Christ was indeed divine, then what *part* of him was divine, or if the whole of him was divine, in what sense was he still human? The dogmatic synthesis (he is "two natures in one person") was worked out at the Council

---

and the relation of the gift of being to the gift of grace see David L. Schindler, *Ordering Love: Liberal Societies and the Memory of the Good* (Grand Rapids, MI: Eerdmans, 2011), 365–70, and also Adrian Walker's chapter on "Constitutive Relations" in Healy and Schindler (eds), *Being Holy in the World*, 123–161.

4. Thus in the Mass we respond to the greeting "The Lord be with you," with the words, "And with your spirit."

5. Saint Irenaeus, *The Scandal of the Incarnation: Irenaeus Against the Heresies*, transl. John Saward (San Francisco: Ignatius Press, 1990), 94.

of Chalcedon in 451, but the theological interpretation of that solution is still under discussion, as Sergius Bulgakov insists in the first part of his work *The Lamb of God*. There he points out that the solution earlier proposed by the heretic Apollinarius, though misunderstood and rejected by his contemporaries, still has something to recommend it. What Apollinarius suggested was that in the man Christ, the Logos or second Person of the Trinity had replaced the third element in man, namely the *nous* or intellect, which is the "hypostatic center" of human personality, or the "face" we turn to God. The solution was rejected in part because it seemed to make Christ incompletely human (missing a part, namely his mind and will), although as Bulgakov shows it could be interpreted differently.[6]

In his important essay on "Tripartite Anthropology" in the collection *Theology in History*, Henri de Lubac traces the rise and fall of this traditional idea that man is composed not simply of body and soul, but of body, soul, and spirit (*soma/psyche/pneuma*) beginning with St. Paul's teaching in 1 Thess. 5:23 ("Now may the God of peace himself sanctify you completely, and may your whole spirit and soul and body be kept blameless at the coming of our Lord Jesus Christ").[7] The idea is alive and well in *The Philokalia*, where the Eastern Fathers frequently contrast the *nous* as spiritual intelligence with the *dianoia* or discursive reason, and in the ascetic traditions of

---

6. In other words, there was a confusion between the *nous* in the sense of the ontological principle of personality, the soul of the soul, and the *nous* as human mind or intelligence. See Sergius Bulgakov, *The Lamb of God,* transl. Boris Jakim (Grand Rapids, MI: Eerdmans, 2008), 7–18, 230. On p. 235 he discusses the Chalcedonian dogma of two natures. According to this, Christ's humanity "is defined as consisting of 'a reasonable soul and body,' which," he says, "presupposes a tripartite structure of man where the third and supreme principle of the spirit is the Logos." Christ, in other words, is a human being but not a human person, since the Logos has taken the place of the "interior face" we turn to God—this is what is meant by the assumption of human nature by the Logos.

7. Henri de Lubac SJ, "Tripartite Anthropology" in *Theology in History* (San Francisco: Ignatius Press, 1996), 117–200. De Lubac tells us that philosophers and theologians have a tendency to reduce the trichotomy to a dichotomy. Mystics, on the other hand, sometimes identify the third element too readily with the divine. (Ephrem, in the hymn quoted earlier, clearly avoids that temptation.)

both East and West right up to our own day, if not in mainstream theology.[8]

For the ascetical writers, the three parts of the human being explain the threefold concupiscence. They correspond to the three archetypal sins, since Eve took the fruit in Eden because it was (1) good for food, (2) a delight to the eye, and (3) desirable for wisdom—sins enveloping respectively body, soul, and spirit—that had to be overcome at their triple root by Christ in the wilderness and by divine grace operating in the Christian life through fasting, almsgiving, and prayer (and through chastity, poverty, and obedience in the religious state).[9]

The human ternary of body, soul, and spirit is assumed by many of the mystics, from Eckhart to St. Teresa of Avila, and the Renaissance Platonists Nicholas of Cusa, Pico, and Ficino. Nevertheless the concept of "human spirit" remains elusive—and is flatly denied by many Thomists, who are concerned that it smuggles a kind of Gnostic dualism into the make-up of the human subject of salvation.[10] The *Catechism* sums up as follows: "Sometimes the soul is distinguished from the spirit: St. Paul for instance prays that God

8. Several of Samuel Zinner's essays in *Christianity and Islam*, especially chapters 4 and 5, are helpful in tracing the distinctions between *Intellectus* and *Ratio* (or *nous* and *dianoia*) in the context of a tripartite anthropology common to Judaism, Christianity, Platonism, and Islam.

9. Jean Borella traces the distinction between body, soul, and spirit back through the Old Testament in *The Secret of the Christian Way*, 75–88, 103–14.

10. Even if St. Thomas does allude to the distinction, for example in his commentary on the Letter to the Hebrews: "the spirit in us is that by which we are akin to spiritual substances; but the soul is that through which we are akin to the brutes." Jacques Maritain examines the place St. Thomas gives to the spiritual or Illuminating Intellect in his *Creative Intuition in Art and Poetry* (London: Harvill Press, 1953), 96–7: "It was the work of St. Thomas to show and insist that, because the human person is an ontologically perfect or fully equipped agent, master of his actions, the Illuminating Intellect cannot be separate, but must be an inherent part of each individual's soul and intellectual structure, an inner spiritual light which is a participation in the uncreated divine light, but which is in every man, through its pure spirituality ceaselessly in act, the primal quickening source of all his intellectual activity." See also Maritain's *The Degrees of Knowledge* (London: Geoffrey Bless, 1937), especially the final chapters on supra-rational knowledge, and the last, on St. John of the Cross.

may sanctify his people 'wholly,' with 'spirit and soul and body' kept sound and blameless at the Lord's coming. The Church teaches that this distinction does not introduce a duality into the soul. 'Spirit' signifies that from creation man is ordered to a supernatural end and that his soul can gratuitously be raised beyond all it deserves to communion with God" (n. 367), adding, "The spiritual tradition of the Church also emphasizes the *heart*, in the biblical sense of the depths of one's being, where the person decides for or against God" (n. 368).

Certainly there is still much confusion over the meanings of "spirit" and "mind" and "intellect," which are used in different ways by different authors. But some kind of naturally supernatural "third element" in man is indispensable. We may view this as the face of the soul that turns towards God rather than to the material world, or as the fundamental will of the soul that is fixed on the Good, or as the capacity of the soul to contemplate truth rather than just give form to the material body. Even before it is "supernaturalized" by the indwelling of God's Holy Spirit at baptism, this spiritual intellect or *apex mentis* is the organ of metaphysics, and the foundation of conscience.

As such it is recognized in all religious traditions. The knowledge of universals that it gives (however distorted and confused after the Fall) is part of the common heritage of humanity. We may think of it as knowledge by a kind of "connaturality" with the truth of things, a (Platonic) "reminiscence" not of previous lives but of Being itself, by virtue of our constitutive relation to God. This is the basis of Cardinal Ratzinger's attempt in 1991 to clarify the doctrine of conscience by distinguishing *conscientia*, or the act by which we apply our knowledge of good and evil to a particular situation, from *synderesis*, which he identifies with the Platonic *anamnesis*. This is the deeper sense of conscience—the "ground of our existence," "the law written on our hearts" (St. Paul), or the "inner spark of love" (St. Basil). As he explains:

> This means that the first so-called ontological level of the phenomenon of conscience consists in the fact that something like an original memory of the good and true (the two are identical) has

been implanted in us, that there is an inner ontological tendency within man, who is created in the likeness of God, toward the divine. From its origin, man's being resonates with some things and clashes with others. This anamnesis of the origin, which results from the godlike constitution of our being, is not a conceptually articulated knowing, a store of retrievable contents. It is so to speak an inner sense, a capacity to recall, so that the one whom it addresses, if he is not turned in on himself, hears its echo from within. He sees: "That's it! That is what my nature points to and seeks."[11]

The Three Presences of God

St. Teresa of the Cross, the philosopher Edith Stein, developed an explicitly tripartite anthropology in her book *Finite and Eternal Being*. "The being of human beings," she writes, "is a composite of body, soul, and spirit."[12] In this case the distinction forms part of a phenomenological analysis of the human person, which she relates both to the cosmos and to the image of the Creator. She argues that every created being must reflect in some degree the likeness of the Trinity in the form of (first) a tendency to formation, (second) a fixed essence or nature, and (third) a possibility of self-transcendence. This corresponds in inanimate matter, for example, to the three natural states of liquid, solid, and gas. But the highest expression of this image is in the person, with the human soul, body, and spirit corresponding to Father, Son, and Holy Spirit respectively.[13]

In her final book, *The Science of the Cross*, completed just before

---

11. Joseph Cardinal Ratzinger, "Conscience and Truth," *Communio* 37:3 (Fall 2010), 535. The article first appeared in 1991 and has been reprinted in several collections.

12. Edith Stein, *Finite and Eternal Being: An Attempt at an Ascent to the Meaning of Being*, trans. Kurt F. Reinhardt (Washington, DC: ICS Publications, 2002), 363. See especially for what follows 423–63. Note however that, like St. Teresa of Avila, she does not make the spirit a separate faculty from the soul, but describes the spirit as the soul's "innermost essence" (460).

13. See ibid., 463. Stein also discusses Augustine's more famous "psychological" trinity of human faculties (memory, understanding, and will corresponding to Father, Son, and Spirit), but refines it by adding that the Trinitarian image in man is multi-faceted: memory, feeling, knowledge, will, and love each possess a Trinitarian structure of their own.

she was taken to be killed by the Nazis, St. Teresa returned to the tripartite theme, describing the human spirit as the inmost region of the soul (St. Teresa of Avila's "seventh dwelling place") where God lives "all alone" as long as the soul has not reached the perfect union of love.[14] At this depth the life of the soul "precedes all splitting into different faculties":

> There the soul lives precisely as she is in herself, beyond all that will be called forth in her through created beings. Although this most interior region is the dwelling of God and the place where the soul is united to God, her own life flows out of here before the life of union; and this is so, even in cases where such a union never occurs. For every soul has an inmost region and its being is life.[15]

This life in the spirit is hidden even from the soul herself, and often our "I" dwells outside it, having been drawn out from this ground of the soul to a more superficial existence by the lure of all that is less than God. Yet the spirit or interior castle remains as the deepest point in us, the place where God is (and not simply in the way he exists within everything created). It is the place of the soul's true freedom—the only place she can "collect her entire being and make decisions about it." Only from there can she find the place in the world intended for her. "The angels have the task of protecting it. Evil spirits seek to gain control of it. God himself has chosen it as his dwelling."[16]

St. Teresa Benedicta goes on to clarify a point that she says is not totally clear in St. Teresa of Avila and St. John, namely the three types of divine presence in the soul. The first is that by which the Creator accompanies everything in existence and sustains it in being. The second, which is an actual "indwelling" of the person, is the indwelling by sanctifying grace. This we associate with baptism and the life of faith. The third is mystical union, in which "the *locked inner region* of God opens up" (178), within the ground of the

---

14. Edith Stein, *The Science of the Cross* (Washington, DC: ICS Publications, 2002), 162. In that sense the spirit could be called the "Sabbath" of the soul.

15. Ibid., 157.

16. Ibid., 160.

soul. In this, not only does the soul give herself to God, but God gives himself to the soul (179):

> John of the Cross gives clear expression to this when he says that the soul can now give God *more* than she is herself: she gives to God, God himself in God. So it is that there is something in *essence* that differs from the union in grace: a being drawn to the utmost limit within the divine being. This divinizes the soul herself. It is a union of persons that does not end their independence, but rather has it as a prerequisite, an interpenetration that is surpassed only by the cicumincession [the mutual indwelling] of the divine persons upon which it is modeled.

Structurally, in other words, the human person is a material body, but it possesses an interiority, a spiritual side, which we call a soul. This is like a tunnel or shaft that has no bottom but is open at the far end (as it were) to the infinity of God. It is in this sense that Meister Eckhart and other mystics have spoken of the human spirit or intellect as the "uncreated" (and unfallen) ground of the soul in which is the divine spark.[17] And this helps to explain the confusion over whether the higher intellect is part of the creature or something more, something eternal. For if the *nous* is less like the component in a mechanical system easily disassembled, than it is like a shaft or well or channel, one may identify it with any number of points along its length, and give it names such as "active intellect" or "*lumen gloriae*," deeming these in some sense created, but only in the far distance discerning the uncreated light entering it from above.

At that "far end of the soul" God dwells, indeed (as Eckhart says) it is there that the Son is born of the Father. But as Edith Stein tells us, that place deepest within is "locked" to us for as long as we dwell in the shallower parts of ourselves. Even the sanctifying grace of baptism, which brings the Holy Spirit into our souls, does not unlock that inner room. The Holy Spirit comes to meet us outside it, just as the Son has come to meet us in the world through his Incarnation, but we have not yet made the ascent within ourselves

---

17. See Kelley, *Meister Eckhart on Divine Knowledge*, 133–9 concerning the divine "spark."

to the innermost sanctuary where both Son and Spirit are one with the Father.

Henri de Lubac loves to quote Paul Claudel's description of that "innermost" room: he calls it "the sacred point in us that says *Pater noster*," and Georges Bernanos writes:

> His will is ours, and when we revolt against it, it is only at the price of an uprooting of our whole inner being.... Our will has been united to his since the beginning of the world.... What sweetness to think that even while offending him, we never cease completely to desire what he desires at the depths of the Sanctuary of the soul![18]

Louis Massignon found this teaching about the "Virginal Point" (*point vierge*), the secret holy place or inner heart, in the Islamic mystic al-Hallaj, and convinced Thomas Merton of its existence. Merton in turn describes it as "a point of nothingness which is untouched by sin," "a point or spark which belongs entirely to God," "the pure glory of God in us . . . like a pure diamond, blazing with the invisible light of heaven. It is in everybody."[19]

Freedom and Creativity

For the philosopher who became John Paul II, the "spirit" in man is equivalent to the characteristic reflexivity of human consciousness by which we experience the drama of our existence as acting persons.[20] He sees this consciousness of our own agency as lying at the heart of our experience of freedom, securing our "liberty from total immersion in the world of objects" and receptivity to grace.[21]

According to Joseph Ratzinger: "He who can merely choose between arbitrary options is not yet free. Only he who takes the measure of his action from within and need obey no external con-

---

18. De Lubac, *Theology in History*, 176. St. Thomas says that conscience or *synderesis* is not extinguished even in the damned. It is the inclination to good that is intrinsic to our nature. On this see Pearlman, *A Certain Faith: Analogy of Being and the Affirmation of Belief* (Lanham, MD: University Press of America, 2012), 193–8.

19. Thomas Merton, *Conjectures of a Guilty Bystander* (New York: Doubleday Image, 1968), 158.

20. Cited in Schmitz, *At the Center of the Human Drama*, 74.

21. Ibid., 76.

straint is free. Therefore, he is free who has become one with his essence, *one with the truth itself.* For he who is one with the truth no longer acts according to external necessities and constraints; essence, willing, and acting have coincided in him."[22]

Pope Benedict threw further light on this question in his commentary on Jesus' prayer on the Mount of Olives in his book *Jesus of Nazareth.* Discussing the response of St. Maximus the Confessor to the heresy of monotheletism (the belief that Christ can have had only one will), he explains that in Jesus, who has two natures, there must also be two wills, a human and a divine will. But these two are united in the person of the divine Son. "And this is possible without annihilating the specifically human element, because the human will, as created by God, is ordered to the divine will. In becoming attuned to the divine will, it experiences its fulfillment, not its annihilation."[23] For human beings, consenting to God's will is their opportunity to become fully themselves.

This union of the human and divine will is the fulfillment of the divine image and likeness. The mystery takes place in the depths of the spirit, where the ground or wellspring of freedom in man touches the source of freedom in God. At a certain depth the human spirit touches or even merges with the groundless ground of God (Eckhart), the *Ungrund* of Jacob Boehme, the divine interiority or darkness brighter than light, in which Divinity is at rest in the eternity of the Divine Trinity. As Nicolas Berdyaev wrote: "Freedom is the ultimate: it cannot be derived from anything: it cannot be made the equivalent of anything. Freedom is the baseless foundation of being: it is deeper than all being. We cannot penetrate to a rationally perceived base for freedom. Freedom is a well of immeasurable depth; its bottom is the final mystery."[24]

---

22. Ratzinger, "Freedom and Liberation: The Anthropological Vision of the Instruction 'Libertatis Conscientia,'" *Communio* 14 (Spring 1987), 55–72.

23. Joseph Cardinal Ratzinger, *Jesus of Nazareth*, Part Two: Holy Week (San Francisco: Ignatius Press, 2011), 160.

24. Nicolas Berdyaev, *The Meaning of the Creative Act* (London: Gollancz, 1955), 145. Nicolas Berdyaev was born in Kiev in 1874, broke with Marxism in 1909 (with his friend Sergius Bulgakov), and was exiled in 1922, settling eventually in Paris where he published and lectured extensively until his death in 1948.

Yet, he reminds us, this does not imply that freedom is arbitrariness, or mere indifference; it is not freedom *from*, but freedom *for*. It is "penetrated by universal love"; it is identical with love—which in turn, we might add, is identical with divine knowledge, or the unlimited will to know. This freedom is, according to Berdyaev, the real "nothing" out of which the world was made: "God created the world out of nothing, but it would be equally true to say that He created it out of freedom. Creation must be grounded upon that limitless freedom which existed in the void before the world appeared. Without freedom creation has no value for God."[25] It

Unfortunately, as we can see from the preceding quotation, Berdyaev too easily sets freedom and being in opposition to each other, in his haste to distance himself from what he calls the "static ontologism" (115) of Greek philosophy. His misinterpretation is influenced by postmodernism. Freedom is not opposed to being; it reveals its deeper meaning. Freedom is the radiance of being. This recalls the distinction between being and beyond-being. Beyond-being is not something other than being, but is being resting in its own ground, or rather "groundlessness."

The misinterpretation leads him to give a decisive importance not to the ontological or spatial structure of the world but to the dynamic pattern of its history, and to the emergence of something new within it, the Logos, or God-Manhood. But the false opposition of freedom to being is not the only possible basis for a positive valuation of the historical process. History unfolds as a result of the forces released by freedom, as Balthasar shows.[26] The opposition to God stirred up by the cosmic Enemy elicits the response of the Incarnation, and this injection of Eternity into time provokes history to its climax in the "Battle of the Logos," drawing all of mankind and the whole of nature into a final unveiling (apocalypse) of the Alpha and Omega, the heart of the Passion itself.

This is the Liturgy at the heart of the world, the eternal drama of

---

25. Nicolas Berdyaev, *Freedom and the Spirit* (London: Geoffrey Bles, 1935), 165.

26. In *Theo-Drama*, II, 189–334, Balthasar described how God stands back from man in order to make with him a Covenant and to enter as a player into human history.

the Trinity reflected in time and space as the drama of human and divine will, culminating in the victory of the "new heavens and the new earth" and the City descending like a Bride. This much is foreseen in Scripture, but the realities to which these symbols refer remain obscure until the end. In this sense we can accompany Berdyaev in taking a step that at first seems too far, too shocking. He claims that freedom in its deepest sense allows the possibility of bringing about something truly new, something (from a certain point of view) "additional" to God. "At the end of the Christian path there dawns the consciousness that God expects from man such a revelation of freedom as will contain even what God Himself has not foreseen. God justifies the mystery of freedom, having by His might and power set a limit to His own foreseeing."[27] Freedom is part of our make-up, beginning with Christ the new Adam, so that through us, Berdyaev dares to say, God himself awaits a revelation, the revelation of our creativity.

Balthasar quotes G. K. Chesterton's *Orthodoxy*: "According to most philosophers, God in making the world enslaved it. According to Christianity, in making it, he set it free. God had written, not so much a poem, but rather a play; a play he had planned as perfect, but which necessarily had been left to human actors and stage-managers, who had since made a great mess of it." And as Balthasar makes very clear, there are such things as surprise and wonder, as well as reciprocal petition, within God. The world is "created 'for nothing,' that is, out of a love that is free and has no other reason behind it," and God opens up to us "his own realm of freedom so that, in it, we can attain the fulfillment of our own freedom" (260).

This theme of creative freedom as the deepest reason and purpose of creation is developed in the final volume of the *Theo-Drama*, "The Last Act." There it is made plain that "existence in God, who will remain for all eternity the 'mystery laid bare in holiness' (Goethe), will be no less full of tension and drama than earthly

---

27. Berdyaev, *The Meaning of the Creative Act*, 159. Notice that even for Berdyaev there must be a sense in which God knows all, even the things that Berdyaev here supposes he has permitted to be "hidden" from himself.

existence with its obscurities and freedom of choice."[28] It cannot be a mere standing still and gazing. In fact all persons, the created human person as well as the divine, possess an unknown depth because they *have no ground* other than freedom itself (and this must be so if God is love).

Berdyaev's rhetoric is sometimes alarming, and sometimes one is unclear exactly what he is proposing. Examining the relationship of the saint to the creative genius, he concludes that in the way of creative genius a "new type of monasticism" might arise, more radically ascetic and world-renouncing than the "moderate [*bourgeois*] asceticism" of the monasteries.[29] But in this new kind of Christian existence, artistic endeavor will give way to "theurgy," which is "art creating another world, another being, another life" (247), "man working together with God," overcoming "the tragic opposition of subject and object" (248).[30]

> Theurgy is the final liberty of art, the inwardly-attained limit of the artist's creativeness. Theurgy is an action superior to magic, for it is action together with God; it is the continuation of creation with God. The theurge, working together with God, creates the cosmos; creates beauty as being.... Art must become a new, transfigured nature. Nature itself is a work of art and the beauty in it is creativeness. (249)

"Working together with God." These are the four words that secure Berdyaev's lifeline to Christian orthodoxy. Behind them lies the paradoxical relationship of nature and grace that we have already discussed. The creative, "theurgic" action of man is the fulfillment of nature, raised up by grace. The apparent opposition between obedience and creative freedom is overcome in Christ himself, who is fully man as well as fully God. His Passion is both an

28. Balthasar, *Theo-Drama*, V, 410. Cf. 406–7.
29. Berdyaev, *Freedom and the Spirit*, 178–9.
30. I cannot help connecting what he says about theurgy with the English writer J.R.R. Tolkien, for whom, too, the image of God in man is attained through the (sub-) creation of worlds. As Jim Maroosis once said to me, "Perhaps when Tolkien came up with the idea of the Hobbit, God said to his closest advisers, 'Why didn't I think of that?'!" Although maybe he did, judging by the bones of a race of one-meter-high human beings discovered in Indonesia.

act of obedience to his Father, and the supreme expression of his own freedom, both as man and as God.

Radiating outwards from this central point, the same divine-human freedom, the same divine-human creativity, is seen in the Blessed Virgin Mary, God's work of art, whose own masterpiece is the Son conceived in her womb. He is her own work, not brutally forced upon her, but brought to life by her and raised with love, belonging both to her and to the Father of all. And she, the model Christian, divinized by grace, is the one who surprises God when the "hour" has not yet struck, by telling the stewards at the wedding, "Do whatever he tells you" (John 2:5).

God in Man, Man in God

For Balthasar, no *philosophy*, as such, can explain the "Why and Wherefore" of creation. "Only a philosophy of freedom and love"— that is, a philosophy transformed by theology—"can ever justify our existence—though not unless it at the same time interprets the essence of finite being in terms of love." We have seen already how this enables Balthasar to see the world as truly a *free act* on God's part—and yet not pointless. No gift of love between lovers is pointless, and every creature is fundamentally a *gift of love*—a gift not only to itself, but also a gift from God to God.[1]

We have seen how, in their different ways, Berdyaev and Balthasar are among those who redefine the *nihil* out of which the world is made. For Balthasar, creation takes place in the nothingness that is not "outside" but "within" God: that is, in the infinite spaciousness of the divine Trinity. Encompassed by that distance established in God between "I" and "Thou"—the space of freedom and love—each created person can participate in a unique way in the uniqueness of the divine Son.[2]

---

1. Once again we return to the theme of a previous chapter. "It is a gift, because the world acquires, through the different activity of each of the persons, an intimate participation in the divine exchange of life; what the world has received of the divine from God, in addition to its creaturely being, thus comes back to God as a divine gift" (Balthasar, cited by Marc Ouellet in "The Message of Balthasar's Theology," *Communio*, Summer 1996, 294). Ouellet highlights Balthasar's dramatic conception of a God who is no longer static perfection but "supra-mutable," and thus able to receive from man, and even to make himself in a sense dependent on man, without ceasing to be God. This conception is discussed at length and in depth, critically but not unsympathetically, by G.F. O'Hanlon SJ in *The Immutability of God in the Theology of Hans Urs von Balthasar*, especially in relation to the Thomist tradition and some of its modern exponents.

2. He writes: "the 'nothing-out-of-which' the world came into being can only be sought in infinite freedom itself: that is, in the realms of creatable being opened up by divine omnipotence and, at a deeper level, by the trinitarian 'letting-be' of the

218

But, again we come to the question, why does God create us, by his magic, and what does he expect of us? The *Catechism* tells us that: "The ultimate purpose of creation is that God 'who is the creator of all things may at last become "all in all,"' thus simultaneously assuring his own glory and our beatitude" (CCC, 294). He freely gave it being for the sake, ultimately, of *our beatitude*. But do we have any conception what that beatitude might mean?

We may speak of an "eschatological ontology," because while nothing that can be swallowed up by death is ultimately "true," things acquire truth *from the future*, from the final goal of creation which is the "recapitulation in the Son" and *theosis* (becoming divine). This means that ultimately it is only the Incarnation and Resurrection that can show us the reality of creation in the Trinity. Through Christ and through the Church the whole world becomes "real" in the end, by being "hypostasized" in the Son. Mary incarnates the *ecclesia* that is redeemed creation ingathered in God. Until it is subsumed into the love of God through being offered in the eternal sacrifice of the Son to the Father in the divine Liturgy, the cosmos can have only a shadowy existence. The act of creation, in a sense, is incomplete. And so, while God is the same yesterday, today, and tomorrow, this does not mean that nothing at all happens for God. History is the process of finding out what that is.

---

hypostatic acts. The 'not' which characterizes the creature—it is 'not' God and cannot exist of itself—is by no means identical with the 'not' found within the Godhead. However, the latter constitutes the deepest reason why the creaturely 'not' does not cause the analogy of being between creature and God to break down. The infinite distance between the world and God is grounded in the other, prototypical distance between God and God." This is from *Theo-Drama*, II, 266 (but see whole section 260–77). The Greek Orthodox theologian Philip Sherrard, in *Human Image: World Image* and in *Christianity: Lineaments of a Sacred Tradition*, identifies the failure of Western theology with the doctrine of creation *ex nihilo* interpreted to mean that God creates *ad extra* or "outside" himself. Many of Sherrard's legitimate concerns—and those of the mystics he discusses—are answered, directly or indirectly, by Balthasar. As we shall have occasion to mention again, without adopting the Palamite distinction between essence and uncreated energies in God (or what God *is* and what he *does*), Balthasar maintains the paradox that God reveals himself yet always remains unknown. The Holy Spirit is in a sense the "personalization" of the *ever-more* of the divine essence within the Trinity itself: even God cannot exhaust the divine infinity (*Theo-Drama*, V, 78, 82).

Only as part of the God-Man can creation begin to share God's own life. Within the Liturgy it is brought within the Trinity, where all of reality is eternally present in glory. It is this unity with Christ to which everything in creation is called, because it was for this purpose that it was made in the beginning. The more diverse and varied are the productions of nature, the more seemingly distinct from human life and from each other, the more exotic and bizarre, the more nature reveals herself as fragmentary. But every incomplete fragment implies a whole. The modern discovery of ecological interdependence is itself only a pointer towards the mystical whole to which all creatures belong. This completeness has a center, which like all centers is smaller than the whole but encompasses and projects everything else. The center, which is Man in God and God in Man, is insignificant in physical scale, but supplies a key by which the whole can be understood.

Balthasar, for all his strictures against "Platonism," which he sees as dualistic (that is, as separating ideal forms from their instantiations) presents us with a kind of christocentric Platonism, within which the classical tradition may be retrieved: "If we call the incarnate Son God's primal Idea in creating the universe . . . (Col. 1:16), this all-embracing primal Idea contains the (primal) ideas of the individual creatures. In the one, exemplary, primal Idea, the incarnate Son, raised from the dead (1:18), all creatures, especially those endowed with freedom, have their own exemplary idea."[3]

Through the Church, the world becomes the "body" of a God who takes up into union with himself all the forms of creation in their ordered hierarchy—as the Church Fathers saw clearly—and brings them to unexpected perfection through his death and Resurrection. "If the cosmos as a whole has been created in the image of God that appears—in the First-Born of creation, through him and for him—and if this First-Born indwells the world as its Head through the Church, then in the last analysis the world is a 'body' of God, who represents and expresses himself in this body, on the basis of the principle not of pantheistic but of hypostatic union."[4]

---

3. Balthasar, *Theo-Drama*, II, 302–3.
4. Balthasar, *The Glory of the Lord*, I, 679.

Pope John Paul II articulates this vision in *Dominum et Vivifi-cantem* (n. 50):

> The Incarnation of God the Son signifies the taking up into the unity with God not only of human nature, but in this human nature, in a sense, of everything that is "flesh": the whole of humanity, the entire visible and material world. The Incarnation, then, also has a cosmic significance, a cosmic dimension. The "first-born of all creation," becoming incarnate in the individual humanity of Christ, unites himself in some way with the entire reality of man, which is "flesh"—and in this reality with all "flesh," with the whole of creation.

In the end it is love that explains everything. It is love that unites God and man. We have seen that the spirit in man can be identified with the love by which we are ultimately divinized. But as love, the spirit is not a particular element in man, but rather the whole person *qua* person, for the *person* is precisely the *face* that the whole body-soul unity turns towards God; and indeed it constitutes that unity, that hypostasis, which is called into existence by love. Or one might say that the *heart,* constituted by love given and received, in the end (in the saint, that is) is nothing less than the whole person—body as well as soul—gathered into one, made into a gift for the Father.

The result is that "I live, yet not I, but Christ in me" (Gal. 2:20). The phrase is in keeping with the many writings of the mystics who assure us that we must eventually become nothing, melting into God who alone is truly real. Yet "becoming nothing" is not quite right either. Judging from the universality and unanimity of this testimony, the experience of extinction in God (*fana* in Sufism) is evidently very real. Some aspects of this problem have been discussed in earlier chapters. And yet other phrases of Holy Scripture make it very clear that there is also diversity in heaven: "In my Father's house are many rooms; if it were not so, would I have told you that I go to prepare a place for you? And when I go and prepare a place for you, I will come again and will take you to myself, that where I am you may be also" (John 14:2–3); "I am in the Father and the Father is in me" (John 14:10); "He who abides in me, and I in him, he it is that bears much fruit" (John 15:5); "As the Father has loved me, so I have loved you; abide in my love" (John 15:9). What these quotations seems to imply is that far from being extinguished, we will in fact "abide"—becoming if anything more real rather than less.

In fact even in Sufism it is taught that beyond the state of *fana* is the state of *baqa*, involving rebirth and subsistence in God. This is consoling to those of us who feel instinctively that God would never "throw away" those things that make us, or those we love, both unique and lovable. It cannot *merely* be our (very slight) resemblance to his Son that causes the Father to welcome us into heaven at the last. When the mystics talk in this way, they must be referring rather to our need to turn our faces from ourselves and towards God, for it is not by our gazing at our own image or loving ourselves that we will be sustained in being. As the Buddhists have taught us to say, we must be detached not from our human state of existence but from the *false self* that is constituted by our ideas and imaginings.

Self-knowledge is a delusion, until we know ourselves in the self-knowledge of God. God knows us better than we know ourselves, and knows the unique person he is hoping we will become. When we love someone, it is a glimpse of that true self that we see and love. It is that true self which husband and wife vow to nurture in the other, till death brings their time to an end, and opens a new state of existence.

We do indeed, as we approach God, lose interest in thinking of ourselves, our own hopes and desires, the memories of our achievements and our dreams of glory. But anything that is real in us, anything worth preserving or fulfilling, is already known by God. We do not need to see it and think about it, if we trust him as we should. And we become more authentically ourselves the more we gaze on him and the beauty that we see in him.

Incarnation

The beauty of God, of the love of God, is fully revealed by Jesus Christ. But how is that possible? Perhaps we need to probe more deeply into this question. Is Jesus just a good example, a demonstration, of how to love as God loves? Or is he, as the Church teaches, the actual incarnation of that love—and what might that mean, in any case?

Light is thrown on these questions by David C. Schindler in a penetrating article about Christ as the "concrete analogy of being."[5] The being of God and the being of creatures (the way they "are") are related analogously; which is to say, there is both similarity and difference. The idea of "analogy" connects the three orders of being: that of God, firstly, who is self-subsistent and eternal; secondly, that of created being common to all things, as an act of existing that does not subsist in itself but is dependent on God; and thirdly, that of created individual things, all of which participate in that common act of being.

We will return to this difficult notion of "common being" later, but the point to note here is that it refers to something, or rather to an *act*, that depends on both what comes before (God) and what comes after (creatures), since the act of existing has no reality in itself but only in the creatures who share in it. Furthermore the creatures depend upon it as much as it depends upon them. This is possible because it is situated not temporally "before" but in a sense (if we use space rather than time as the metaphor here) "above" things. They express the meaning of being in time—spread out through a series of moments—whereas as far as being is concerned, all of that meaning is present supra-temporally. Thus things in time depend on being for their act of existing, but the act of existing depends for its meaning on whatever unfolds in time. It is *action* that gives meaning to being, but being that gives actuality to the things that act.

In the case of Jesus Christ, who enters into the world of individual things not just as a perfect exemplar but as divine Person, being eternal he precedes even the supra-temporality of being, and so gives meaning to being from above even as he does so also from below. He reveals the relationship between God and being, embodying this in the temporal form of one man living among other men. And the meaning he gives to being is love, in that he shows that love

---

5. D.C. Schindler, "'Ever Ancient, Ever New': Jesus Christ as the Concrete Analogy of Being," *Communio* 34 (Spring-Summer 2012), 33–48.

is the basis of the *similarity* in the analogy between God's own being and the actions that unfold below, in time. This implies

> not only that things open up from within to an ever higher meaning, but also that the ultimate meaning of being always has room for another contribution "from below" ("Let the children come to me," Jesus said). Jesus Christ not only *is* the ultimate meaning of things, but at the same time truly *gives* meaning to things, and perhaps the most radical form of this gift is to receive meaning *from* them. This is the essence of analogy, and it is also an essential aspect of love. Indeed, we might say that the analogy of being *is* love, translated into the terms of metaphysics."[6]

The gift that Jesus both is and exemplifies, in other words, flows both ways (up and down), because it is the act of the Trinity and of a Father who gives all things in such a way that he is also able to receive all things.

In fact, the very *highest* archetype of the analogy of being is found within the Trinity itself, and is well expressed by John Zizioulas (though he does not call it this). In God, he says, "the substance never exists in a 'naked' state, that is, without hypostasis, without a 'mode of existence.' And the one divine substance is consequently the being of God only because it has these three modes of existence [the Persons], which it owes not to the substance but to one person, the Father."[7] Thus, in divinity, being depends upon the Persons, just as the Persons depend upon being.

At the lower level, which is that of creation, the analogy of being is expressed in the hypostatic union between the divine and human natures in Christ—that is, this union, though unique, is the supreme form of the relation between God and creature, or between God's being and creaturely being. At the same time, since the Son is defined by his relations with the Father and Spirit, this form discloses the intra-Trinitarian relations to our gaze, and thus the higher version of the analogy of being.

---

6. Ibid., 46. He calls this a recovery of the Platonic understanding of analogy within a Trinitarian context.

7. John D. Zizioulas, *Being as Communion: Studies in Personhood and the Church* (London: DLT, 1985), 41.

The existence of Jesus as a man on earth, from his Mother's womb, is the perfect gift of the Creator to his creation, and because the Spirit of Love eventually unites all of creation to the Son, it enables that creation to be given by the Son along with himself to the Father. This enables us to consider each action of Jesus during life as itself an instance of his gift of himself, and ultimately of the divine nature, to the degree we can be accommodated to receive it. This is the basis of saying that the sacraments are "founded" by him, through his actions on earth, and that they "extend the Incarnation" through time and space, by carrying the Holy Spirit and his will to save us with them, thereby constituting the community of the Church.

Of all these gifts of self, which are the everyday actions of Christ acting both as God and as man, those that are most deliberately intended to be received by all believers are the basis of the formal sacraments of the Church, anchored in the Passion which is the earthly incarnation and fruit of the heavenly liturgy. Thus the Cross is the link between earth and heaven, and by anticipation of the Cross at the Last Supper its meaning is applied to the Mass, the supreme act of theurgy: God and man acting together as one. But at the heart of the Mass is a mystery that we still need to explore, namely the transformation of the bread and wine into the actual (and now resurrected) Body and Blood of the Son of God.

Transubstantiation

Modern science, as we saw at the very beginning of this book, raises metaphysical questions, such as the nature of existence and the relationship between appearance and reality, between infinity and nothingness, questions that some would rather have ignored in their pursuit of "knowledge as power." But it should be clear by now that the metaphysical cannot be ignored, and neither can it be subsumed by science.

Science assumes that the "substance" or "what it is" of something is simply what it is made of—the atoms and energies that are its various elements. However, the Greek philosophers were reaching for other than material composition when they first used the term *ousia*. Furthermore, something deeper is implied by the Catholic Christian belief in what is termed the "real presence" of our Lord in the Blessed Sacrament. For no one suggests that the host would look any different under an electron microscope before and after its consecration, and yet the Church still teaches that its "substance" has been transformed. To be more precise, she says that during the Mass, as a result of the priest's words of consecration, the *substances* of the bread and wine are changed into the *substances* of Christ's Body and Blood.[8]

According to Aristotle, the world is made up of "substances" and their "accidents." A substance is, roughly speaking, any entity that exists in itself, while its "accidents" are whatever properties happen to attach to it (and which may vary without changing the thing it is). But if we take literally the words of Christ spoken at the Last Supper and now repeated by the priest in his name ("This is my Body.... This is the chalice of my Blood"),[9] what continues to look and taste like bread and wine after that point is no longer what it seems. The properties (appearances or "species") that are normally associated with the substances of the bread and wine are preserved,[10] but the substances themselves must have ceased to exist, having been

8. Aristotle, endeavouring to bring Plato's forms down to earth, argued that the essences can exist only in individual things, but lacked an account of how they came to be—something that would have to wait for the doctrine of creation, where the God whose essence is *to be* deliberately brings these essences into existence. See *Aristotle's Metaphysics*, trans. Joe Sachs (Santa Fe: Green Lion Press, 2002), 126, and on this whole subject David B. Burrell's fascinating article "Mulla Sadra's Ontology Revisited," in *Journal of Islamic Philosophy*, 6 (2010), 45–66. Aristotle did not envisage the possibility of "creation" (as distinct from a cause of all things). For Aquinas, a God who is Creator is necessarily able to transform the substances of things once created.

9. I won't go into the reasons for taking these scriptural words literally, when so many others are taken figuratively, but only note that there are good arguments for doing so, not least the fact that Christ himself appeared in John 6:52–8 deliberately to exclude a merely figurative interpretation, even to the extent of losing some disciples as a result of this insistence.

10. Except in a Eucharistic miracle, of which there are several well-authenticated examples. For example in Lanciano in Italy (where road-signs in the surrounding countryside point the way to "Miracolo Eucaristico"), a glass chalice and a monstrance display the congealed AB blood and a cross-section of heart tissues that replaced the appearances of wine and bread at a Mass in the 8th century and have remained incorrupt ever since, exposed for the veneration of the faithful. If it was the appearances that were changed, one assumes that the blood and muscle are also mere appearances, lacking substance in the sense about to be discussed.

converted by the power of the Word into the Body and Blood of Christ.

In the account of his departure from the Catholic priesthood, the philosopher Anthony Kenny describes this teaching that he was taught at the Gregorian University in the early 1950s as follows:

> All material bodies, we were told, were made up of substance and accidents; the substance appeared to be an invisible metaphysical core around which the accidents clustered like a wrapping. The doctrine of substance was presented thus in order to make room for the doctrine of transubstantiation. According to that doctrine, in the Eucharist the substance of the bread and the wine changes into the substance of the body and blood of Christ; the appearances of bread and wine remain but they are merely accidents inhering in no substance. The notions of substance and accidents were taken from Aristotle, and may well be coherent; but for Aristotle the notion of accidents adhering in no substance would be a contradiction in terms.[11]

Kenny's departure from the priesthood was related to his philosophical difficulties with this doctrine (which are not untypical of the period). He was repelled by the misuse of philosophy in the service of dogma by St. Thomas Aquinas. But can we discover something deeper and more convincing in the Catholic transformation of Aristotle's philosophy? A growing number of scholars see in St. Thomas Aquinas more of a Platonist than an Aristotelian, and in his philosophy a more radical reconfiguration of the notion of substance.

Appearances "Without a Subject"

Let us first examine St. Thomas's treatment of transubstantiation in more detail, because it contains several interesting features that are often overlooked.

One might assume that the appearances of bread and wine after their consecration attach to, or rest upon, the substance that has taken the place of their own; that of Christ. But this is not the case, according to Aquinas. For Christ, being resurrected and ascended, is currently located in heaven with his own appearances, his own

---

11. A. Kenny, *A Path from Rome* (Oxford University Press, 1986), 72.

properties—those of a man, possessing a body, albeit one in a new state of existence we can barely imagine. This fact is unaffected by transubstantiation. The appearances of bread and wine therefore cannot inhere in *him*. To put it more simply: while the bread ceases to be bread and becomes Jesus Christ, our Lord remains in heaven, and does not suddenly start to look like a piece of bread. The appearances, which by nature must inhere in a certain substance, have ceased to do so; on the other hand, the substance of Christ is "sacramentally" present, but not present in the normal way a substance is present to its accidents.

St. Thomas explains in Article 1 of Question 77 of the *Summa Theologiae* that the appearances are in effect floating free, for "the accidents continue in this sacrament without a subject." This is possible by the power of God, who can directly produce an effect without its normal cause if he so wills (just as we might speculate that in the case of Christ he formed a male human body out of Mary's ovum without using the seed of man to supply the y-chromosome). But in the second article of Question 77, St. Thomas introduces a refinement. He proposes a distinction between two types of accident. On the one hand there are the accidents of how a thing appears to our unaided senses—round, white, smooth, and so on. Let's call these simply "appearances." On the other hand, there are its quantitative or "dimensive" properties—the fact, for example, that it is a single piece of bread, one inch across, weighing one gram, or whatever. Of these he writes that they are "related to their subject through the medium of dimensive quantity." So that, when transubstantiation occurs, even though these dimensive properties of the bread are left without a "subject" in which to inhere (because it is not Christ who is one inch across, etc.), they can nevertheless *serve in place of* a subject for the other properties. So the dimensive properties are a kind of intermediary between the appearances of the bread and the substance of Christ, which the bread's own substance has been converted into.

The notion of "dimensive properties" is intriguing. From the time of Galileo it has been the job of science to separate "primary" from "secondary" qualities, or quantities from qualities—the former being the mathematical and measurable characteristics that are used to explain the latter. Aquinas mentions that already in his day "some have maintained that dimensions *are the substances* of bodies" (referring the reader to *Metaphysics* 3). The emphasis is mine. In fact, modern science is nothing but a systematic exploration of this dimensive realm of quantitative relations. It discovers there the particles and forces that underpin all other observed properties, such as color, shape, weight, and so on. Thus what Aquinas claims is the case, uniquely, with the Eucharist—namely that its apparent physical reality is founded on dimensive properties rather than "substance"—seems to be what modern science has come to affirm of *all things* without exception.[12]

We may set this refinement of the doctrine aside, intriguing though it is, since it makes little difference to the main problem. What mainly strikes us as strange is the idea that appearances or accidents normally caused by a particular substance can become like a veil floating over another substance entirely, which itself naturally possesses other appearances that do not appear. The *disappearance* of the actual substances of the bread and wine is rather disconcerting. We have to ask not only whether this is the best way to preserve the doctrine of the Real Presence, but also what it implies about the nature of substance.

In Search of Substance

Remember that while a "substance" for Thomas is that which exists "in itself," in the end this is only fully true of God, the one purely self-subsistent being. Joseph Ratzinger writes:

> With the insight that, seen as substance, God is One but that there exists in him the phenomenon of dialogue, of differentiation, and of relationship through speech [i.e., the Logos or Word who "is God"], the category of *relatio* gained a completely new significance for Christian thought. To Aristotle, it was among the "accidents," the chance circumstances of being, which are separate from substance, the sole sustaining form of the real.... It now became clear that the dialogue, the *relatio*, stands beside substance as an equally primordial form of being.[13]

12. See, for example, Schmitz, *The Recovery of Wonder*, 66.
13. Ratzinger, *Introduction to Christianity*, 182–3.

In *Metaphysics*, Adrian Pabst argues that Aquinas may be distinguished from Aristotle by his "Platonist metaphysics of relationality," and from Plato by the fact that (building on Augustine and Boethius) he "accounted for the relationality of being itself in terms of the substantial relations of the Trinity and of the relationality of created [being] in terms of God's outpouring love."[14]

Thomas describes the "Persons" in God as subsistent relations, which do not multiply or divide him, and are based purely on action (ST 1, q. 28, a. 4). This "action" of God can only be self-gift, for *God is love* (1 John 4:8), which means he is *circumincession*: giving and receiving, receiving and giving. This also means that the act by which some created entity exists, dependently on God's act and analogous to it, must also be an act of receiving and giving, giving and receiving (of receiving first, and then of giving).[15]

Prime matter or "pure potency to receive form" becomes in Aquinas simply the receptivity of the created individual itself (which is individuated not by matter but by God's creative intention)—it does not exist separately or prior to created things (like the primordial chaos in mythology), but exists only in things and therefore is created with them. In fact this prime matter or receptivity is the exact equivalent or receptive counterpart of the universal or "common being," the non-subsistent being of created things that is the "initial created effect of the first cause."[16]

Thus all the things that exist "reflect in particular and diverse ways the universal triunity of their Creator whose goodness individuates all beings relationally" (horizontally to each other and vertically, as it were, to himself as the Creator of being).[17]

One of the difficulties many people feel with the doctrine of transubstantiation is that it seems to conflict with the great Scholastic

---

14. Pabst, *Metaphysics*, 257. See also, for a good account of "constitutive relationality," Adrian Walker, "Constitutive Relations: Toward a Spiritual Reading of *Physis*," in Healy and Schindler (eds), *Being Holy in the World*, 123–161.

15. An earlier chapter considered self-gift and the Trinity in more detail. See also David L. Schindler, "The Embodied Person as Gift and the Cultural Task in America: Status Quaestionis," *Communio* 35 (Fall 2008), 397–431.

16. Pabst, *Metaphysics*, 248.

17. Ibid., 251.

intuition that "grace does not destroy but perfects nature"—that nature is destined (through man) for a supernatural fulfillment. What makes us uneasy is that the substances of the bread and the wine seem to have been destroyed (which is hardly a completion). And yet Aquinas is very concerned to show that this is not the case: the substances are not destroyed but converted. I think once we realize the relational or gift-nature of substance it becomes obvious that this does imply a supernatural fulfillment of the substances in question. For the conversion of each of these substances is not its replacement by another; it is the absorption of a more limited intention and gift by a less limited one, in keeping with the analogy that links the two.

In the case of the bread and wine, this *less limited* gift that they have become is the self-gift of God himself, which the bread and wine in any case always represented in a figurative manner.[18]

In Search of Accidents

This also gives us a way of understanding the appearances as more than a mere "veil" hanging over the new substance. Accidents, we said, are whatever properties happen to attach to a thing which may vary without changing the thing it is—so a man may be short or tall without ceasing to be a man, for example. But the more we think of the world as a Trinitarian place, the more we think in terms of rela-

---

18. This could be dubbed an "intentionalist" theory of substance, in the sense that the substance of a thing is "whatever God intends to give." God is giving what he intends in that thing, in the very act of giving it existence. The "whatever he intends to give" is the *substance* of the thing. This might be what Maurice Blondel was reaching for after 1893 in the use he made of the Leibnizian idea (itself inspired by the notion of transubstantiation as a way of solving the problem of organic or composite unities in a monadic system) of the *vinculum substantiale* or "substantial bond." Blondel describes this as "not only a physical nature, a metaphysical essence, an immanent finality," but as "the supreme magnet, which attracts and unites from above, step by step, the total hierarchy of distinct and consolidated beings," so that the substitution by the *vinculum* of Christ for that of the bread and wine becomes a prelude to the eventual incorporation of all things into the "new earth and heaven" (J. A. Lyons, *The Cosmic Christ in Origen and Teilhard de Chardin* (Oxford University Press, 1982), 162–3). The *vinculum* idea is discussed by Oliva Blanchette in *Maurice Blondel: A Philosophical Life* (Grand Rapids, MI: Eerdmans, 2010), 346–353.

tions. And we notice that appearances or accidents, too, are not arbitrary ("stuck on," as it were), but relational. That is, they are part of the fabric of how substances relate to each other. The shortness of one man compared to another, the whiteness of the bread and its weight, are caused not just by substances, but by substances in relation to each other. In fact I would not be who I am were I not shorter than you, and paler than him, or weaker than that tiger over there. These relational properties are more intimately bound up with my substance than Aristotle's account might at first seem to make them.

Even the particular appearance of something is therefore a result of the gift-nature of things in themselves. Appearances are an *expression* of the gift that is being given in each case, with the further limitation that they concern the effect of the gift on others, or its meaning for them. An appearance is always an appearance (at least potentially) *to* someone, to an observer of that object. The appearance is not arbitrary. It is tied to the substance not just by being the appearance *of* that substance (as subject), but by being expressive of that substance in its relation to other things. That is to say, the appearance is "brought out" of the thing by those relationships that it has with other things together making up the fabric of the world.

The whiteness and weight of the host is, it is true, not the whiteness and weight of Jesus Christ, who is not the "subject" of these properties in that particular sense. But the properties of bread (and similarly the properties of wine) are not "floating free" because they still represent and express the meaning of the gift that is being given in them, in terms of its effect on others. In this case the gift is no longer limited to an imitation (of a certain aspect of) the divine nature, or a particular "form." It is the whole divine nature itself, which is present in the Son as "Form of forms," and is poured out for us on the Cross, and in the Eucharist.

But the *appearances* of bread and wine are still the perfect language in which to express the way in which God wishes to give himself to us—a language that has always been built into creation, waiting for its fulfillment. The ingredients of bread have always existed in order to become the Eucharist. The accidents are a language perfectly suited and ready to express God's new intention.

The Eucharist Makes the Church

Christ intends to give himself completely, in order to unite himself as closely as possible with those who will receive him, just as intimately as food and drink are united with us when we eat and drink. "For my flesh is real food and my blood is real drink. Whoever eats my flesh and drinks my blood remains in me, and I in him. Just as the living father sent me and I live because of the Father, so one who feeds on me will live because of me" (John 6:55–7). Thus we do not have to worry too much about the details. We know that *whatever Christ refers to when he says "I"* is the substance that is now given to us in Holy Communion. It is given under the form of bread and wine, which symbolize God's purpose in giving himself in this way: that is, to nourish and sustain the (eternal) life that is already growing in us.

All of this helps, I think, to illuminate the meaning of Henri de Lubac's insight that "the Eucharist makes the Church." For without the Eucharist there would be no Church. If Christ were to be joined with us in a symbolic sense only, or by means of a purely spiritual communion, there would be no Church, and no New Covenant. But since what is received in Communion is the *whole* Christ—the "I" of the second divine Person, in other words the actual "substance" that is Christ—what takes place in Communion is a welcoming, a reception into myself, of that entire Person. That is to say, Eucharistic communion, which takes the form of a sacrifice and a meal, is also like a marriage, for marriage is based on a merging of two lives together in a physical sense. The Holy Spirit binds the spouses together in one flesh, and a new life is created in which both are reflected. If the Eucharist did not contain the whole substance of Christ—that is, his body, soul, and person—there would be no "marriage" between myself and God, between human and divine nature, no Bride of Christ, no Church. It is therefore the very reality of the Church, and of our salvation, that is at stake in the doctrine of transubstantiation.

Conclusion

To understand substance in terms of gift, and accidents as the way that gift is transmitted and received, is to enter a contemplative state. In the things we see around us and which we touch, we see

God making himself partially visible and tangible in multiple ways. The essence of each thing affords us a glimpse into the nature of God; its existence is the actual presence of God in that thing, creating and sustaining it in love.[19]

But the Eucharist is more than this. It is like white light compared to these fragmentary colors, a warm embrace compared to these finger-tip contacts and evocative breezes. All things are divine speech referring indirectly to God, but in the Eucharist as in Jesus Christ himself the Divinity says "I."

The Church teaches and faith assures us that the reality of the bread and wine have been converted into the body and blood of the risen Christ in heaven, which are inseparable from his entire Person. In the Eucharist, as Pope John Paul II used to say, we "digest" the secret of the Resurrection. We receive that Person, whose nature is love or entire self-gift, through the accidents of a creation that has been intended from eternity to serve this purpose—to communicate God.

Along these lines, Nicholas J. Healy is able to describe the Eucharist as the "consummation" of the analogy of being—in that "the unity of the Holy Spirit and the Eucharistic flesh of Christ" constitute "the concrete gift of the totality of Christ's human and divine life" and thus "provide the medium and form of the relation of deification" (a notion we shall approach more directly in the final chapter).

> Taken in their unity, the Holy Spirit and the Eucharist represent both a divine self-communication to mankind *and* a human self-communication to God. Grace is essentially the life and body of Jesus Christ assumed by the Son and universalized by the Holy Spirit.[20]

---

19. Everything is gift. My skin may even serve as God's way of giving himself to the mosquitoes and the fleas. There is nothing sentimental about contemplation.

20. Nicholas J. Healy, *The Eschatology of Hans Urs von Balthasar: Being as Communion* (Oxford University Press, 2008), 178.

Time, Eternity, Hell

God is the pure act of being. By that we mean that his "to be" (*esse*) or existence is identical with his essence, or "what he is." In other words, his existence is infinite, unrestricted. It is everything it could be, perfectly "in act" with nothing remaining merely "potential." What makes a thing real is its participation in the existence of God.[1] One of these creatures, these things brought into existence by the Word of God, is Time. Or if we prefer not to call it a "thing" that has been made—because that is too crude a way of describing a container that is nothing without its contents—we could say it is a dimension of what is made.

Time is the dividing of reality moment by moment across this dimension we call temporal. We can say further that this dimension is not simply flat, but has a structure, a pattern to it—a beginning, middle, and end. Like a circle, or the turn of a spiral, its form reflects the unity of the center from which it radiates. For time is, like all creatures in their own way, an image, in this case an image of eternity. Ananda Coomaraswamy, in his book on time and eternity in the various traditions, writes that time "is an imitation of eternity, as becoming is of being, and as thinking is of knowing."[2] Eckhart writes:

> Heaven is untouched by time and place. Corporeal things have no place there, and whoever is able to read the scriptures aright is well

1. In Islamic terms, the divine utterance of the word *Kun* (Be!) is necessary to call the *mumkin* (possible things) into actuality, sending the "immutable entities" (*al-ayan ath-thabitah*) into cosmic existence, "from an existence which we do not perceive to an existence which we do perceive." William C. Chittick, *The Sufi Path of Knowledge* (State University of New York Press, 1989), 87. Coomaraswamy informs us that the Arabic *Kun* can just as well mean "Become" (*Time and Eternity*, 98 fn), which better captures the fact that what is being created is a "world of becoming."

2. A. K. Coomaraswamy, *Time and Eternity* (Munshiram Manoharlal Publishers, 1993), 4.

aware that heaven contains no place. Nor is it in time: its revolution is incredibly swift. The masters say its revolution is timeless, but from its revolution, time arises. Time and place are fractions, and God is *one*. Therefore if the soul is to know God, she must know him above time and place: for God is neither this nor that as these manifold things are: God is one. When we have got beyond time and temporal things, then we are free and always happy, and *then* there is the "fullness of time," and then God's Son is born in you.[3]

In a sense, the Trinity is not motionless. True, there is nothing for God to "become." But it is misleading to depict this by analogy with a stone that lacks movement. God is moving at super-speed. It is not that he does nothing, it is more accurate to say that he has already done everything, just as he is always *about* to do everything, and furthermore that he never runs out of things to do, so that he is always not only one jump ahead of us, but also one jump ahead of himself. Balthasar writes: "Our notions of time are deceptive: eternal life is not a continuation of transitory life; it does not begin 'after death' but is perpendicular to it; it is the manifest face of a totality that, for the present, is accessible only in veiled form."[4] So that, "For the dimension of time, eventually, the moment comes when its movement is taken up into God's eternal super-movement."[5]

The unity that pertains to eternity is lost in the division of the image into a series of successive moments, but a resemblance to that unity is established by this return of the series upon itself. And there are other ways in which time resembles eternity. For example, if we consider the distinction between past, present, and future we notice

---

3. Eckhart, *Meister Eckhart: Sermons and Treatises*, 168 (Sermon 69).

4. Balthasar, *Theo-Drama*, V, 499.

5. Ibid., 520. A more detailed study of the Trinitarian processions and the relationship between Eternity and time may be found on pp. 61–109 of the same volume. For Balthasar, the eternal *nunc* is not a "single unmoving point" but a "trinitarian process," "eternal *being*" is "eternal *event*" (91–2), otherwise there would be no archetype of creative self-realization in God. Like Eckhart, whom he nevertheless criticizes for collapsing the analogical distance between God and creation, Balthasar is here straining the very limits of language.

that there is a sense in which only one moment ever really exists. We live always in the *now*, the *nunc*, even if for us it is always changing. The past is for us only a memory that exists in the present, and the future that we think we can almost grasp is only imagined by us in the present. This "now" is different from the eternal "now" of God's Eternity, yet by its quality of absolute inescapability resembles it in an important respect.

Dom Sylvester Houédard discusses this in his *Commentaries on Meister Eckhart Sermons* (5–6). There he explains that since we only exist in the present moment, which is non-time, we cannot say "I am" because that would take two moments or more to pronounce. The "I," you could say, is *in via*, it is "travelling" down the timeline, but has not yet become complete, has not fully become itself. As creatures we can only say "I will be." God can say, "I AM" because he is not becoming, but simply is. He already is all that he could ever be. Yet the present moment in which we exist so fleetingly, and so inescapably, is also in its way an image of God, and is an essential part of the self-gift of God that makes us what we are, makes us "be." This is what he means by speaking of the "kiss," of the coincidence of the two *nunc*'s, the *now* that is flowing and the *now* that is always standing still and around which the world moves.

Our progress through time is the passage from potentiality to actuality, to full actuality in God. It is the completing of the circle (or spiral) of *exitus* and *reditus*, of creation and return, that makes time an image of eternity. In the case of human beings, it is the unique "signature" that we scrawl through time, the pattern of a life composed of freedom interacting with necessity, an interaction that makes the story that we are.

The point is to recognize what we actually are, beings continually created by God; to accept the reality of our situation, which is that everything we have is received from him. We are to become receptive towards God, in order to allow him to act through us. But if he acts through us, it is only to affirm our own truest identity. There is no loss of self, although there may be a welcome loss of self-consciousness. The ability to act, that freedom which is the power to act, is magnified in us. But now we act out of receptivity. We do not presume or pretend to act out of ourselves, as though we could create our own ground to stand on, for we are not self-subsistent.

In Between

In order to understanding the human situation, we must acknowledge that there is also something that exists "between" time and eternity, in which we ourselves participate. The Christian tradition gives it the name *aevum*, or eviternity, or sempiternity, and it is the region or dimension, the "in-between" world, inhabited by the angels—and also, in a slightly different way, by human souls. While the body is in time, the soul transcends time to some degree, otherwise we could not experience a succession of discrete moments as a unity (such as the unity and form we observe in a piece of music or a dramatic play, that necessarily takes time to unfold).

Everything in time has a beginning and an end. It is subject to entropy, which means a tendency to the dissipation of energy and the decline of order. In fact, in physical terms entropy defines the very direction of time. Locally, of course, order can be restored and chaos reversed by taking energy from outside, as biological life takes energy from the sun and uses it to maintain the complex order of its own dynamic existence, or as a new invention or even an entire civilization may spring out of some seminal inspiration. Furthermore the photons of light and other basic elements of nature—while they exist—are not subject to entropy in the same way, existing in a sense "out of time." But if we look at the system as a whole, the scientists tell us there is no such thing as a free lunch. The overall trend of time is one of decline, as in the ageing process with which we are all too familiar, and when our personal time runs out we will find ourselves standing in sempiternity. This is where we have to locate purgatory.

There are living creatures that are not subject to the law of entropy, creatures that do not ever exist in time as we know it, for whom sempiternity is a way of life.[6] The angels have a beginning

---

6. According to St. Denys and St. Bonaventure, the angelic creation is divided into three hierarchies corresponding to the Trinity, and each hierarchy also contains three types of angel, making nine in all. The names of the nine choirs are derived

but no end. They do not experience change, though they may manifest differently at different points in time.[7]

It would be too crude, but it may nonetheless be helpful, to imagine time as a circle, along the periphery of which we are traveling. Eternity is the point at the center of the circle, equidistant from each moment. From this position God is able to see all that will happen in past, present, or future. Sempiternity would then be the space between the two, or if you like a series of radii linking the center with each point on the circle. The presence of this intermediary world of angelic time makes it possible to see how the messages and guidance of eternity are normally conveyed to us here below.[8] John Henry Newman refers to "Spiritual Intelligences which move those wonderful and vast portions of the natural world which seem to be inanimate.... Every breath of air and ray of light and heat, every beautiful prospect, is, as it were, the skirts of their garments, the waving of the robes of those whose faces see God in heaven" (*Parochial and Plain Sermons*).

What this picture does not convey is the extraordinary reversal brought about by the Incarnation of God. Christianity claims that the divine center of the circle has placed itself through the Blessed Virgin Mary on the periphery, as it were, creating an entirely new order of things—an order divinely envisaged and anticipated from the very beginning. Or, to look at it another way, it is as though one point on the circle had been drawn inwards to the center, allowing

from St. Paul: Seraphim, Cherubim, and Thrones; Dominions, Virtues, and Powers; Principalities, Archangels, and Angels.

7. There are different theological opinions here, concerning the relation of the angels to duration, as well as to bodiliness. But certainly the Christian tradition speaks of at least two "moments" in the life of an angel: the moment of creation, and the moment of decision, in which the angel exercises its free will. For some angels, this will be the occasion of a "fall from grace," to be discussed below. These moments are coincident if viewed from a certain perspective, but separate when viewed from "below."

8. The idea of the angel as the radius of a circle finds support in the experience described by Tolkien of seeing the Guardian Angel as a ray of light, as it were God's attention "personalized." Elsewhere he writes of the Angel as a kind of "umbilical cord." See *The Letters of J. R. R. Tolkien*, ed. Humphrey Carpenter (London: Allen & Unwin, 1981), 66, 99.

the circle of time to enter into a new relationship with eternity. In a sense the mediation of the angels has been by-passed, and they too are drawn through this one point into a new relationship with God, seeing in Christ and his Church things that had previously been hidden even from them. St. Gregory of Nyssa writes of this as follows:

> Dare I say it? Perhaps the angels, as they beheld in the Bride the beauty of the Bridegroom, have come to marvel at him who is invisible and incomprehensible to all. He, whom no one has seen or can see, has made the Church into his Body, has formed the Church into his image, so that, by turning to her, the friends of the Bridegroom have perhaps seen the Invisible more clearly in her.[9]

It seems inconceivable, yet nothing less is implied by the description of the Church as the extended body of Christ.[10]

Origin of Evil

Extended—but how far? Will demons and the damned be excluded from the reach of God's mercy by their own rejection of it? In order to approach this question, we need first to give some thought to the nature of damnation, and where evil fits in the scheme of things. It is hard to think of, because evil is, in a sense, *un*thinkable, being the destruction of order and meaning. It is not mere limitation—though some may have thought that matter and its limits were themselves evil as such. According to Christianity, there is nothing evil about material existence. Moral evil is something different from this. It is the destruction or reduction of a good that *ought to have been there* but now isn't. How does this, this inherent absurdity, come about?

The Fall of man is hard enough to understand, since we are told that unfallen man possessed such natural gifts and such a well-ordered soul that it is hard to conceive of him deliberately disobeying his maker. But even harder to understand is the prior fall of the

---

9. Cited by Hans Urs von Balthasar, *The Glory of the Lord*, I, 676–7.

10. Balthasar writes: "The time of revelation is the relationship of God to the world in Christ, now transposed to the horizontal plane, and this transposition is the impressing of form upon the continuity of time" (*The Glory of the Lord*, 645–6).

serpent and his angels, without whom we assume there would have been no temptation in the Garden. Yet the angels—and especially Lucifer, who was by most accounts the highest of the angels—are the most powerful of created intelligences, and incapable of acting out of ignorance. How are we to explain the fact that they chose a course that they knew would lead to eternal frustration and punishment?

The possibility of evil does not exist in God, but it does in creation. Why? If creation is the image of God, this is because its essence is distinct from its existence, whereas in God these are identical. Creation is not necessary existence but posited in freedom, in order to show forth what is in God in the form of an image. God is love, and creation is an image of love, but it is not *necessary* love. That is, in God, freedom and necessity are not separated, whereas in creation they are. This implies that a possibility must exist within creation of what we might call not-love, or of the rejection of love. That is where the possibility of evil comes from. Evil originates not in God, but in the rejection of something that God wishes to give the creature, or (what amounts to the same thing) in the refusal of the creature to give to God what would be required to make room for that gift.

In the case of Lucifer, the rejection of God is prompted by pride; and indeed, he has the most reason of any creature to be proud, since his nature is so high and splendid. He does not rebel against his existence, which is the first gift of God. Nor does he reject his unique position and role in the cosmos, by which the angels have been likened to the stars in the sky. In fact, it is this singular position that he wishes to preserve. What he rejects is a second gift, the gift of sanctifying grace in which he was created and yet which requires him to cooperate with others, even creatures of lesser degree than himself. He takes his stand without passion, and without ignorance of the consequences, since as a pure intelligence he can have neither passion nor ignorance.[11] It is the most cold-blooded and conscious decision ever made, and for that reason appears to be definitive—

11. Anscar Vonier elucidates the Thomistic teaching thus in his book on the human soul in *Collected Works of Abbot Vonier*, III, 177–84.

Catholic theology does not envisage any possibility of repentance or salvation for the fallen angels.[12]

The intimate union with God requires the complete gift of self, which implies obedience, submission, service of the other. Though Lucifer is by nature part of the image of God's love, he refuses to assume the likeness of God's kenotic nature—and he is not compelled to do so because love ceases to be itself when compelled by another. Nor is God the only good to which the will can cleave.

Once we have accepted the existence of angelic sin, it is easier to understand the fall of man, since in many ways human nature is dependent upon or entangled with the angelic, and not just with the angelic guardians who are assigned to protect and assist us on the way to heaven. Human beings may be deceived or manipulated in ways that angels cannot, even if to be confirmed in sin they must take responsibility for their evil actions in their own way. It also becomes easier to understand the conflict and warfare in nature herself, beginning with universal entropy and extending to natural disasters such as earthquakes and plagues, since, although all of these apparent flaws in nature (from our point of view) result from a consistent set of physical laws, the whole order of nature that we observe and which is defined by these laws is influenced by the separation of the evil spirits from the good, which together form the spiritual order on which the physical is based or in which it participates. In the words of Sergius Bulgakov, "*Everything in the world* is preserved by angels, and everything has *its* angel and its *correlation* in the angelic world,"[13] something that the pagans intuited and expressed in the statement that "everything is full of gods."

Eternity of Damnation?

It is *de fide* in the Catholic religion (in other words, the Church teaches) that there is an eternal hell, involving perpetual separation

---

12. There is a more radical Christian view, expressed by some of the Eastern Church Fathers and in modern times by Sergius Bulgakov, that even the devils may be saved, in a dispensation about which the Church is silent, but this is more difficult to reconcile with the sense of Scripture.

13. Bulgakov, *Jacob's Ladder*, 24. This was touched upon in Part One.

from God, awaiting those who join the fallen angels in making a definitive choice against the divine will during their earthly lives. From that choice there can be no release, since time and with it the freedom to repent has come to an end at death.[14] Yet God foreknows the decision of the damned, and permits their existence in a state of suffering to which there is no possible end. In fact Aquinas suggests that the just in heaven will rejoice at the pain inflicted forever upon their fellow human beings, since they will see these sufferings as an expression of divine justice—as God himself sees them. There will be no sorrowing, in heaven, over the damned. Nor will the damned themselves regret their choice, since they are now completely identified (if not "happy") with it. They have what they want.[15]

14. And what of reincarnation? Here the author of *Meditations on the Tarot* comes to our aid. For him the search for evidence and assurance of some kind of reincarnation in this world is unhealthy: "One ought during earthly life to prepare for this meeting with a fully awakened consciousness, which is purgatory, and for the experience of the presence of the Eternal, which is heaven, and not to prepare for a future terrestrial life" (361). To do so would amount to *"replacing one immortality by another,* namely that of God by that of the serpent" (362), a "vertical" immortality by a "horizontal" one. It is not in phantoms and ghosts, or prolongations through reincarnation, that we can find assurance of immortality, but only "in the experience of the kernel of the human being and his relationship with the breath, light, and warmth of God" (363). It is the *person as a whole* who is raised up by God, in whom is an eternal life altogether different from that life promised by the serpent in Eden.

15. Ibn Arabi says something similar: "The folk of the Fire will . . . find pleasure from being in the Fire, and they will praise God that they are not in the Garden" (cited in Chittick, *The Self-Disclosure of God,* 227). The problem is not quite so acute in Islam, however, since a *hadith* hints that hell—vividly depicted in the (chronologically) earliest *surahs* of the Qur'an—will not last forever, or rather that its flames will eventually grow cold, because God's Mercy takes precedence over his Wrath. On this see Murata and Chittick, *The Vision of Islam,* 209–10. Ibn Arabi's writings on the "cooling of the fire" are summarized and quoted in Chittick, *Imaginal Worlds,* 113–19. For Ibn Arabi, while the chastisement of hell's inhabitants comes to an end, they will never experience the vision of God. Frithjof Schuon discusses the "problem of the afterlife" in *Dimensions of Islam* (Allen & Unwin, 1969), 136–41. There he suggests that it is not hell that comes to an end, but the "end" which in a sense does away with hell, since the dimension in which hell exists (endlessly) must itself be absorbed into the Essence. As the Qur'an states, "Everything is perishing except His face" (28:88).

To many people, this seems an inhuman doctrine, and metaphysically nonsensical, since surely an eternity both without God *and* without time is hardly to be conceived. Blessed John Henry Newman is one of those Christian writers who has tried to soften the doctrine somewhat, by suggesting that, while it may be everlasting, it need not "be attended by a consciousness of duration and succession, by a present imagination of its past and its future, by a sustained power of realizing its continuity."[16] In other words, the experience of torment in hell might be that of a moment, even if that moment should last forever.

The eternity of damnation is suggested by the Gospel itself, where Jesus refers to the "sin against the Holy Spirit," which "shall not be forgiven, neither in this world, nor in the world to come" (Matt. 12:32). Christianity takes the freedom of man to refuse God's grace extremely seriously, and resists any suggestion that with the passing of a sufficient quantity of years that freedom may be somehow worn away, so that the sinner collapses back into the arms of God.

It has always seemed to me that this "problem" of hell in Christianity, which leads many to reject Christianity altogether, is really caused by our inability to understand the relations of time, eternity, and sempiternity, and by the popular equation of the everlastingness of hell with that of heaven. Neither hell nor purgatory can be measured in years. The state of the angels, though it is said to have no end, is not simply one that is indefinitely prolonged. St. Maximus the Confessor, after exploring the Scriptural references to "ages" and "ages of ages," speaks of the Kingdom of God as the "final goal of those who long for that which is the desire of all desires. Once they have reached it they are granted rest from all movement whatsoever, as there is no longer any time or age through which they need to pass. For after passing through all things they will come to rest in God, who exists before all ages and whom the nature of ages cannot attain."[17] Newman was surely correct in his intuition

16. John Henry Newman, *An Essay in Aid of a Grammar of Assent* (South Bend, IN: University of Notre Dame Press, 1979), 328.

17. "Second Century on Theology," 86, in Nikodimos and Makarios, *The Philokalia*, II, trans. G.E.H. Palmer, Philip Sherrard and Kallistos Ware (London:

that the state of the blessed is one of infinite fullness, whereas that of the damned is one of emptiness, akin to non-existence.

But will any human being *in fact* end up in the vortex of hell? Will hell turn out to be empty? That is a question that has perplexed recent theologians, none more than Hans Urs von Balthasar, who took as his guide in this matter the remarkable modern visionary to whom he acted as confessor, Adrienne von Speyr. Von Speyr, among other things, was allegedly able to visit both hell and heaven and converse with the saints, which perhaps gives Balthasar something of an advantage over theologians who need to rely on more conventional methods. In the second volume of his series *Theo-Logic*, he unpacks some of her teaching on this topic. He writes: "So long as the world endures, there remains for us the unresolvable contradiction between the atemporality of the Cross, the different atemporality of hell, and the yet altogether atemporality of heaven. This cannot be neatly calculated, much less be forced into a theory (of 'universal redemption', say). No one can try to anticipate the judge and look at the cards."[18] And yet, he adds, "if the Lord brings the marks of his wounds into his victory . . . it is surely not in order to integrate the contradiction of sin and hell into his heaven."

The way in which Balthasar, guided by Speyr, resolves this *aporia* is by making hell itself "a trinitarian event."[19] On Holy Saturday—the period between the Crucifixion on Good Friday and the Resurrection on Easter Sunday—the Church speaks of Christ's "descent into hell." Most theologians and the *Catechism of the Catholic Church* itself assume that this descent was not into a realm of intense punishment but into some shallower region where the good pagans and patriarchs were awaiting liberation. But Scripture tells us that Christ went into hell to preach not to the good, but to those who "formerly

Faber & Faber, 1981), 159. For the (notional) distinction between "kingdom of God" and "kingdom of heaven" see 161.

18. Balthasar, *Theo-Logic*, II, 359. But a theory of "universal redemption" is precisely what Balthasar appears to be offering, as critics such as Alyssa Pitstick have pointed out. For Balthasar's position see his *Dare We Hope "That All Men be Saved"? with a Short Discourse on Hell* (San Francisco: Ignatius Press, 1988).

19. Ibid., 352.

did not obey" and were lost in the time of Noah (1 Pet. 3:19–20). The Hebrew *Sheol* refers simply to the land of death (the Greek Hades), without making these distinctions. At any rate, Balthasar has no qualms about holding that the descent was into complete darkness, to experience on behalf of sinners the punishment even of apparent separation from God. This is the final frontier of Redemption, and one that is necessarily obscure (or "esoteric") to us.

Hell is, as Newman saw and Adrienne here confirms, "something that is at once atemporal-eternal and self-destroying, perishing, 'dragged down', 'eddying down.'"[20] But it is also

> the preserve of the Father, in the sense that, as Creator (indeed as generator of the Son, in whom he has always already conceived every possible world) he foresaw, and took responsibility for, the possibility of the creature's freedom and, given the abuse of this freedom, of its eternal perishing: "a chaos of sin . . . like a mirror image of the chaos at the beginning of creation."[21]

God the Father, be it noted, *takes responsibility for* this state of hell, and the same passage goes on to tell us that the Father,

> so to say, "draws back" in order to admit the incarnate Son into this ultimate darkness, which the Father discloses to him, as Redeemer of sinners, only here, at the end of the way of redemption. In this sense, the Son's "way" into the no-way-out of sin is, without his perceiving it, at the same time the most direct and, in Trinitarian terms, the most intimate way into the Father.

Hell is a Trinitarian event because everything that is created, hell not excepted, must have its archetype in the eternal Principle. Von Speyr tells us that:

> Hell thus serves the intradivine mysteries and their revelation: it vividly exhibits and demonstrates the supreme distinction of the Persons and their unimaginable unity. At the point where the Son believes he is most abandoned by the Father, abandonment becomes the means to break open the prison of abandonment,

---

20. Ibid., 351.
21. Ibid., 352.

hell, and to admit the Son, along with the redeemed world, into the heaven of the Father.[22]

In the "Thirteenth Revelation" of her *Revelations of Divine Love*, the great fourteenth-century mystic Julian of Norwich reflects on the Lord's promise to her that the "blessed Trinity shall make well all that is not well." She questions him, saying that if, as she had been taught by Holy Church, "many creatures shall be condemned . . . to hell without end," then surely it is impossible "that all manner of things should be well." To this she receives the reply that, "*That which is impossible to thee is not impossible to me: I shall save my word in all things and I shall make all things well.*" Her part is simply to believe what the Church teaches, but also to believe the seeming contradiction that she has received from God, and await the "Great Deed that our Lord shall do, in which deed He shall save His word and He shall make all well that is not well," a Deed that none shall know until it is done.

Balthasar has been accused of teaching the (officially rejected) doctrine of universal salvation, or *apokatastasis*. Like Lady Julian, he pulls up short, however, from teaching that we can know for certain that all will be saved—though he drops a heavy hint or two, and he is quite clear that we also cannot know for certain, either from Scripture or from Church teaching (leaving aside private revelation), that anyone *will not*.[23] It may be that the Church rejected the doctrine of *apokatastasis* because at this level, the level of formal beliefs, it can never be expressed with the depth and subtlety that its truth requires. There is also the practical question of the possible effect on human behavior of announcing an effective "abolition of hell" (since that is how it would inevitably be interpreted by the religious press).

22. Ibid., 353. Thus "The Son gropes his way through the darkness of hell into the mystery of the origin," where "In the 'chaos' of love [i.e., in its unfathomable depth] the chaos of sin becomes possible in the first place." It should be noted that this idea of the Son "groping his way" towards the Father is not accepted without protest by other theologians!

23. Except demons, since his speculations are concerned only with humanity and he appears to accept the eternal damnation of the fallen angels.

The Hebrew *Gehenna*, as distinct from *Sheol* meaning simply the state of death, refers to the refuse-dump in which waste from the city was discarded and burned. Used as a symbol of damnation, the analogy may be useful in shedding light on this final mystery. Balthasar writes of the "work of the Cross" as the separation of the sinner from his sin.[24] In this way, it may be possible to conceive of the salvation of those who in life rejected God's love as a kind of stripping-away of the false self they had constructed out of sin. The idea becomes even clearer in an exposition of Gehenna by Pavel Florensky:

> The "for itself" therefore burns ceaselessly in the inextinguishable flame of hate. . . . It is the empty self-identity of "I" which cannot transcend a single, eternal moment of sin, torment, and fury directed at God, at one's own impotence, a single moment of insane epoche, which has become an eternity.[25]

The self-made existence "for itself" is ultimately without a subject, because the only real subjectivity is "for another." This false self is like a "husk" or empty skin. The human beings in hell are not persons but zombies, empty shells, phantoms; the truth that was the basis of their reality having been stripped away in a "surgical procedure" by the Holy Spirit, who is like a sharp sword that divides even the soul from the spirit (Heb. 4:12). What is left by this procedure is the holy essence of the person, the barest subjectivity. Of course, to be reverted to this state is hardly salvation in the normal sense of the word (one would not strip a canvas bare to save the painting). But it is only the extreme version of something that takes place in all of us when we pass through death and resurrection to be united with our uncreated Idea.

One of the objections felt by orthodox Christians to the idea of "universal salvation" is that it makes salvation much too mechanical, too automatic. This is a serious objection, but Balthasar's theological approach (at least in my interpretation) offers a possible answer to it. His implied "redemption of hell" is not one that overrides

---

24. Balthasar, *Theo-Drama*, V, 314–16.
25. Pavel Florensky, *The Pillar and Ground of the Truth* (Princeton University Press, 1997), 157. See the whole section on Gehenna, 151–89.

human freedom or takes sin less seriously than it deserves. The pages on damnation, based upon the mystical experiences of Adrienne von Speyr, are harrowing to read. Hell is real enough, as Christ discovers to his cost; and hell would have the "last word" were it not for the freely-willed presence of the Word himself within it, at the very deepest level. In this way the doctrine of the Trinity may yet enable us to wrest a kernel of metaphysical truth from the heart of an age-old heresy.[26]

26. In addition to his book *Dare We Hope?*, see the section "Can Hope Deceive?" in *Theo-Drama*, V, 316–21, where Balthasar describes the history of the doctrine of *apokatastasis* after the condemnation of Origenism. As he remarks, several Church Fathers who openly taught the doctrine after Origen, such as Clement of Alexandria and Gregory of Nyssa, were not condemned for doing so. (Not that it is necessary to be condemned by the Church in order to be mistaken!) A good way to approach Balthasar's writing on the last things is via Healy, *The Eschatology of Hans Urs von Balthasar.*

Visions of Sophia?

Lo, there, whence love, life, light are pour'd,
    Veil'd with impenetrable rays,
Amidst the presence of the Lord
    Co-equal Wisdom laughs and plays.
Female and male God made the man;
    His image is the whole, not half;
And in our love we dimly scan
    The love which is between Himself.
                            Coventry Patmore[1]

I have tried to show how our theological understanding of the revealed doctrine of the Trinity illuminates cosmology and anthropology. Now I want to venture further into the realm of the esoteric and the visionary in order to glean some insight into the topic of this book from Christian hermeticism. I will look at Jacob Boehme, Vladimir Solovyov, Oscar Milosz, and Valentin Tomberg, and then return to theology with the help of Sergius Bulgakov.

The history of hermetic and esoteric Christian writings and movements is complex and fascinating. It begins with the Wisdom books of the Bible and takes in the development of Jewish Kabbalah on the one hand, and the classical philosophies through Neoplatonism on the other, intertwined with influences from Egypt and the Far East.[2] These writings have an uneasy relationship with orthodoxy, even if they cannot always be easily dismissed as simply

---

1. Coventry Patmore, "The Prototype," from "The Angel in the House" in *Collected Poems*.

2. For much more on this whole "Christian Hermetic" tradition, including the figures I have not discussed, see Antoine Faivre, *Access to Western Esotericism* and *Theosophy, Imagination, Tradition: Studies in Western Esotericism* (State Univ. of New York Press, 2000). See also Antoine Faivre and Jacob Needleman (eds), *Modern Esoteric Spirituality* (London: SCM Press, 1992), esp. Pierre Deghaye's essay on 210–47.

heretical. They certainly offer considerable challenges even to the most well-informed and intelligent reader.

It would not even necessarily make things clearer if we could identify in each case, historical-critical fashion, the sources and influences that have shaped the imagination of these writers and given them their vocabulary. It does not matter to me a great deal whether the Zohar (the great text of Kabbalah), so influential on most subsequent esoteric writers, originated in the third or the thirteenth century, and was the invention of Moses de Leon or a long oral tradition, any more than I worry over the identity of Denys the Areopagite or Hermes Trismegistus. I am more interested in the "ring of truth" that one may hear in these texts. I am besides convinced that the "new evangelization" will fail if it does not appeal to the wise imagination, to the spiritual senses, to the eye of the heart, and to our yearning for the beauty that is Sophia.

Jacob Boehme

A contemporary of Francis Bacon and follower of Paracelsus, Jacob Boehme (1575–1624) was a gentle and devout Lutheran. A family man and shoemaker with little education, he received two illuminations around 1600 and later which became the basis for his obscure but influential visionary writings. Although he never broke from his church, the Lutheran authorities deemed him unorthodox, and as a result he was forced into an itinerant life. Boehme was an influence not only on William Blake but even on Isaac Newton, and on Catholics and Protestants alike, from Franz von Baader and F.C. Oetinger to William Law and Hegel (who took from him the dialectic but appears to have misunderstood the rest), Solovyov, and Berdyaev.[3] The following sketch is partially guided by one commentator in particular: Hans L. Martenson (1808–1884), Bishop of Denmark, who struggled manfully to salvage from Boehme whatever could be reconciled with Christian orthodoxy.

Boehme's writings are not understood correctly (indeed, they are

---

3. See Nicolescu, *Science, Meaning and Evolution*, and Wolfgang Smith, *Christian Gnosis: From St Paul to Meister Eckhart* (Tacoma, WA: Angelico Press/Sophia Perennis, 2011), 119–47.

wildly misleading) when they are confused with philosophy or theology. We have to remember what was said about the active imagination turned wholly towards God, and by Ian Davie about the
theological use of mythological and poetic speech.[4] In his account
of creation, Boehme is trying to describe structural elements that lie
deep within the visible world, below the surface of nature; but he
represents these as *story*, applying temporal categories to eternity
and inventing mythical events within the life of God in a way that
is hard to disentangle. According to Wolfgang Smith, Boehme is
viewing "from below," or through the lens of nature, realities that
in the Kabbalah are treated "from above," through commentary
on revealed Scripture.[5] Nor should we assume that Boehme, just
because he was a visionary, was always correct either in what he saw
or in the way he interpreted and expressed it. His work is something
of a stylistic mess, and full of real or apparent self-contradictions. In
his later writings he found in alchemy and in Kabbalah many terms
and concepts that helped him in the expression of his insights.

For Boehme, cosmogony recapitulates theogony. That is, creation
is preceded by, and echoes, the primordial "birth of God." In a
"beginning before the beginning," there is only the primal Abyss or
chasm of the *Ungrund*, the womb of God, containing the unorigi-
nated divine Will. This Will generates a Son, and breathes forth its
energies as a Holy Spirit. Of these three principles the first (unorigi-
nated Will) is a principle of darkness or mysterious fire in the
"Unground" of God's mystery. The second (the Son) is a principle
of light, corresponding to the Will's apprehension of itself as truth.
The third is a reconciling force, in which the previous two are
united—the radiation of the fire in the light.[6]

---

4. It should be noted that Hans Urs von Balthasar lumps Boehme with the
"many forms of post-Christian Titanism" that lead to the "total perversion" of the
Christian tradition in *Theo-Drama*, II, 420. I agree that this is a danger if Boehme's
writings are treated as theology.

5. Smith, *Christian Gnosis*, 142–4.

6. Bear in mind that even in orthodox theology, defended by St. Maximus
against the monothelites, there is only one divine will, not three, so that the will
pertains to the Godhead as such—which is the same as to say that it belongs to the
divine nature that is perfectly shared in the circumincession.

Through this third principle, which describes the operation of the Holy Spirit, the fullness or content of the divine nature is sent out into the void and (having nowhere to go) "reflected back" from it as though in a mirror. To this illuminated reflection Boehme gives the name Wisdom, and in his later writings, Sophia, making him the father of Western sophiology. A dream of the divine Imagination, Sophia clothed by the desire of God in an eternal, imperishable body becomes "Uncreated Heaven," the Kingdom of Beauty or Body of God, Eternal Nature, in which his Glory is forever manifested.

Heaven or Sophia is the model for all subsequent creation—the creation described in the Seven Days of Genesis.[7] It is "constructed" through a separation and reconciliation of darkness and light within the divine will. The dark forms a "Wheel of Life" consisting of three archetypal energies, which he calls by the alchemical terms Salt (contraction), Mercury (expansion) and Sulphur (rotation). The light consists in another wheel of three forces. A fourth energy called the "Lightning Flash" marks the transition between darkness and light, or the point where Love overcomes the darkness of the first wheel, transfiguring it into the Wheel of Light or Spirit-Will. This makes seven forces in all, making possible a comparison with the Kabbalah's seven "*sefiroth* of construction," and the Seven Days of Genesis that culminate in the Sabbath rest or Kingdom of God. In language that is less alchemical and more theological, one might say that in this eternal process, the Trinitarian Will of God has entered into the knowledge of itself by reconciling in Love the "otherness" of Father and Son. God eternally "becomes" *what he eternally already is*: a Trinity of Persons enthroned in an Uncreated Heaven full of peace and beauty.

Boehme described this vision in the work known as *Aurora* (finally published in 1656). While not a theological work, it contains

---

7. Each and every creature that God makes is modeled in its own way on Heaven, and its life imitates the same balance of forces, but in divided and temporal form. Martenson writes: "Boehme's fundamental idea is that every life has a double *center*, a *Nature-Center* and a *Life-* or *Light-Center*; that it begins with the first, and is perfected in the second; and that every life, in order to realize its destiny, must be born twice" (124–5).

the following fine description of the Christian Trinity, showing that
at that time Boehme believed all he had said to be perfectly in keeping with orthodox Christian teaching:

> Now when we speak or write of the *three Persons* in the deity, you
> must *not conceive* that therefore there are three Gods, each reign-
> ing and ruling by himself, like temporal kings on earth.
>
> No: such a substance and being is not in God; for the divine being
> consisteth in power, and not in body or flesh.
>
> The Father is the whole divine power, whence *all creatures* have
> proceeded, and hath been always, from eternity: He hath neither
> beginning nor end.
>
> The Son is in the Father, being the Father's Heart or light, and the
> Father generateth the Son continually, from eternity to eternity;
> and the Son's *power* and splendor shine back again in the whole
> Father, as the sun doth in the *whole* world.
>
> The Son is also *another* Person than the Father, but not externally,
> without or severed from the Father, *nor* is he any other God than
> the Father is; his power, splendor, and omnipotence, are *no less*
> than the whole Father.
>
> The Holy Ghost *proceedeth* from the Father and the Son, and is the
> *third* self-subsisting Person in the Deity ... he is nothing less or
> greater than the Father and the Son; his *moving power* is in the
> whole Father."[8]

God's own nature, according to Boehme, is not the seemingly
static perfection implied by medieval scholastic philosophy under
the influence of the Greeks. It is a *dynamic process*, yet outside time,
eternally fulfilled and complete in itself without the need of a creation. It is as if he were seeing into the Trinitarian relations and
conceiving them afresh, rather than using the conventional theological formulations. To create the world, according to Boehme,
was an act of divine freedom motivated by love alone. The word he

---

8. John Sparrow's seventeenth-century translation of *The Aurora* is reproduced
in Nicolescu's *Science, Meaning and Evolution.*

uses is "Magic," referring to an outbirth of God's eternal nature formed by the divine Will through the divine Imagination. The Mirror of Wisdom contains all angels and souls as eternal "possibilities." God imbues these with actuality through his Word (the *Fiat lux*).

> 15. And herein we understand the eternal Essence of the triad of the Deity, with the unfathomable wisdom. For the eternal will, which comprehends the eye or the mirror, wherein lies the eternal seeing as its wisdom, is Father. And that which is eternally grasped in wisdom, the grasp comprehending a basis or center in itself, passing out of the ungroundedness into a ground, is Son or Heart; for it is the Word of life, or its essentiality, in which the will shines forth with lustre. 16. And the going within itself to the center of the ground is Spirit; for it is the finder, who from eternity continually finds where there is nothing. It goes forth again from the center of the ground, and seeks in the will. And then the mirror of the eye, viz., the father's and Son's wisdom, becomes manifest; and wisdom stands accordingly before the Spirit of God, who in it manifests the unground. For its virtue, wherein the colors of the wonders shine forth, is revealed from the Father of the eternal will through the center of his Heart or Ground by the forthgoing Spirit.... 19. Thus the essence of the Deity is everywhere in the deep of the unground, like as a wheel or eye, where the beginning hath always the end; and there is no place found for it, for it is itself the place of all beings and the fullness of all things, and yet is apprehended and seen by nothing. For it is an eye in itself, as Ezekiel the prophet saw this in a figure at the introduction of the spirit of his will into God, when his spiritual figure was introduced into the wisdom of God by the Spirit of God; there he attained the vision, and in no other way can that be.[9]

Boehme is neither a pantheist nor an emanationist: the world is made by the seven archetypal forces, the "seven spirits of God" that form the Heavenly Sophia, in continual creative and unpredictable interaction with the three Principles emerging from the *Ungrund*; it is made out of Fire and Light woven together by divine Eros ("all

9. Jacob Boehme, *Six Theosophic Points and Other Writings* (Ann Arbor, MI: University of Michigan Press, 1958), 8–10.

things stand in the wisdom in a spiritual form in the attraction of the Fire and Light, in a wrestling sport of Love").[10]

Vladimir Solovyov

The Russian visionary philosopher and friend of Dostoevsky, Vladimir Solovyov (1853–1900), is sometimes known as the "Russian Newman." Hans Urs von Balthasar discusses him with great sympathy and interest in the third volume of his series on theologi-

---

10. The first strictly *created* reality is the Heaven of the Angels. There are three Angels—Michael, Lucifer and Uriel—symbolic of the divine Ternary, each ruling a kingdom of lesser angels that include seven Thrones. Angelic life is a partial or derived eternity, free of space and time; it is not divided up into a succession of moments or locations but is simultaneous and everywhere present. (Martenson struggles with this idea, but it is simply a rediscovery of the medieval Catholic notion of the *Aevum*, an intermediary state between God's eternity and our time.) The freedom of the Angels consists in the ability to choose between nature and grace—or, in Boehme's terminology, to sacrifice the Wheel of Nature (self-centered existence) in the fourth natural energy for the sake of the Wheel of Light (the life of Love). Boehme believed that the Fall of Lucifer affected his entire subordinate kingdom, which happens to be the world of our own Earth, reducing this to a fiercely burning Chaos. The Angel Lucifer "fell" by choosing to dwell in his own nature, and so the Fire was transformed not into Light but into Anguish. The Hell in which he suffers, and into which he drags the rest of creation, is caused not by God but by his own choice. (However, the *possibility* of Hell lies in the natural imperfection of a created reality, which must be distinct from eternity and therefore cannot be perfect in itself.) It was the Fall that initiated the war of Light against Darkness that we call time and space. God's merciful reaction to this first Fall was to submerge the Earth in water and begin a new creation. The process (recapitulated later in the story of the Flood) is described in the early chapters of the Book of Genesis—an account not of the first or Angelic creation but the re-creation from Chaos, and specifically the attempt to establish a new harmony based on Man. Adam is made in God's image, tripartite. He is body, soul, and spirit; his body drawn from that created world that is a copy of Uncreated Heaven, his soul and spirit reflecting respectively the Father (Fire) and Son (Light). Even the human soul is tripartite, in that it can turn towards one or other of the three primordial worlds of the Ternary. Indeed, Man was created with a view to his becoming (in Christ) the Consummator of the creation and Mediator between heaven and earth. But to be made imperishable in blessedness and to bring the Light out of the Fire in himself he must first overcome temptation. This, as we know, he did not do. Time as we understand it—let us call it "entropic time," meaning time that is measured by decay and death—began with the Fall of Man, as a secondary cycle of reparation and restoration centered on the Cross.

cal aesthetics. Whereas the Gnostic Valentinus tried to integrate the doctrines of Incarnation and salvation into the surrounding alien systems of pagan thought, thus denuding them of their real significance, Solovyov (Balthasar claims) largely succeeds in integrating *true gnosis* into Christianity. His researches into the Jewish Kabbalah and spiritualism led him not into a new form of the old heresies but to a deeper orthodoxy, a synthesis of philosophy with theology in the "theosophy" that reveals Christ as the inner unity of all things, the living flesh of the Logos at the center of the cosmos and of history.

Three visions of Divine Wisdom as a beautiful and mysterious female figure (in Moscow, London, and Egypt) revealed to Solovyov the feminine/receptive principle in both God and creation. The first took place during a church service as the doors of the iconostasis opened ("Azure around me, azure within my soul"). The second took place in the reading room of the British Museum in 1875, when the face of Sophia appeared to him and commanded him to seek her in Egypt. The third vision, as he describes in his poem *Three Meetings*, took place in 1876 out in the desert, after he had nearly been killed by Bedouins who mistook him—dressed in his black European top hat and overcoat—for a demon.

> Then I fell into a deep sleep; and when I waked
> The fragrance of roses wafted from earth and heaven.
>
> And in the purple of the heavenly glow
> You gazed with eyes full of an azure fire
> And your gaze was like the first shining
> Of universal and creative day.
>
> What is, what was, and what will be were here
> Embraced within that one fixed gaze. . . . The seas
> And rivers all turned blue beneath me, as did
> The distant forest and the snow-capped mountain heights.
>
> I saw it all, and all of it was one,
> One image there of beauty feminine. . . .
> The immeasurable was confined within that image.
> Before me, in me, you alone were there.

The Radiance of Being

O radiant one! I'm not deceived by you.
I saw all of you there in the desert. . . .
And in my soul those roses shall not fade
Wherever it is the billows of life may rush me.[11]

Balthasar could be said to have assimilated and translated Solovyov's insight into theological terms—if he did not simply rediscover it for himself on a different path—while at the same time purging it of any lack of balance. He identified Solovyov's Sophia with the Blessed Virgin Mary, whilst incorporating the insight that God contains a "feminine" aspect in his revision of conventional Thomism.[12] But for Solovyov himself, the personal nature of Sophia as she had appeared to him was important. He had fallen in love with the "body of God," with the body of Love itself, with the "guardian angel of the world." It is she, this feminine presence, alluring and transcendental, who inspired his writings on the reconciliation of

11. Vladimir Solovyov, *The Religious Poetry of Vladimir Solovyov*, transl. Boris Jakim and Laury Magnus (San Rafael, CA: Semantron Press, 2008), 105. See also Judith Deutsch Kornblatt, *Divine Sophia: The Wisdom Writings of Vladimir Solovyov* (Ithaca: Cornell University Press, 2009), 15.

12. St. Thomas, adapting Aristotle, had defined God's nature as pure act (*actus purus*). But this rather technical abstraction is totally transformed once we realize that the "act" in question is an *act of love*. It is therefore an act of seeing, of beholding, of giving (revealing), and of receiving (adoring), as we saw in a previous chapter. The tradition that God, being pure act, contained no trace of passivity had become associated with the tendency in Catholic and Christian thought to assign a lower place to woman and to "feminine" virtues. In a society that increasingly valued the hard, driving mechanisms of technological progress and economic competition, theology became entangled with the same attitude. According to Balthasar, on the other hand, to *receive something from another* is not at all a weakness or imperfection, but intrinsic to the nature of what it is to love. This meant that theology was free to revalue the feminine—and the child. Balthasar's theology is thus closely allied with the "alternative" stream of affective and mystical theology flowing through feminine mystics from Teresa of Avila and Margaret Mary Alocoque to Therese of Lisieux and her "Little Way" of spiritual childhood. (Balthasar himself was so closely associated with the mystic Adrienne von Speyr that he claimed their works could never be separated.) See the discussion between Long, Blair, Clarke and Schindler in *Communio*, Spring 1994, reprised in the final chapter of David L. Schindler, *Heart of the World, Center of the Church*. Cf. John S. Grabowski, "Person: Substance and Relation," in *Communio*, Spring 1995, together with articles there referred to.

heaven and earth through the "divine humanity" of Christ—the concept of "godmanhood" (*bogochelovechestve*) being, in Bulgakov's opinion, a much-needed taking up again of the unfinished business of Chalcedon.

In his *Lectures on the Humanity of God*, Solovyov makes the argument that the reality of the individual human being such as me or you depends on the existence not merely of an abstract human "essence" or general concept of man, but on the concrete universal that is Sophia:

> To be actual, such a being must be both one and many and therefore is not merely the universal common essence of all human individuals, taken in abstraction from them. Such a being is universal but also individual, an entity that actually contains all human beings within itself. Every one of us, every human being, is essentially and actually rooted in and partakes of the universal, or absolute, human being."[13]

Thus "all human elements" constitute an

> integral organism, one both universal and individual, which is the necessary actualization and receptacle of the organism of the living Logos. They constitute a universally human organism as the eternal body of God and the eternal soul of the world. Since this latter organism, that is, Sophia, in its eternal being necessarily consists of a multiplicity of elements of which she is the real unity, each of these elements, as a necessary component part of eternal Divine Humanity, must be recognized as eternal in the absolute or ideal order.[14]

And so:

> The deepest essence of every actual human being is rooted in the eternal divine world. Every human being is not only a visible phenomenon, that is, a series of events and a group of facts, but also an eternal and special being, a necessary and irreplaceable link in the absolute whole. Only by recognizing this is it possible to admit rationally the two great truths that are absolutely necessary for

13. Kornblatt, *Divine Sophia*, 184.
14. Ibid.

both theology, that is, for religious knowledge, and human life in general: the truths of human freedom and human immortality.[15]

Oscar Milosz

O.V. de L. Milosz (1877–1939), a Lithuanian poet and visionary, is the author of a series of poetic writings that flowed from a vision in 1914.[16] In these we glimpse another intriguing mysticism of light, nothingness, and Sophia.

Milosz grasped that *relationship* is the fundamental law of all phenomena. This makes him a mystic especially for our own time, the Age of Relativity. Space, time, and indeed matter are for him different aspects of a single Movement (David Bohm would perhaps call it the Holomovement), which he identifies mystically with "Blood," the essence of life. According to him it was the crucial metaphysical mistake of modern science to abstract them one from another, in an attempt to subject them to mathematical analysis, to the fictitious procedures of division and multiplication—with the result that we came to believe that we are situated somewhere other than God. The world is situated *not* in space and time, that is, materially, but spiritually, in the Nothing. "The Nothing is the code word of the Noble Travelers. It is the entrance and the exit of the labyrinth."[17]

For Milosz, the materialization of thought in the modern period is associated with the loss of a sense of the eternal simultaneity of past, present, and future. It amounts to the identification of the infinite (which is properly a spiritual concept) with space, with an infinite void or "soul-shuddering vacuum."[18] As he writes, "The

15. Ibid., 184–5.
16. O.V. de L. Milosz, *The Noble Traveller*, ed Christopher Bamford (Hudson, NY: Inner Traditions/Lindisfarne, 1985), 277.
17. Ibid., 281.
18. "Our true, unadulterated idea of the infinite is identical with what is purest and deepest in our being and is nothing other than the idea of the knowledge which God has of himself. The idea of the infinite is that of the consciousness of God. What God perceives when he broods over his consciousness is the infinite.... Adam, the Master of our Freedom, has changed the infinite—that is, his idea of the knowledge that God has of himself—into a space without end, an eternally fleeting result of ceaseless multiplication: Adam has lost his way in the universal darkness which followed the extinction of the Sun of Memory" (Milosz, 334–5).

Nothing, only intelligible container of a universe which is as free and pure as God's thought, the Nothing superior to any notion of the finite and the infinite, was repudiated by man. . . . Adam's consciousness of the primordial relationship grows dim. The human spirit is driven from the paradisal light, the transmutation of which occurs in the holy, holy idea of an exterior, lucid region of exaltation, or sacrifice, of charity, and of freedom; of freedom, blessed may it be."[19]

The origin of cosmic movement lies in incorporeal light. This as-yet unmanifested Universe is the "knowledge that God has of himself." Into this Nothing, which is the "idea-archetype of an exterior" (contained in God), the "inconceivable spiritual fire" projects this incorporeal light as an archetypal world equivalent to the plenitude of Platonic Forms: *Fiat lux*. The world then exists as a mathematical point, containing in itself the whole of space-matter-time (an "initial singularity" in terms of modern physics). The Universe now appears to God "as if from outside in its clothing of physical light transformable into electricity, that essence of bodies" (i.e., electromagnetic energy). It appears "in its form of Beauty, of Bride" (344). The God of omniscience has become the God of "universal sacrifice and inexpressible love." (The parallels with Boehme are very clear.)

The following visionary description of the "Big Bang" was published in 1927, before the scientific hypothesis of Georges Lemaître (first published in an obscure scientific journal in that year) had become generally known:

> The unique Being who is one with his law, God, in an emission of incorporeal light, exteriorized the archetypal world of his thought so that he could love it no longer inside but somehow outside his being. . . . (Jacob Boehme in an outburst of holy rapture exclaims: Our Lord is magical!). . . . Projected upon the Nothing which is synonymous with the non-existence of the void and the full, it transmuted itself into the first mathematical point of space-matter

---

19. Ibid., 399. (By contrast, for Hans Urs Balthasar creation takes place in the nothingness that is not "outside" but "within" God: that is, in the infinite spaciousness of the divine Trinity.)

and, blazing up, emitted in turn the first ray of physical light, transforming into electricity and creator of the universe through expansion. The universe of matter thus formed took on in its entirety, which can be embraced only by the eye of God, the likeness of a Bride of Glory.[20]

Milosz continues: "Do we know of any freedom other than that of sacrifice? The Father creates the universe so that the law of necessity which he is should be transmuted into love, so that holy beauty should call him from outside. The Son gives his *blood* just as the Father spilled his *light*, so that the descendants of the guilty man might return to the possession of their rights, so that the regenerated Adam would renounce infinite space, his kingdom of darkness, and, grasping the identity of blood and of physical light in the first movement of incorporeal brightness, would situate the universe in this brightness alone" (347)—a "spiritual light" that cannot be separated "from the fire that sheds it forth." "In this act of manifestation, beauty, the Bride, detached herself from the Bridegroom without breaking the indivisible unity; for she detached herself as an image separates itself from its object" (349).

This is not pantheism, Milosz explains, nor some doctrine of the Supreme Identity of the many and the One. In Christian esotericism, the highest spiritual unity is based on the Otherness of Bride and Groom and on Sacrifice, that mystery of the "conjugal principle": the "holy arcanum of Conjugal Love, the subject of Solomon's Song of Songs"; about which Milosz feels himself constrained to silence by "the Legions clad in gold" (353).

Even as he asserts the supremacy of the "spiritual and political truth" belonging to the "Catholic, Apostolic and Roman Church" (350), and its absolute difference from non-Christian mysticism, Milosz dares to say things that look very like formal heresy in the cold light of day. For example: "God could not but create the world, because His law had to be transmuted into love; God could not do otherwise that be born into this world to suffer, because the Jewish law, the harsh law of man, had to be succeeded by Love exalted in

20. Ibid., 310–311.

Woman, in Mary, in nature glorified once again through its original virginal maternity" (358).

But then, Milosz is not writing "in the cold light of day," but in the heat of a passionate vision that reveals the necessity at the heart of absolute freedom, of absolute Love. Love is that absolute freedom that binds itself absolutely. "The incorporeal light of beauty detached itself from the being which is identical with the law and is the hidden spiritual fire. It detached itself in order that just as the first relationship was established between this fire and this light, between this bridegroom and this bride, so love should be exalted above the law" (373).

Valentin Tomberg

In the light of all the above, we can understand better the following passage from the author of *Meditations on the Tarot*, a hermeticist and former anthroposophist who by the time of writing his masterpiece had become, like Milosz, a devout Catholic. (It should be noted that the Tarot cards here are not treated by Tomberg as a system of divinization but as a collection of symbols representing different aspects of truth, each of which is here explored in a series of chapters written as "letters" to an unknown friend.)

> It is not a matter of seeing the Holy Trinity with human eyes, but rather of seeing with the eyes—and in the light—of Mary-Sophia. For just as no one comes to the Father but by Jesus Christ (John 14:6), so does no one understand the Holy Trinity but by Mary-Sophia. And just as the Holy Trinity manifests itself through Jesus Christ, so *understanding* of this manifestation is possible only through intuitive apprehension of what the virgin mother of Jesus Christ understands of it, who not only bore him and brought him to the light of day, but who also was present—present as mother— at his death on the Cross. And just as Wisdom (Sophia)—as Solomon said—was present at the creation ("when he established the heavens, I was there, when he drew a circle on the face of the deep ... then I was at work beside him"—Prov. 8:27–31) and "built her house ... set up her seven pillars" (Prov. 9:1), so Mary-Sophia was present at the redemption and "was at work beside him," and "built her house ... set up her seven pillars," i.e., she

became Our Lady of the seven sorrows. For the seven sorrows of Mary correspond, for the work of redemption, to the seven pillars of Sophia for the work of creation. Sophia is the queen of the "three luminaries"—the moon, the sun and the stars—as the "great portent" of the Apocalypse shows. And just as the *word* of the Holy Trinity became flesh in Jesus Christ, so did the *light* of the Holy Trinity become flesh in Mary-Sophia—the *light*, i.e. three-fold receptivity, the threefold faculty of intelligent reaction, or *understanding*. Mary's words: *mihi fiat secundum verbum tuum* ("let it be to me according to your word"—Luke 1:38) are the key to the mystery of the relationship between the pure act and pure reaction, between the word and understanding—lastly, between Father, Son and Holy Spirit on the one hand and Mother, Daughter and Holy Soul on the other hand. They are the true key to the "seal of Solomon."[21]

For Tomberg, as for Boehme, the world of creation is a projection from nothingness into nothingness, an act which he is not afraid of calling "magical." But this is not mere emanation of the divine substance, or pantheism, any more than it is a monistic form of Advaita, or a disguise for Western idealism. He writes that:

[P]antheistic, emanationist and demiurgic doctrines deprive creation of its magical sense. Pantheism denies the independent existence of creatures; they live only as parts of the divine life and the world is only the body of God. Emanationism attributes only a transitory, and therefore ephemeral, existence to creatures and the world. Demiurgism declares that *ex nihilo nihil* ("out of nothing comes nothing") and teaches there must exist a *substance* co-eternal with God, which God uses as *material* for his work of craftsmanship.

And he sees a way these apparently rival doctrines can be fitted within the broader vision of a Christianized Kabbalah:

In the doctrine of the ten Sephiroth, it teaches first the mystery of eternal *mysticism*—AIN SOPH, the Unlimited. Then it expounds the *gnostic* doctrine of eternal emanations from the womb of the Divine, which precede—*in ordine cognoscendi*—the act of

21. Anon., *Meditations on the Tarot*, 547.

creation—the latter being a conscious act and not impulsive or instinctive. Then it speaks of pure creation or creation *ex nihilo*—the act of magical projection of the ideas of the plan of creation, i.e., the Sephiroth. This creative, magical act is followed—*in ordine cognoscendi*, always—by the activity of formation in which the beings of the spiritual hierarchies participate, including man." [22]

Sergius Bulgakov

In order to see what a systematic theologian can do with the data gleaned from the visions of Sophia, we should look at the work of Sergius Bulgakov (1879–1944). Though he remains highly controversial, he has been the most successful at reconciling the sophianic tradition as developed by Solovyov and slightly later by Pavel Florensky with mainstream Orthodox theology.

For Bulgakov, as for Boehme and Solovyov, the Sophia spoken of in the Wisdom books of the Old Testament cannot simply be identified with the Virgin Mary. Nor is she a purely allegorical figure as she often appears in the West. The greatest cathedral of Byzantium was dedicated to Sancta Sophia, and other churches and cathedrals likewise. There are icons of her seated on a throne with wings unfurled, holding a scroll. It is such images—as well as the three visions of her that were so important to Solovyov—that inspire Russian sophiology; even if the original icons most likely were intended by their makers to represent wisdom as an aspect or attribute of Christ, rather than a distinct feminine entity.[23]

The notion that Sophia is a fourth divine person (*hypostasis*) is plainly heretical, and the idea that she is both the eternal body of God and the eternal soul of the world (let alone the Eternal Feminine), somewhat confused. Bulgakov thought Solovyov's writings

22. Ibid., 47.
23. Based on the fact that St. Paul refers to Christ as the "wisdom" of God in 1 Cor. 1:24. For the gradual transformation of this idea in Russia see Judith Deutsch Kornblatt, *Divine Sophia*, e.g., 48–60. Solovyov sees this as a particular manifestation of the "Russian genius" in religion. It should also be noted that for some writers, especially Berdyaev, the femininity of Sophia is less important than her virginity. Sophia is the "Eternal Virgin" and therefore can be equally masculine and feminine. In the Kabbalah, each of the *sefiroth* is feminine (receptive) to the one above and masculine (active) in relation to the one below.

too syncretistic, the work of a poetic visionary seeking antecedents for his own ideas in Kabbalistic and Gnostic teachings. Closer to Florensky, it seems that Bulgakov sought and found a new level of clarity. In his book, *Sophia: The Wisdom of God*, he comes to the conclusion that Sophia is, in her divine form, to be identified with the *ousia* of God, that substance which is common to the three Persons, or which is possessed in equal measure by each of them. Sophia therefore, for Bulgakov, is the eternal Nature or self-revelation of God, the secret of the Father disclosed in the Son and Spirit—the beauty or "glory" of God ("Wisdom is the matter of glory, glory the form of Wisdom"[24]). In a certain sense, she is the divine *pleroma* or Godhead. For Bulgakov, in fact, *Sophia is the reality to which the word "consubstantial" refers in the Creed*, when we say the Son is consubstantial with the Father.

But that is the *divine* (and non-hypostatic) Sophia. There is also a "creaturely" Sophia, because the wealth of divine being is manifested outside God in creation. Here Sophia is the "foundation" on which the entire creation is established, when the Father created all things in the Son and the Spirit brought them to completion. She is at first nothing more than a "seed" containing the potentiality of the perfect divine image and likeness. But in her all the ideal forms or divine ideas contained in the Son are reflected through creation— that is, through a process of temporal becoming, at the end of which they are brought to the fullest possible likeness of divine glory by the Holy Spirit.

In this way, "Sophia unites God with the world as the one common principle, the divine ground of creaturely existence."[25] In a special way, she unites God with man as the center and sum of creation, for "Divine-humanity is the unity and complete concord of the divine and created Wisdom, of God and his creation, in

24. Sergius Bulgakov, *Sophia: The Wisdom of God* (Hudson, NY: Lindisfarne, 1993), 50. See also 30–36. This book was published in 1937. The trilogy where his theology of Sophia and divine humanity was worked out, beginning with *The Lamb of God* and *The Comforter*, culminated in *The Bride of the Lamb*, completed in 1939 but not published until 1945.

25. Bulgakov, *Sophia: The Wisdom of God*, 74.

the person of the Word."[26] This is a retrieval of Solovyov's idea of "godmanhood." In the Holy Trinity, "the Son and the Holy Spirit together constitute Divine-humanity," as the self-revelation of the Father in the Holy Trinity.[27]

For Bulgakov, the Incarnation of God as man is only possible because of this "Divine-humanity," the fact that from eternity the Word or Son of God was somehow already "human." This means that the uniting of the two natures in Jesus Christ is not the forcing together of two "alien principles" in some kind of chimera, but supernaturally natural or appropriate—even, in a sense, "expected," being the fulfillment of the divine design in nature.[28] Becoming a human creature, the Word relinquishes the Glory that he has with the Father in the beginning (a sacrifice even the angels wonder at), but "remains in the nature of God" in order to "raise the creaturely up to the heavenly in the state of his glorification."[29] This salvation of the created world in Christ, which is the realization of Sophia as divine Glory, is known by the Eastern Fathers as *theosis*, and in the West as "divinization by grace."

Divinization

The notion that our ultimate destiny is to "become divine" is held in common by Eastern and Western Christianity. One of its foundations is this passage from the First Letter of John (1 John 3:2), which indicates that we are to become "like" God—and that this state is something *more* than the state of being a child of God. The second letter of Peter also speaks of our becoming "partakers of the divine nature" (2 Peter 1:3–4).

---

26. Ibid., 95. He goes on to say that the Eucharistic change "denotes the inclusion of the 'elements' of this world in the glorified body of Christ," since the whole world is now "a potential extension of his body" (96–7). Transubstantiation, too, is made possible by Sophia.

27. Ibid., 80. In fact, he sees in the relationship between Second and Third Hypostases—the Son and the Spirit—the archetype of the relationship between the sexes in creation, and between Christ and the Church (81, 99).

28. Ibid., 87. See Bulgakov, *The Lamb of God*, 196–7.

29. Bulgakov, *Sophia: The Wisdom of God*, 89–90.

Theosis or divinization is based on the prior union of divine and human natures in Christ, as defined at the Council of Chalcedon in 451. The God-Man is there "acknowledged in two natures which undergo no confusion, no change, no division, no separation; at no point was the difference between the natures taken away through the union, but rather the property of both natures is preserved and comes together into a single person and a single subsistent being." He is "consubstantial with the Father as regards his divinity, and the same consubstantial with us as regards his humanity."

In order to unfold what this might mean, Thomas Aquinas concentrated on the phrase "we shall see him as he is," and developed a theory of the Beatific Vision. In his view, since the creature cannot know its Creator, we can only be beatified and attain the knowledge of God if he shares with us his knowledge of himself. The place of the "idea" in ourselves by which we recognize a thing to contain that form and to be that thing is to be taken by the Essence of God himself, or we might say by the Son who is the self-knowledge of the Father. We shall see God "as he is" because we shall be able to know him as he knows himself—though (Aquinas is careful to stress) never in the *degree* to which he knows himself.

The Christian East took a different approach. After St. Gregory Palamas, it tended to distinguish the unknowable "essence" of God from the knowable and participable "energies." It is through the latter that creatures are divinized, while the former remains eternally mysterious. Yet both are divine, both uncreated, and both Trinitarian.[30]

The mystery remains intractable if God and creature are so

---

30. Councils in Constantinople in 1341, 1351, and 1368 affirmed the teaching of Gregory Palamas that it is impossible for a creature to see the essence (*ousia*) of God. Deification takes place not *via* a Beatific Vision of the essence but a mystical union with the divine energies. I find convincing Balthasar's comment on this in *Theo-Logic*, summing up the views he had laid out in detail earlier. "The triune God's self-transcendent relation lies, not in his essence, but in his freedom" (*Theo-Logic*, III, 130). In perfect self-giving, there can be no "remainder" that is not given. But the unknowability of God is preserved even in self-gift, for God reveals himself precisely as inexhaustible, as infinite depth. It seems to me that the place of the uncreated energies of Palamas is occupied by Sophia.

different that there can be no common measure between them. How can oil and water mix, how can God and man become one, how can the creature be divinized? To say that we become divine "by grace," or by some kind of participation or sharing in God's life, rather than divine by nature, is no solution. What is this "grace" that unifies us? Is it created or uncreated? And how is the distinction to be preserved, once we become one with God? (For Balthasar, the grace that unifies is itself the concrete analogy of being, fully divine and fully human—whether this be the embryo in Mary's womb or the Eucharist offered "for all.")[31]

For Bulgakov, as we have just seen, the solution to the question of *theosis* also lies in the analogy of being, in his case interpreted in terms of Sophia and godmanhood. "The real basis for the union of the two natures in Christ seems to lie in their mutual relationship as two variant forms of divine and created Wisdom. It is conceivable only because humanity is the created form of divine Wisdom, which is simply God's nature revealing itself."[32] He goes on to say that without the "analogy of being" between divine and created Wisdom, the union of natures would be a "metaphysical absurdity." The likeness between them makes it possible for human nature to "receive and make room for the divine person of the Word together with, or, more precisely, in the stead of the human person."[33]

We have seen in our discussion of the human spirit that, as Bulgakov says, "human personality is itself supernatural, and stands for the divine principle in the human makeup."[34] The analogy, or the similarity, that links the human and divine natures therefore rests on this common factor, the spirit of personality, which in man is a *created openness to the uncreated*. It is this that "makes room" in the human being for the presence of the uncreated—and in the case of Jesus of Nazareth, enables the personality of the Word to assume the entire nature of humanity.

31. See Healy, *The Eschatology of Hans Urs von Balthasar*, 214.
32. Bulgakov, *Sophia: The Wisdom of God*, 88.
33. Ibid., 85.
34. Ibid., 87.

Who Is Sophia?

I am inclined to think that in Bulgakov we are looking at an authentic theological development that illuminates our understanding of nature and creation. But before closing I want to explore a bit further this notion of Sophia as, on the one hand, the "being" or "nature" of God, and, on the other, as "creaturely Sophia," a feminine figure possessing the attributes of personality.

First, the identification of Sophia with "being." I have to confess that I don't feel entirely comfortable with this. My discomfort may have something to do with the fact that so many theologians have warned against abstracting the divine "nature" from the Trinity, as though it was something prior to or other than the nature of the Father, which is shared (and not duplicated) through the other Persons. Of course, there is a temptation to abstraction when we are talking about God as such, for example in apologetics. St. Thomas does this, and in fact it is impossible to avoid if we want to make clear that the three Persons subsist in a single nature. Yet to equate the divine or heavenly Sophia with this unity of nature, or with divinity *per se*, seems to confuse things. Bulgakov himself says that *ousia* is not hypostasized.

What of creaturely Sophia? Hans Urs von Balthasar treats the difference between worldly and divine being according to St. Thomas in the fourth volume of *The Glory of the Lord*, where he describes *esse commune* as "*creaturely reality in so far as it is seen and conceived as the all-embracing manifestation of God*" and the "kingdom of beauty" (374–5); in terms, that is, very similar to those that Bulgakov applies to creaturely Sophia. And at the end of the fifth volume Balthasar describes it again as "Nothing substantial and subsistent, therefore, but the radiant fullness of God's Being in the condition of its being given to the finite recipient."[35] This makes it possible to identify creaturely Sophia with the common being of created things, or *esse non subsistens*. But this does not immediately enable us to identify a personal reality, a "she." No more than the *ousia* of

---

35. Balthasar, *The Glory of the Lord*, V, 631.

God can this "common being" be identified as an existent entity in its own right, since it is only realized in existing things.

So where does the feminine and "personal" quality of Sophia come from? Pavel Florensky hints at the answer when he says that "being for the Triune Divinity one and the same, she, in herself, is different in her relation to the Hypostases. The idea of Sophia acquires one shade or another depending upon toward what Hypostasis [Father, Son, or Holy Spirit] we predominantly direct our contemplation."[36] And Bulgakov writes, "The Divine Sophia can be defined both in relation to the entire Holy Trinity in its unity (which is without separation) and in relation to each of the hypostases (which are inconfusable and inseparable)."[37] One may think therefore of Sophia either in the abstract in relation to Divinity as such (but does she exist "in abstract"?), or in the concrete in relation to one or other of the divine hypostases. It is in the latter case that she assumes her personal identity, just as we ourselves assume an eternal personal identity only by virtue of our relationship to the Son of God and thus through our inclusion in the life of the Trinity, "between" the Persons.

In the end, it seems, nothing can exist except persons, and things incorporated in persons. That goes for mankind and for the universe as a whole. We may say, with Bulgakov, that Sophia is "hypostasized" as the Dyad of Son and Spirit within the Trinity, as the self-revelation of the father. But perhaps one may also say more than this. Perhaps one may say that, just as the individual human being is raised up into an eternal person by the love of God, creaturely Sophia is hypostasized in a series of stages, by each of the divine Persons in turn, until she incorporates the entire creation and is reunited with (or becomes) the divine Sophia.

The first face adopted by Sophia—that is, worldly substance—(through her direct relationship to the Persons of the Trinity) is that of the Virgin Mary, the so-called spouse of the Holy Spirit and Mother of the Son at the Annunciation. As such Mary is the first

36. Florensky, *The Pillar and Ground of the Truth*, 252.
37. Bulgakov, *The Lamb of God*, 110–111.

face, the personality, of creaturely Sophia. But as new members are added to the Church and the body of the faithful grows, Sophia acquires a second "face," a second personality; that of *Ecclesia*, the Church. No longer the spouse of the Holy Spirit, Sophia as *Ecclesia* is the Bride of the Lamb (as glimpsed at the end of the Book of Revelation). Here we must appeal to the fact that the Church is no mere fellowship or society of individuals, as we tend to think of her, but *by virtue of the very real unity in Christ brought about by the Holy Spirit, the "soul" of the Church,* she is a genuine personality, a corporate person.

There is a third stage, however; and this is the eschatological fulfillment of the process. Once united with her spouse in the Passion, *Ecclesia* and Christ together form a genuine unity that is not identical with either of them, a new unity or person that we might now call the "Bride of the Father." This is Sophia in her highest manifestation. As the Son united with the Church, and in that unity offered to the Father through the Spirit, she is able to clothe the Father and give him a home in the new heavens and the new earth, being now indistinguishable from *Shekinah* (Glory), foreshadowed in the epiphany of the Burning Bush and in the cloud that filled the Lord's Temple to manifest his presence:[38]

> Wisdom is therefore the glory which was the Son's at the side of the Father before the creation of the world, a glory the Father bestows on him through his crucifixion in historical time, a glory which the glorified Son will then impart to the faithful when he gives them the Spirit, the Spirit of filiation, the Spirit of the Father and of the Son. Or rather, Wisdom tends through its whole being, in God as in ourselves, toward that divine glory which God gives

---

38. This connects with St. Paul's otherwise strange description of woman as "the glory of the man" in 1 Corinthians 11:7, a phrase whose depths have been noted by the Victorian poet Coventry Patmore, for example in *The Rod, the Root, and the Flower* (London: Bell & Sons, 1923). See also Bulgakov's own comments in *The Comforter*, transl. Boris Jakim (Grand Rapids, MI: Eerdmans, 2004), 366–7, where he says that just as the Logos is Sophia (but not vice versa), and the Holy Spirit is Sophia (but not vice versa), so the Father is Sophia (but not vice versa), because she reveals him "in all the power of divine Fatherhood." Ultimately, "Sophia, as Divine-humanity, *belongs* to the Father; she is *His* revelation."

to no other, but which is nevertheless destined to clothe all things, since all things . . . derive from the Father through the Son only to return to him in the Spirit.[39]

Sophia is not, therefore, a fourth hypostasis in relation to the Trinity, but is the creation, or let us say, the divine Imagination, hypostasized in relation to each of the three Persons in turn.[40] And if she were not this, in fact, there would be no hope for us, because Sophia is simply the corporate *theosis* in which we are called to participate as individuals. She is in her own person the totality of "what God gains from the world." She contains nothing that is not in God, no ideas but those that are already part of the Logos or Son of God, and yet is eternally distinct from God as he exists in himself, being what we might call the eternal *blazing out* of his glory, of which he himself is the eternal witness.

The White Rose

Paradoxes and confusions are unavoidable, since we are talking from within the world of time-and-limitation of eternity, infinity, and nothingness. The idea of creation *ex nihilo* simply means that God needed no pre-existing matter, even chaotic matter or prime matter, to make the world. Nor was he determined to create the world by anything other than his own will. But that does not exclude a creation *ex deo et in deo*. Uncreated Nature or Sophia can be said both to precede creation and to follow it, to be its perfection.[41] Created

---

39. Bouyer, *Cosmos*, 192. On all of this see also Bouyer's fine work, *The Seat of Wisdom: An Essay on the Place of the Virgin Mary in Christian Theology* (New York: Pantheon Books, 1962).

40. This in fact is very close to what John Zizioulas says in *Communion and Otherness*, 66–76. But for him it is in Christ that the Church and the whole of nature is hypostasized and rendered eternal, whereas the sophiologist emphasizes the reality of the nuptial relationship through which the creature is hypostasized in God. For both, "There is no escape from personhood in Christian cosmology" (66). In Western terms, the *actus completus non subsistens* is realized only in individual beings, but such beings include those "persons" in whom Sophia acquires a personal identity: the Blessed Virgin Mary, and *Ecclesia*.

41. "All of creation has in God a supratemporal foundation and through this foundation participates in eternity, for creaturely Sophia is the image of the Divine

nature is separated from the Uncreated by the process of time, but when time is completed then the creature is "divinized" and the two are one. The overcoming of the separation is not an automatic process but is brought about by the exercise of freedom. In no other way could the world be a manifestation of love.

Why is all this important (apart from the fact that getting to the truth is the most important thing there is)? It is important because, as John Milbank recognizes, sophiology by-passes or undercuts or even solves the whole nature-grace dynamic in Western thought, which is the root of modern secularism and many of the problems of our civilization.[42] As Henri de Lubac argues, from soon after the time of Aquinas, "nature" had been constructed by theologians as a backdrop for the drama of salvation and soon achieved a kind of notional autonomy, allowing a mentality to flourish in which reference to God became increasingly unlikely, the "hypothesis" of God unnecessary. The challenge of explaining the universe passed to science, and the result was a drastic narrowing of human reason. Meanwhile, faith was reduced to a set of dogmatic and moral assertions and a cultural heritage all too easily dispensed with. By contrast, the sophiologists offer something that our times need: a potentially coherent account of nature intrinsically related to God, and humanity as called to a divine destiny.

In the final Canto of Dante's Paradiso we see that divine destiny embodied in the white rose, above the *Primum Mobile*, an image of the Empyrean, the unmoving sphere of living light or "heaven of divine peace" within which all the others revolve. It is here that Dante finds first his beloved Beatrice and then—at its golden heart —the Blessed Virgin Mary, before glimpsing the Trinity and the mystery of the divine-human Son. Here is the bliss that lies beyond our laughter and our tears. It is a vision of Sophia, the Kingdom for

Sophia" (Bulgakov, *The Bride of the Lamb*, 123). The descent of the Lamb's bride at the end of the world in the Book of Revelation (Rev. 21:2) represents the reintegration of creaturely with divine Sophia.

42. John Milbank, *The Suspended Middle* (London: SCM, 2008), and "Sophiology and Theurgy: The New Theological Horizon" (2007), a working paper at http://theologyphilosophycentre.co.uk/online-papers/.

whose coming we pray in every *Paternoster*, to which each of us is connected in the deepest recesses of our soul, in the spirit that makes us persons, where God's love waits for us in glory and peace.[43]

43. See Christian Moevs, *The Metaphysics of Dante's Comedy* (Oxford University Press, 2005). The Empyrean in turn is compared to the spirit as center of the soul, by Teresa of Avila in *The Interior Castle*, VII, 2, 9 (in *Collected Works*). The spirit is for the microcosm what Sophia or the Empyrean is for the world as a whole. Cf. Plotinus, *Enneads* 5, Tractate 1, transl. Stephen MacKenna (London: Faber & Faber, 1969), 10–12.

Conclusion

I begin this final summary with a quotation from Joseph Ratzinger, not as an appeal to authority, but because I recognize in these particular words so many of the themes that I tried to explore in the preceding chapters, and a vision similar to the one I have glimpsed in writing them.

> We have to make evident once more what is meant by the world's having been created "in wisdom".... Only then can conscience and norm enter again into proper relationship. For then it will become clear that conscience is not some individualistic (or collective) calculation; rather it is a "*con-sciens*," a "knowing along with" creation and, through creation, with God the Creator. Then, too, it will be rediscovered that man's greatness does not lie in the miserable autonomy of some midget proclaiming himself his one and only master, but in the fact that his being allows the highest wisdom, truth itself, to shine through. Then it will become clear that man is so much the greater the more he is capable of hearing the profound message of creation, the message of the Creator. And then it will be apparent how harmony with creation, whose wisdom becomes our norm, does not mean a limitation upon our freedom but is rather an expression of our reason and our dignity. Then the body also is given its due honor: it is no longer something "used," but is the temple of authentic human dignity because it is God's handiwork in the world. Then is the equal dignity of man and woman made manifest precisely in the fact that they are different. One will then begin to understand once again that their bodiliness reaches the metaphysical depths and is the basis of a symbolic metaphysics whose denial or neglect does not ennoble man but destroys him.[1]

---

1. Joseph Cardinal Ratzinger, "Fundamental Characteristics of the Present Crisis of Faith," *L'Osservatore Romano*, July 24, 1989.

A symbolic metaphysics that ennobles man and the entire natural cosmos, the world of nature, that was my goal.

The world is in God. The cosmos is one, being an image of the One God, subsisting in God, and everything in it is related to everything else, analogously to the way each Person in God is related to each other. At the center of this analogy of being and holding it together is man, or rather the Man-God, in whom all the elements are reflected and to whom they are given—who is the "concrete analogy of being."

Through man, nature has a direct link to God deeper than its own creation, namely the intellect or spirit, like a shaft or opening connecting him to the Infinite, which appears like a spark deep inside him. This is the uncreated and unfallen element in man, which makes it possible for him to be united with God in his own ground. It is the source of his freedom and identity, from which he is exiled by sin.

This "seventh chamber" of the soul (as described by St. Teresa of Avila) opens onto the "tenth heaven" or Empyrean around which the universe turns. This is the world blossoming in eternity like Dante's white rose. It is the Glory and Wisdom of God (Sophia), the world perfected, the Virgin Mary crowned in heaven, and all in her divinized by grace.

The only mediator between heaven and earth is Jesus Christ, true man and true God. In the heart of man and of human history (which in an unfallen world would still have been located in Eden) he assumes our nature. Into the womb of Mary and with her consent, instead of breathing the limited spirit of a man, he breathes the Holy Spirit, the divine nature, making Jesus the Son of God.

This introduces eternity into the midst of time, and makes the finite a sacrament of the infinite. It makes the son of Mary the one fully human being who is also a divine Person. This does not leave the rest of the world unaffected, not least because, the world being fallen, Jesus Christ is now its only hope of passage back to the world of heavenly Sophia from which we were exiled. The bridge or "magnetic field" that draws all men to Christ is the Holy Spirit of divine love, arousing the love of man and giving it a direction. It leads all of creation through the Cross to resurrection and ascension.

Earthly Sophia is the nature of creation fallen in Eve and born again in Mary, growing by the grace of the Holy Spirit into the Church, united on the Cross with all creation in the eternal offering of the Son to the Father, ultimately to be reunited with the heavenly Sophia who waits outside time for the fulfillment and joy of all things.

The Radiance of Being

Chesterton points out that when respectable people objected to the acclamation of Jesus by guttersnipes in the streets, he answered, "*I tell you, if these were silent, the very stones would cry out*" (Luke 19: 40). And so it proved, for "[u]nder the impulse of his spirit arose like a clamorous chorus the facades of the mediaeval cathedrals, thronged with shouting faces and open mouths. The prophecy has fulfilled itself: the very stones cry out."[2]

Even the undressed stones cry out, for those who have ears to hear their voices and their groaning. For those who have ears to hear the parables of Jesus, it is clear that the whole world speaks of God, and calls us to him. Those whose ears can hear the music, and whose eyes are open to the light that cascades from on high, flooding up from within all things, are blessed. *They shall see God*, for their hearts are pure:

> Whoever, therefore, is not enlightened by such splendor of created things is blind; whoever is not awakened by such outcries is deaf; whoever does not praise God because of all these effects is dumb; whoever does not discover the First Principle from such clear signs is a fool. Therefore open your eyes, alert the ears of your spirit, open your lips and apply your heart, so that in all creatures you may see, hear, praise, love and worship, glorify and honor your God, lest the whole world rise against you.[3]

One of the most appealing features of the Asian religious traditions is the intense appreciation of the *radiance of being* that we see

---

2. G.K. Chesterton, *Collected Works*, Vol. I, 307 (from *Orthodoxy*).
3. Bonaventure, *The Soul's Journey Into God, The Tree of Life, The Life of St Francis*, transl. by Ewert Cousins, Classics of Western Spirituality (London: SPCK, 1978), 67–8.

expressed, for example, in Chinese landscape painting or Japanese Haiku poetry. Mountains and waterfalls half-emerge from the mist, an echo in the forest evokes memories of spring. The fragility and transience of life is perfectly realized, along with the infinite value of each moment, partly because it hangs over an abyss of non-existence. The poignancy of this realization is something true and valid. It must be preserved, and deepened if possible, in any Christian account of Being.

Now that Christ has come, we see the depth of creation. Now that Christ has come, we can see everywhere the exchange of love by which the world was made, and is, and becomes; each thing and each person taking what is given by every other thing and person; and, if it does not give back, descending into darkness. And in the end, we shall see all things in God, as he does.

The world is entirely relational, constituted (that is) by its relation to God, all substance being the gift of God, received and given back to God by ourselves, and by God to himself. I who receive and am given, am in God receiving and giving, God being within me as the gift of myself and yet not myself, loving that which is in me that is not himself, the Father loving the Son in the Spirit.

The world is born in darkness as light, in the womb of the Trinity that is entirely luminous because the act of loving is all act and entirely act, being that which is given and received. All peace and all beauty are found in that darkness. The darkness is the light that cannot be seen because it sees all things, and it is the freedom to be, just as it is the freedom to love, because to be is to love and to love is to be.

Bibliography

Alexander, Christopher. *The Timeless Way of Building*. Oxford University Press, 1979.

Anon. [Valentin Tomberg]. *Meditations on the Tarot: A Journey into Christian Hermeticism*, trans. Robert A. Powell. Amity, NY: Amity House, 1985.

Aquinas, Saint Thomas. *Catena Aurea: Commentary on the Four Gospels*, Vol. 4, Part 1. Oxford: John Henry Parker, 1845.

_____. *Summa Contra Gentiles*, Books 1–4, trans. Anton C. Pegis FRSC. University of Notre Dame Press, 1975.

_____. *Thomas Aquinas: Selected Writings*, ed. M.C. D'Arcy. London: Dent, 1939.

Aristotle. *Aristotle's Metaphysics*, trans. Joe Sachs. Santa Fe: Green Lion Press, 2002.

Augustine, Saint. *Augustine: Later Works*, ed. John Burnaby. Philadelphia: Westminster Press, 1955.

Balthasar, Hans Urs von. *Cosmic Liturgy: The Universe According to Maximus the Confessor*. San Francisco: Ignatius Press, 2003.

_____. *Dare We Hope "That All Men be Saved"? with a Short Discourse on Hell*. San Francisco: Ignatius Press, 1988.

_____. *Explorations in Theology*, II, "Spouse of the Word," trans. John Saward. San Francisco: Ignatius Press, 1991.

_____. *The Glory of the Lord: A Theological Aesthetics*, Volumes I–VII. Edinburgh and San Francisco: T&T Clark and Ignatius Press, 1982–91.

_____. *Theo-Drama: Theological Dramatic Theory*, Volumes I–V. San Francisco: Ignatius Press, 1988–98.

_____. *Theo-Logic: Theological Logical Theory*, Volumes I–III. San Francisco: Ignatius Press, 2000–2005.

Barr, Stephen M. *Modern Physics and Ancient Faith*. University of Notre Dame Press, 2003.

Berdyaev, Nicolas. *Freedom and the Spirit*. London: Geoffrey Bles, 1935.

_____. *The Meaning of the Creative Act*. London: Gollancz, 1955.

Berman, Morris. *The Reenchantment of the World*. Cornell University Press, 1981.

Blanchette, Oliva. *Maurice Blondel: A Philosophical Life*. Grand Rapids: Eerdmans, 2010.

Boehme, Jacob. *Mysterium Magnum: An Exposition of the First Book of*

Moses Called Genesis. London: John M. Watkins, 1965.
_____. *Six Theosophic Points and Other Writings.* Ann Arbor: University of Michigan Press, 1958.
Bohm, David. *Wholeness and the Implicate Order.* London: RKP, 1980.
Bolton, Robert. *The Order of the Ages: World History in the Light of a Universal Cosmogony.* Ghent, NY: Sophia Perennis, 2001.
Bonaventure, Saint. *The Soul's Journey Into God, The Tree of Life, The Life of St Francis,* trans. by Ewert Cousins, Classics of Western Spirituality. London: SPCK, 1978.
Borella, Jean. *Guénonian Esoterism and Christian Mystery.* Hillsdale, NY: Sophia Perennis, 2004.
_____. *The Secret of the Christian Way: A Contemplative Ascent Through the Writings of Jean Borella.* SUNY Press, 2001.
_____. *The Sense of the Supernatural.* Edinburgh: T&T Clark, 1998.
Bortoft, Henri. *The Wholeness of Nature: Goethe's Way of Science.* Hudson, NY: Lindisfarne and Edinburgh: Floris Books, 1996.
Bouyer, Louis. *Cosmos: The World and the Glory of God.* Petersham, MA: St. Bede's Publications, 1988.
_____. *The Invisible Father: Approaches to the Mystery of the Divinity.* Edinburgh: T&T Clark, 1999.
_____. *The Seat of Wisdom: An Essay on the Place of the Virgin Mary in Christian Theology.* New York: Pantheon Books, 1962.
Brague, Rémi. *The Law of God: The Philosophical History of an Idea.* Chicago University Press, 2007.
Brooke, John, and Geoffrey Cantor. *Reconstructing Nature: The Engagement of Science and Religion.* Edinburgh: T&T Clark, 1998.
Bulgakov, Sergius. *The Bride of the Lamb,* trans. Boris Jakim. Grand Rapids: Eerdmans, 2002.
_____. *The Comforter,* trans. Boris Jakim. Grand Rapids: Eerdmans, 2004.
_____. *Jacob's Ladder: On Angels,* trans. Boris Jakim. Grand Rapids: Eerdmans, 2010.
_____. *The Lamb of God,* trans. Boris Jakim. Grand Rapids: Eerdmans, 2008.
_____. *Sophia: The Wisdom of God.* Hudson, NY: Lindisfarne, 1993.
Burrell SJ, David B. *Knowing the Unknowable God: Ibn-Sina, Maimonides, Aquinas.* University of Notre Dame Press, 1986.
_____. *Towards a Jewish-Christian-Muslim Theology.* Oxford: Wiley-Blackwell, 2011.
Caldecott, Stratford. *All Things Made New: The Mysteries of the World in*

Bibliography

Christ. San Rafael, CA: Angelico Press/ Sophia Perennis, 2011.

————. *Beauty for Truth's Sake: On the Re-enchantment of Education*. Grand Rapids: Brazos, 2009.

————. editor. *Beyond the Prosaic: Reviving the Liturgical Movement*. Edinburgh: T&T Clark, 1998.

————. *Catholicism and Other Religions: Explaining Interfaith Dialogue*. London: CTS, 2008.

Capra, Fritjof. *The Tao of Physics: An Exploration of the Parallels between Modern Physics and Eastern Mysticism*. London: Fontana, 1983.

————. *The Web of Life*. London: HarperCollins, 1996.

Carey, John. *A Single Ray of the Sun: Religious Speculation in Early Ireland*. Andover, MA: Celtic Studies Publications, 1999.

Chesterton, G.K. *Collected Works*, Vol. I. San Francisco: Ignatius Press, 1986.

————. *Collected Works*, Vol. II. San Francisco: Ignatius Press, 1986.

————. *Generally Speaking*. London: Methuen, 1928.

Chittick, William C. *Imaginal Worlds: Ibn al-'Arabi and the Problem of Religious Diversity*. SUNY Press, 1994.

————. *The Self-Disclosure of God*. SUNY Press, 1998.

————. *The Sufi Path of Knowledge*. SUNY Press, 1989.

Clément, Oliver. *The Roots of Christian Mysticism*. London: New City, 1993.

Coomaraswamy, A.K. *Coomaraswamy 2: Selected Papers, Metaphysics*, edited by Roger Lipsey, Bollingen Series LXXXIX. Princeton University Press, 1977.

————. *Hinduism and Buddhism*. New Delhi: Munshiram Manoharlal Publishers, 1975.

————. *Time and Eternity*. New Delhi: Munshiram Manoharlal Publishers, 1993.

————. *The Vedas: Essays in Translation and Exegesis*. Beckenham: Prologos Books, 1976.

Cunningham, Conor. *Darwin's Pious Idea: Why the Ultra-Darwinists and Creationists Both Get it Wrong*. Grand Rapids: Eerdmans, 2010.

Davie, Ian. *Jesus Purusha: A Vedanta-Based Doctrine of Jesus*. New York: Inner Traditions/ Lindisfarne Press, 1985.

D'Costa, Gavin, ed. *The Catholic Church and the World Religions: A Theological and Phenomenological Account*. London: T&T Clark International, 2011.

————. *Theology and Religious Pluralism*. Oxford: Blackwell, 1986.

Deane-Drummond, Celia. *Christ and Evolution: Wonder and Wisdom*. London: SCM Press, 2009.

————. *Eco-Theology*. London: Darton, Longman & Todd, 2008.

Dennett, Daniel. *Darwin's Dangerous Idea: Evolution and the Meanings of Life*. Harmondsworth: Allen Lane, The Penguin Press, 1995.

DiNoia, J.A. *The Diversity of Religions: A Christian Perspective*. Washington, DC: Catholic University of America Press, 1992.

Dupré, Louis. *Passage to Modernity*. New Haven and London: Yale University Press, 1993.

Eckhart, Meister. *Meister Eckhart: The Essential Sermons, Commentaries, Treatises, and Defense*, trans. Edmund College OSA and Bernard McGinn. New York: Paulist Press, 1981.

————. *Meister Eckhart: Selected Treatises and Sermons*, trans. James M. Clark and John V. Skinner. London: Faber & Faber, 1958.

————. *Meister Eckhart: Sermons and Treatises*, Vol. 1 and 2, trans. and edited by M.O'C. Walshe. Shaftesbury: Element Books, 1987.

Ephrem the Syrian, Saint. *Hymns on Paradise*, trans. Sebastian Brock. Crestwood, NY: St. Vladimir's Seminary Press, 1990.

Faivre, Antoine. *Access to Western Esotericism*. SUNY Press, 1994.

————. *Theosophy, Imagination, Tradition: Studies in Western Esotericism*. SUNY Press, 2000.

Faivre, Antoine, and Jacob Needleman, editors. *Modern Esoteric Spirituality*. London: SCM Press, 1992.

Florensky, Pavel, *The Pillar and Ground of the Truth*. Princeton University Press, 1997.

Francis of Assisi, Saint, and Saint Clare of Assisi. *Francis and Clare: The Complete Works, Classics of Western Spirituality*. London: SPCK, 1982.

Gawronski SJ, Raymond. *Word and Silence: Hans Urs von Balthasar and the Spiritual Encounter between East and West*. Edinburgh and Grand Rapids: T&T Clark and Eerdmans, 1995.

Gilson, Etienne. *History of Christian Philosophy in the Middle Ages*. London: Sheed & Ward, 1955.

Goodwin, Brian. *How the Leopard Changed its Spots*. London: Weidenfeld & Nicolson, 1994.

Gould, Steven J. *The Panda's Thumb*. New York: W.W. Norton, 1980.

Grant RSCJ, Sara. *Toward an Alternative Theology: Confessions of a Non-Dualist Christian*. University of Notre Dame Press, 2002.

Guardini, Romano. *The Lord*. Chicago: Regnery Gateway, 1954.

Healy, Nicholas J., and D.C. Schindler, eds. *Being Holy in the World: Theology and Culture in the Thought of David L. Schindler*. Grand Rapids: Eerdmans, 2011.

————. *The Eschatology of Hans Urs von Balthasar: Being as Communion*. Oxford University Press, 2008.

Bibliography

Hodgson, Peter. *Science and Belief in the Nuclear Age*. Ann Arbor: Sapientia Press of Ave Maria University, 2005.

Houédard OSB, Dom Sylvester. *Commentaries on Meister Eckhart Sermons*. Roxburgh: Beshara Publications, 2000.

Ibn Al-'Arabi. *Ibn Al-'Arabi: The Bezels of Wisdom*, trans. R.W.J. Austin. New York: Paulist Press, 1980.

Irenaeus, Saint. *The Scandal of the Incarnation: Irenaeus Against the Heresies*, trans. John Saward. San Francisco: Ignatius Press, 1990.

Izutsu, Toshihiko. *Sufism and Taoism: A Comparative Study of Key Philosophical Concepts*. University of California Press, 1983.

Jaki, S.L. *The Road of Science and the Ways to God*. University of Chicago Press, 1978.

John Paul II, Pope. *Redemptor Hominis*. Vatican City: Vatican Press, 1979.

Jones, Deborah. *The School of Compassion: A Roman Catholic Theology of Animals*. Leominster: Gracewing, 2009.

Journet, Charles. *The Dark Knowledge of God*. London: Sheed & Ward, 1948.

Keeble, Brian. *God and Work: Aspects of Art and Tradition*. Bloomington, IN: World Wisdom Books, 2009.

Kelley, C.F. *Meister Eckhart on Divine Knowledge*. New Haven: Yale University Press, 1977.

Kenny, Anthony. *A Path from Rome*. Oxford University Press, 1986.

Kornblatt, Judith Deutsch. *Divine Sophia: The Wisdom Writings of Vladimir Solovyov*. Ithaca: Cornell University Press, 2009.

Le Fanu, James. *Why Us? How Science Rediscovered the Mystery of Ourselves*. London: Harper Press, 2009.

Lewis, C.S. *The Abolition of Man*. London: Geoffrey Bles, 1946.

Lings, Martin. *Muhammad: His Life Based on the Earliest Sources*. Cambridge: Islamic Texts Society, 1991.

Lodahl, Michael. *Claiming Abraham: Reading the Bible and the Qur'an Side by Side*. Grand Rapids: Brazos Press, 2010.

Long-ch'en Rab-jam-pa; H.H. Dudjom Rinpoche; and Beru Khyentze Rinpoche. *The Four-Themed Precious Garland: An Introduction to Dzog Ch'en*, The Library of Tibetan Works and Archives of His Holiness the Dalai Lama. Dharamsala, 1979.

Lubac SJ, Henri de. *Aspects of Buddhism*. London: Sheed & Ward, 1953.

———. *Theology in History*. San Francisco: Ignatius Press, 1996.

Lyons, J.A. *The Cosmic Christ in Origen and Teilhard de Chardin*. Oxford University Press, 1982.

MacDonald, George. *The Wind from the Stars*. London: HarperCollins, 1992.

Majid, Shahn ed. *On Space and Time*. Cambridge University Press, 2008.

Maritain, Jacques. *Creative Intuition in Art and Poetry*. London: Harvill Press, 1953.

————. *The Degrees of Knowledge*. London: Geoffrey Bless, 1937.

Maximus the Confessor. *On the Cosmic Mystery of Jesus Christ*. Crestwood, NY: St. Vladimir's Seminary Press, 2003.

McGinn, Bernard. *The Mystical Thought of Meister Eckhart: The Man From Whom God Hid Nothing*. New York: Crossroad, 2001.

Mersch SJ, Emile. *The Theology of the Mystical Body*. St Louis: Herder, 1951.

Merton, Thomas. *Conjectures of a Guilty Bystander*. New York: Doubleday Image, 1968.

————. *Seeds of Contemplation*. London: Hollis & Carter, 1949.

Midgely, Mary. *Evolution as a Religion: Strange Hopes and Stranger Fears*. Methuen, 1985.

Milbank, John. *The Suspended Middle*. London: SCM, 2008.

Milosz, O.V. de L. *The Noble Traveller*, ed. Christopher Bamford. New York: Inner Traditions/Lindisfarne, 1985.

Moevs, Christian. *The Metaphysics of Dante's Comedy*. Oxford University Press, 2005.

Monk of the West. *Christianity and the Doctrine of Non-Dualism*. Hillsdale, NY: Sophia Perennis, 2004.

Morris, Simon Conway. *Life's Solution: Inevitable Humans in a Lonely Universe*. Cambridge University Press, 2004.

Murata, Sachiko, and William C. Chittick. *The Vision of Islam: The Foundations of Muslim Faith and Practice*. London: I.B. Tauris, 1996.

Murphy, Francesca A. *Christ the Form of Beauty*. Edinburgh: T&T Clark, 1995.

Nasr, Seyyed Hossein. *The Encounter of Man and Nature*. London: George Allen & Unwin, 1968.

————. *The Heart of Islam: Enduring Values for Humanity*. Harper SanFrancisco, 2004.

————. *Religion and the Order of Nature*. Oxford University Press, 1996.

Naydler, J., editor. *Goethe on Science: An Anthology of Goethe's Scientific Writings*. Edinburgh: Floris Books, 1996.

Nebelsick, Harold P. *Renaissance and Reformation and the Rise of Science*. Edinburgh: T&T Clark, 1992.

Nesteruk, Alexei V. *Light from the East: Theology, Science and the Eastern Orthodox Tradition*. Minneapolis: Fortress Press, 2003.

Newman, John Henry. *An Essay in Aid of a Grammar of Assent*. University of Notre Dame Press, 1979.

Nichols OP, Aidan. *A Key to Balthasar: Hans Urs von Balthasar on Beauty, Goodness, and Truth*. London: Darton, Longman & Todd, 2011.

Nicolescu, Basarab. *Science, Meaning and Evolution*. New York: Parabola Books, 1991.

Nikodimos of the Holy Mountain, Saint, and Saint Makarios of Corinth. *The Philokalia*, II, trans. G.E.H. Palmer, Philip Sherrard and Kallistos Ware. London: Faber & Faber, 1981.

Norbu, Namkhai. *The Crystal and the Way of Light*. London: Routledge & Kegan Paul, 1986.

O'Collins SJ, Gerald, and Mary Ann Meyers, editors. *Light from Light: Scientists and Theologians in Dialogue*. Grand Rapids: Eerdmans, 2012.

O'Hanlon SJ, G.F. *The Immutability of God in the Theology of Hans Urs von Balthasar*. Cambridge University Press, 1990.

Pabst, Adrian. *Metaphysics: The Creation of Hierarchy*. Grand Rapids: Eerdmans, 2012.

Panikkar, Raimundo. *The Vedic Experience Mantramanjari: An Anthology of the Vedas for Modern Man and Contemporary Celebration*. London: DLT, 1977.

Patmore, Coventry. *The Poems of Coventry Patmore*, ed. Frederick Page. Oxford University Press, 1949.

_____. *The Rod, the Root, and the Flower*. London: Bell & Sons, 1923.

Pearlman, Barry R. *A Certain Faith: Analogy of Being and the Affirmation of Belief*. Lanham: University Press of America, 2012.

Pegis, Anton C. *St Thomas and the Greeks*. Marquette Univ. Press, 1980.

Philippe OP, Marie-Dominique. *Wherever He Goes: A Retreat on the Gospel of John*. Laredo, TX: Congregation of St John, 1998.

Pickstock, Catherine. *After Writing*. Oxford: Blackwell, 1998.

Pieper, Josef. *Living the Truth*. San Francisco: Ignatius Press, 1989.

Plato. *Plato: Complete Works*, ed. John M. Cooper. Indianapolis: Hackett, 1997.

_____. *Timaeus and Critias*, trans. Robin Waterfield. Oxford University Press, 2008.

Plotinus. *The Enneads*, trans. Stephen MacKenna. London: Faber & Faber, 1969.

Polanyi, Michael. *Personal Knowledge: Towards a Post-Critical Philosophy*. University of Chicago Press, 1958.

Ratzinger, Cardinal Joseph. *Introduction to Christianity*. San Francisco: Ignatius Press, 2004.

_____. (Pope Benedict XVI). *Jesus of Nazareth*, Part 2: Holy Week. San Francisco: Ignatius Press, 2011.

_____. *Salt of the Earth: The Church at the End of the Millennium*, An Interview with Peter Seewald. San Francisco: Ignatius Press, 1997.

Rose, Seraphim. *Genesis, Creation and Early Man: The Orthodox*

Christian Vision. Platina, CA: Saint Herman of Alaska Brotherhood, 2000.

Rowland, Tracey. *Benedict XVI: A Guide for the Perplexed*. London: T&T Clark, 2010.

Russell, Robert J., William R. Stoeger SJ and George V. Coyne eds. *John Paul II on Science and Religion: Reflections on the New View from Rome*. The University of Notre Dame Press, 1990.

Schall SJ, James V. *The Regensburg Lecture*. South Bend, IN: St Augustine's Press, 2007.

Scheffczyk, Leo. *Creation and Providence*. London: Burns & Oates, 1970.

Schindler, D.C. *Hans Urs von Balthasar and the Dramatic Structure of Truth: A Philosophical Investigation*. NY: Fordham Univ. Press, 2004.

Schindler, David L., editor. *Beyond Mechanism: The Universe in Recent Physics and Catholic Thought*. Lanham, MD: University Press of America, 1986.

———. *Heart of the World, Center of the Church*. Grand Rapids and Edinburgh: Eerdmans and T&T Clark, 1996.

———. *Ordering Love: Liberal Societies and the Memory of the Good*. Grand Rapids: Eerdmans, 2011.

Schmemann, Alexander. *For the Life of the World*. Crestwood, NY: St. Vladimir's Seminary Press, 2000.

Schmitz, Kenneth L. *At the Center of the Human Drama*. Washington, DC: Catholic University of America Press, 1993.

———. *The Gift: Creation*. Marquette University Press, 1982.

———. *The Recovery of Wonder: The New Freedom and the Asceticism of Power*. McGill-Queen's University Press, 2005.

Schuon, Frithjof. *Dimensions of Islam*. London: Allen & Unwin, 1969.

———. *From the Divine to the Human*. Bloomington, IN: World Wisdom Books, 1982.

———. *The Fullness of God: Frithjof Schuon on Christianity*, ed. James S. Cutsinger. Bloomington, IN: World Wisdom Books, 2004.

———. *Survey of Metaphysics and Esoterism*. Bloomington, IN: World Wisdom Books, 1986.

———. *The Transcendent Unity of Religions*. Wheaton, IL: Theosophical Publishing House, 1984.

Schurmann, Heinz, Joseph Ratzinger, and Hans Urs von Balthasar. *Principles of Christian Morality*. San Francisco: Ignatius Press, 1986.

Serretti, Massimo, editor. *The Uniqueness and Universality of Jesus Christ: In Dialogue with the Religions*, trans. Teresa Talavera and David C. Schindler. Grand Rapids: Eerdmans, 2001.

Shah-Kazemi, Reza. *The Other in the Light of the One: The Universality of the Qur'an and Interfaith Dialogue.* Cambridge: Islamic Texts Society, 2006.

Sherrard, Philip. *Christianity: Lineaments of a Sacred Tradition.* Brookline, MA: Holy Cross Orthodox Press, 1998.

_____. *Human Image: World Image.* Ipswich: Golgonooza Press, 1992.

Shortt, Rupert. *Christianophobia: A Faith Under Attack.* London: Rider, 2012.

Smith, Wolfgang. *Ancient Wisdom & Modern Misconceptions: A Critique of Contemporary Scientism.* Tacoma WA: Angelico Press/Sophia Perennis, 2013.

_____. *Christian Gnosis: From St Paul to Meister Eckhart.* Tacoma, WA: Angelico Press/Sophia Perennis, 2011.

_____. *The Quantum Enigma: Finding the Hidden Key.* Tacoma, WA: Angelico Press/Sophia Perennis, 2011.

Solovyov, Vladimir. *The Religious Poetry of Vladimir Solovyov,* trans. Boris Jakim and Laury Magnus. San Rafael, CA: Semantron Press, 2008.

Spitzer, Robert J. *New Proofs for the Existence of God: Contributions of Contemporary Physics and Philosophy.* Grand Rapids: Eerdmans, 2010.

Staniloae, Dmitru. *Orthodox Spirituality.* South Canaan, PA: St Thikhon's Seminary Press, 2002.

Stein, Edith. *Finite and Eternal Being: An Attempt at an Ascent to the Meaning of Being,* trans. Kurt F. Reinhardt. Washington, DC: ICS Publications, 2002.

_____. *The Science of the Cross.* Washington, DC: ICS Publications, 2002.

Teresa of Avila, Saint. *The Collected Works of St Teresa of Avila,* Vol. II, trans. Kieran Kavanaugh OCD and Otilio Rodriguez OCD. Washington, DC: ICS Publications, 1980.

Thunberg, Lars. *Man and the Cosmos: The Vision of Maximus the Confessor.* Crestwood, NY: St. Vladimir's Seminary Press, 1985.

Tolkien, J.R.R. *The Letters of J.R.R. Tolkien,* ed. Humphrey Carpenter. London: Allen & Unwin, 1981.

_____. *Morgoth's Ring: The Later Silmarillion, Part One.* Boston: Houghton Mifflin, 1993.

Vonier, Dom Anscar. *The Collected Works of Abbot Vonier,* III. London: Burns Oates, 1953.

Watkin, E.I. *Catholic Art and Culture.* London: Hollis & Carter, 1947.

Weinandy OFM (Cap.), Thomas. *The Father's Spirit of Sonship: Re-conceiving the Trinity.* Edinburgh: T&T Clark, 1995.

Wilber, Ken, editor. *Quantum Questions: Mystical Writings of the World's Great Physicists.* Boulder, CO: Shambhala, 1984.

Zajonc, Arthur. *Catching the Light.* New York: Bantam, 1993.

Zinner, Samuel. *Christianity and Islam: Essays on Ontology and Archetype.* London: Matheson Trust, 2010.

Zizioulas, John. *Being as Communion: Studies in Personhood and the Church.* London: DLT, 1985.

————. *Communion and Otherness: Further Studies in Personhood and the Church.* London: T&T Clark, 2006.

————. *Remembering the Future: An Eschatological Ontology.* London: T&T Clark International/ Continuum, 2013.

INDEX OF NAMES

Index of Names

Hubble, Edwin 17
Hume, David 42, 64, 93
Huxley, Aldous 154

Ibn Arabi 134–137, 153, 187, 243
Ibn Hazm 122–123
Ibn Sina/Avicenna 175, 193
Irenaeus, Saint 79, 205
Isaac 118, 133

Jaki, Stanley 28, 34
Jakim, Boris 55, 206, 258, 272
John of Ruysbroeck 171
John of the Cross, Saint 207, 211
John Paul II 43, 57–58, 80–81, 85, 89, 101, 111, 125, 162, 192, 212, 221, 234
John the Baptist, Saint 138, 141, 158
Jones, Deborah 80
Journet, Charles 176
Julian of Norwich 247

Kant, Immanuel 88, 196
Keeble, Brian 60
Kelley, C. F. 23, 172–174, 177, 184, 211
Kenny, Anthony 227
Kepler, Johannes 11
Kow, James P. 25

Law, William 259
Le Fanu, James 53
Lemaître, Georges 17, 261
Leo XIII 22
Levée, Alphonse 161
Lewis, C. S. 38, 76, 166
Locke, John 42
Lodahl, Michael 125
Long-ch'en Rab-jam-pa 147
Lovejoy, Arthur 194

Lubac SJ, Henri de 25, 144, 147, 203, 206, 212, 233, 274
Lucifer 54, 192, 241–242, 256
Lyell, Charles 31
Lyons, J. A. 231

MacDonald, George 186
Mahoney, Timothy A. 156
Majid, Shahn 27–28
Maturana, Humberto 48
Maritain, Jacques 207
Martenson, Hans L. 251, 253, 256
Mary, Blessed Virgin 113–114, 127, 135–137, 173, 179, 217, 219, 228, 239, 258, 263–265, 269, 271, 273–274, 278–279
Massignon, Louis 129, 212
Maturana, Humberto 37, 48
Maximus the Confessor 54, 82, 84
Maxwell, James Clerk 12–13
McGinn, Bernard 169–170, 176–177
Mersch SJ, Emile 199
Merton, Thomas 15, 154, 212
Michael the Archangel, Saint 256
Midgley, Mary 43
Milbank, John 274
Milosz, Oscar 250, 260, 262–263
Mitchell, Christopher 75
Mivart, St. George Jackson 50
Moevs, Christian 275
Monk of the West, A 161
Moore Jr., Alvin 161
Moses 131, 138, 141
Muhammad 118–119, 121, 124, 126–130, 136, 138
Murphy, Francesca A. 39

Nasr, Seyyed Hossein 29, 124, 154
Naydler, Jeremy 30, 38, 56–57
Nebelsick, Harold P. 30

Made in the USA
San Bernardino, CA
22 February 2015